Selected Writ

JOHN HENRY NEWMAN was born in 1801. When he was fifteen he was profoundly affected by Evangelicalism and Calvinism. In 1817, he went up to Trinity College, Oxford, and was elected a Fellow of Oriel in 1822. At Oriel, he came first under the liberal and latitudinarian influences of Richard Whately and Renn Dickson Hampden, but shortly afterwards, through his friendship with Hurrell Froude, John Keble and Edward Pusey, became a High Churchman. In 1833, when it seemed that the Church of England was under attack from the growing liberalism and secularism of the age, he helped launch the Oxford Movement in the hope of awakening his Church to its Catholic heritage. By 1845, however, he could no longer believe that the Anglican Via Media was the true successor to the Church of the Apostles and he became the nineteenth century's most famous convert to Roman Catholicism. Newman was made a Cardinal in 1879. He died in 1890 and was declared 'Venerable' by Pope John Paul II in 1991.

ALBERT RADCLIFFE was born in Bootle, near Liverpool and trained for the ministry in Birkenhead. He has served in America, Israel and England. In 1991 he became Canon Residentiary at Manchester Cathedral, a post he held until his retirement in 2000.

FyfieldBooks present poetry and prose by great as well as sometimes over-looked writers from British and Continental literatures. Clean texts at affordable prices, FyfieldBooks make available authors whose works endure within our literary tradition.

The series takes its name from the Fyfield elm mentioned in Matthew Arnold's 'The Scholar Gypsy' and in his 'Thyrsis'. The elm stood close to the building in which the Fyfield series was first conceived in 1971.

> *Roam on! The light we sought is shining still.*
> *Dost thou ask proof? Our tree yet crowns the hill,*
> *Our Scholar travels yet the loved hill-side*

from 'Thyrsis'

JOHN HENRY NEWMAN

Selected Writings to 1845

edited by Albert E. Radcliffe

Fyfield*Books*

CARCANET

This edition first published in Great Britain in 2002 by
Carcanet Press Limited
4th Floor, Conavon Court
12–16 Blackfriars Street
Manchester M3 5BQ

A CIP catalogue record for this book
is available from the British Library

ISBN trade paperback 1 85754 545 1
ISBN library edition 1 85754 575 3

The publisher acknowledges financial assistance
from the Arts Council of England.

Set in Monotype Bembo by XL Publishing Services, Tiverton
Printed and bound in England by SRP Ltd, Exeter

Contents

Introduction

Life as quandary: to treat with or to reject modernity

JOHN HENRY NEWMAN (1801–90), once considered 'the most dangerous man in England', and a writer, preacher, poet, prose stylist, controversialist and theologian, was among the most eminent of 'Eminent Victorians', a churchman who, from 1833 to 1845, in twelve tumultuous years, wrote himself out of one church and into another. His account of his conversion, the *Apologia pro Vita Sua*, published twenty years later in 1864, became a classic of Christian autobiography.

Newman believed that the most important problem facing Christians of his day was the struggle between the Church and 'liberalism', by which he meant the attempt to replace faith by reason as the basis of individual and social life. For Newman, faith was prior to reason and in order for it to be real in the real world, it needed to be embodied in a church of whose divine origins there could be no doubt. Was that church the Church of England or the Church of Rome? It was a search that shaped his life and made it one of extraordinary fascination for his contemporaries. At the beginning of the twenty-first century, as the world becomes increasingly polarised between fundamentalists and secularists, Newman's life and writings continue to embody key public concerns in religion, politics and ethics. Was he more than an eloquent reactionary? In what way are his criticisms of liberalism relevant in an age in which it is increasingly obvious that men and women cannot live by reason alone?

For the first half of his life Newman was a member of the Church of England but he spent the second in the Church of Rome. Though he transformed both churches, he was an awkward fit in each. He enriched them spiritually and intellectually in ways the majority of their members, lay and ordained, failed at the time to appreciate. He left the Church of England more 'Catholic' than he found it, its churches better kept and its worship more reverent; and by giving the Church of Rome the best of his Anglican and Oxford inheritance he helped revive its fortunes. It became socially respectable, less Italian and Irish, and almost English. More than for most Christian writers, the public drama of Newman's life holds as much interest as the thought and inner turmoil from which it sprang. In this, he is in the select company of Augustine, Abelard, Luther and very few others.

John Henry Newman was born in the City of London in 1801, the eldest of six children. His mother, Jemima, was from a French Huguenot family. His father, John, was a banker. Until he was seven, Newman was educated at home. The family was well off, middle class and Protestant in a conventionally Bible-centred sort of way, though his father was also something of a freethinker with a common sense, rational outlook. On occasions he warned his son against too much zeal in religion. The home atmosphere was typical of many such moderately evangelical families of the time: close, loving, supportive, and designed to encourage the development of morally serious minds and gentlemanly behaviour.

In 1808, Newman's world changed forever when he was sent to board at Dr Nicholas' private school in Ealing. There he shone academically, especially in the Greek classics. He also played the violin, wrote an opera, acted in Latin plays, won prizes for speeches and edited school journals, though he was no lover of games. His last months at school, however, were marked both by family misfortune and by a deepening of his faith – events which proved to be his making.

At sixteen, full of promise, and with thoughts of becoming a lawyer, Newman went up to Trinity College, Oxford, where through a combination of anxiety, academic distraction and overwork he failed to do well in his final examinations. Yet, in spite of this setback, in 1822 his gifts were recognised and he was elected a Fellow of Oriel College. All thoughts of entering the legal profession were now abandoned and in 1824 he was ordained deacon. He was priested the following year. Newman's teaching and pastoral gifts as a tutor were quickly recognised and in 1828 he was appointed Vicar of St Mary's, the University Church, where he became an influential preacher.

Newman first came to national attention in 1833, when, in response to the government's intentions to reform the Church of Ireland, he and a group of friends began publishing the *Tracts for the Times* and so launched what became known as The Oxford Movement. The aims of the Tracts were to defend the Church of England against parliamentary interference, to awaken it to its true nature as a divine institution and to stress its Catholic heritage over against its current Protestant ethos. They became a publishing sensation, dividing the Church and polarising public opinion. They were also responsible for turning many old-fashioned High Church men into militant 'Tractarians', and unintentionally encouraging the anti-Catholic prejudices of the nation as a whole. Of ninety tracts, Newman contributed twenty-nine. In 1841, the situation became critical with the publication of Tract 90, in which he attempted to reconcile the thirty-nine Articles of the Church of England with the theology of the Council of Trent. The outcome was inevitable: after months of politicking and suspense in Church and State, Newman found himself condemned by his University, the Bishops, and the laity at large. Perplexed but unbowed in spirit he retired to the community he had founded at Littlemore on the outskirts of Oxford. There, to clarify his thoughts and feelings he wrote one of the great theological works of the western Church, his *Essay on the Development of Christian Doctrine,* giving to the Church the one concept that would enable it to cope with a changing faith in a changing world. Finally, on 9 October 1845, after three anxious and uncertain years, during which it seemed the whole Christian world had held its breath, he was received into the Church of Rome by the Passionist priest, Father Dominic Barberi. Newman's dramatic, agonised and very public conversion was a pivotal event in the story of the English Church in the nineteenth century and closed an important chapter in its history.

At his 'Catholic' confirmation, on 1 November 1845, Newman took the name Mary, to emphasise his break with his Anglican past. Following a period of study in Rome, he was re-ordained conditionally on 30 May 1847. The following year he founded the Birmingham Oratory which became his spiritual home for the rest of his life, his new Church being at a loss as to how best to employ its famous convert.

In 1851, Newman was appointed the first Rector of the Catholic University of Ireland, a post he held unhappily until his resignation seven years later. Then, in 1879, the new Pope, Leo XIII, gave public recognition to his spiritual and moral influence, and his standing as a teacher of the faithful, by making him a Cardinal, an action that met with approval far beyond the bounds of the Roman Catholic Church. By the time of his death in 1890, Newman had become a greatly revered national figure. Interest in his life and thought has never waned and to many at Vatican II he was 'The Father of the Council'. In 1991, he was declared 'Venerable'. The case for his being declared a 'Saint' and a Doctor of the Church is presently under examination.

To understand more fully Newman's place in history it is necessary to consider in some detail the unfolding drama of his inner life. His was a complex personality and a subtle intellect. In attempting to say anything illuminating about him it is usually possible also to affirm its opposite; a fact that led Henri Bremond to ask, 'Where is the real Newman?' For Newman was a thinker who was also a man of action; a conservative and reactionary who frequently changed his mind; a scholar who strove after humility, yet could not help but draw attention to himself; a Christian who strove to overcome the clamour of the ego, yet saw life and faith through a profound self-understanding and analysis. Newman was always able to state his opinions and beliefs clearly and forcibly, so that to family and friends his mind invariably seemed to be decided on an issue, but the truth was that its certainty was never simple. It was always a mind in process; and even though, until 1842, or so, it was still largely shaped by Tory prejudice, Oxford snobbery and Protestant priggishness, in the end these were frequently subverted by an unending and costly quest for moral realism, unassailable faith and a spiritual home. Viewed in this way, Newman's inner life was a succession of hard-fought retreats from fixed ideological positions. Its development can best be described in a phrase borrowed from evolutionary biology, as one of 'punctuated equilibrium', that is, of periods of apparent stability followed by others of rapid alteration. These radical changes of opinion were always triggered by some outward event: a serious illness (of which he counted three in his lifetime); the opinion of friends; a disturbing phrase in a book or article; or some personal or national crisis that gave opportunity for the controversies his imagination needed for his genius for thought and leadership to thrive. All it took was for some dearly held principle such as the spiritual independence of the Church or the efficacy of the sacraments to be threatened, for the pen of this once socially shy and tongue-tied scholar to be busy far into the night. On occasions he could work and write for over twenty hours at a stretch.

Newman should be understood primarily as a writer. He needed to write in order to think. He meditated and thought principally on paper, and he took considerable pains to see that most of what he wrote survived. In 1872–3, he copied selections from his journals, and in 1874 burned the originals: 'One can never know what may happen after one's death.' Letters, he thought, made the best biography. He was determined that we should understand him through what he wrote, with all the limitations for a biographer that that implies, especially after he had come to appreciate his own greatness and centrality in the story of the Church of his time. In this way, he still shapes our understanding of him today.

It was the Calvinism of Newman's youth that provided the training ground for the extraordinary self-awareness that is evident in his writings. It encouraged the formation of a principled outlook organised around a few basic feelings, clear ideas and dogmatic attitudes. These can be summarised as a search for personal holiness and the need for consistency and certainty. The Calvinism in which Newman had been nurtured at home was intensified in 1816, which proved to be the turning point of his life, by two events that triggered a profound deepening of his religious outlook. The first was the failure of his father's bank, which threw Newman upon his own resources and caused him to grow up quickly. The second was the first of the 'three great illnesses' of his life. These two events confirmed in Newman his 'mistrust of the reality of physical phenomena', 'making me rest in the thought of two and two only absolute and luminously self-evident beings, myself and my creator'. As a result of this double crisis, Newman was obliged to remain at school over the summer. Needing something to occupy him, his classics teacher, the Revd Walter Mayers, gave him several books of Calvinist theology to read, among them Thomas Scott's *The Force of Truth*. Two phrases of Scott stayed with him and can be seen as characterising his lifelong spiritual formation: 'Growth the only evidence of life' and 'Holiness rather than peace'. 'It made me a Christian', Newman wrote long afterwards, though in reality Newman was never a twice-born Christian, but rather a once-born whose faith had undergone a radical deepening. From Bishop Thomas Newton's *Dissertations on the Prophesies,* Newman also added to his prejudices the belief that the Pope was the anti-Christ. Paradoxically, his reading Joseph Milner's *Church History* that summer also led to a lifelong love of the Church Fathers, a love that would ultimately prove decisive for his faith. Until that summer, Newman had always intended his behaviour to be virtuous and upright. Now he would also be religious. From 1816, his was an ego in search of holiness. His character and personality had taken on their basic form. He would be spiritual and moral by being wholeheartedly religious. He had also made the surprising discovery, for a fifteen-year-old, that it was 'the will of God that he should lead a single life'. Not surprisingly, that and the fact that he spent the remainder of his life in all male communities, and that in each he formed one emotionally intense friendship, has led to much discussion about his sexuality. All that can be said for certain on this matter is that so far the speculations have illuminated nothing about either the man or his thinking.

In June 1817, Newman went up to Trinity College, Oxford, knowing who he was. As a student, he was shy and inclined to be tongue-tied. He made few friends, but those he did make were close. He was thought precocious and abstemious, though a good judge of wine. Not surprisingly for a strong Calvinist, he disapproved of the way most students behaved, and especially of their drinking and frivolity. This temptation to ready disapproval was a characteristic that stayed with him. He saw himself essentially as reserved and cold: 'very much as a pane of glass, which transmits heat, being cold itself'. His closest friends, however, would probably not have agreed. With them he could display a warm and generous and more articulate side.

In appearance Newman was thin and somewhat pale, a slightly feminine figure. Though a good observer and describer of people and places,

he was also short-sighted and needed to wear glasses, behind which his
eyes were large and lustrous. Many thought his nose 'Roman'; others
suspected Jewish ancestry. Some found his gaze 'piercing'. His head was
large. And though he was no sportsman, he enjoyed walking. He walked
quickly; in June 1824, for example, he walked twenty miles to Over
Worton, to preach his first sermon for Walter Mayers. To the surprise of
many, in 1822 Newman became a Fellow of Oriel, then reckoned to be
the most intellectual of Oxford's colleges. There he began to grow consid-
erably in social confidence as his colleagues took him in hand. The
friendship of Richard Whately (1783–1863) in particular helped him break
free from his often debilitating shyness. Newman was to credit Whately
with opening his mind and teaching him how to think for himself. Whately
acknowledged that parts of his *Elements of Logic* were really Newman's
work. And as his circle of friends widened, so did Newman's outlook. He
also discovered the pleasure and power of conversation. It animated a
sometimes disappointing presence. Another Fellow of Oriel, Edward
Bouverie Pusey (1800–82), a High Churchman, prompted him to ques-
tion his evangelicalism, while Charles Lloyd (1784–1829) introduced him
to what would later become a distinction vital to his reconciliation with
the Church of Rome, namely the difference between the Catholicism of
the Council of Trent and that of popular Roman Catholicism. He also
drew Newman's attention to the primitive and medieval components of
the Book of Common Prayer. Prayer was always important for Newman,
though he never found it easy. Thinking, not prayer, was second nature
to him. He often needed to write his prayers down in order to pray them.
The best of them have enriched English devotional literature.

   Although the major influences in his life converged to make Newman
profoundly conservative, this was offset by his capacity for personal growth
and development. His break with Calvinism, for example, began in 1824,
when he was Curate of St Clements. As he reflected on his parish experi-
ence, he realised that there was little correspondence between human
nature and his religious beliefs, especially the Calvinist doctrine of predes-
tination. His parishioners could not be divided easily between the elect
and the damned. They were not 'so good as they should be, and better
than they might be'. Edward Hawkins (1789–1882), another fellow of
Oriel and Vicar of St Mary's, advised Newman that he should follow the
example of St Paul, who did not divide Christians into the converted and
the unconverted. He also lent him John Bird Sumner's *Apostolical Preaching*.
The result was that Newman quickly ceased to think of himself as Calvinist.
Friends noticed too, that he had come round to the Catholic and High
Church belief in the efficacy of the sacrament, in baptismal regeneration.

Nor under the influence of his close friend, Richard Hurrell Froude (1803–36) was he able for long even to think of himself as a Protestant. Froude was particularly scathing too about the benefits of the Reformation.

A number of traditions were now battling for Newman's mind and faith: these were evangelical Calvinism, which was in retreat; the liberal Latitudinarianism of Whately, and the High Church Catholicism of friends like Froude, Keble and Pusey. At this time, 1827, Newman was for a short while something of a liberal. He had been strengthened in this new found freedom of thought by his reading of Bishop Joseph Butler (1692–1752), from whom he learned the importance of analogy in theology, as well as the idea that probability was the 'guide of life'. As a young man Newman had read and enjoyed Tom Paine and felt the strength of the eighteenth century rationalist case against Christianity. For a time, when young, he had even modelled his prose style on that of Gibbon. But his liberal phase was progressively undermined by the opinion of his High Church Catholic friends and did not last long. From Pusey, who had studied in Germany, Newman learned how liberalism and rationalism had devastated the spiritual life of Lutheranism. John Keble (1792–1886), another Fellow of Oriel, was also anti-liberal, while Hurrell Froude believed strongly that Luther and Calvin had been nothing short of a disaster for the western Church. This turning from liberalism proved to be the hinge on which Newman's future as a writer, thinker and Christian leader would turn. He began to see it as the greatest single threat to the survival of Christianity. Its sceptical attitudes and critical techniques would overthrow first the doctrines and then the very existence of the Church. It must be resisted. The fate of the Church in France was a glaring example of what liberalism could do. And with reform in Church and State in the air it was coming to England.

By 1828, Newman had shed the liberal views which, for a short time, had been replacing his weakening evangelicalism. He began, instead, to identify himself as a High Churchman in the tradition of Lancelot Andrewes (1555–1626) and William Laud (1573–1645), men who stressed the continuity of the Church of England with the ancient Church of the west, an understanding that deepened as he read the fine set of Church Fathers given to him by Pusey.

All his life Newman was torn between his head and his heart. Intellectually he gave the priority to the head, his reason to the service of his faith. One explanation for his rejecting the evangelicalism of his youth was that it subordinated doctrine to emotion, as in its preaching of the atonement. Instead, Newman sought facts and objectivity, because these gave him emotional stability and spiritual security. The heart's task was to animate the Church's doctrine. With the liberal option closed to him, there was now nowhere for Newman's theological thinking to go for the security it needed but to the Church of the first centuries.

Newman's pilgrimage to Rome was, in the end, a journey of seven stages: his break with Calvinism, his ceasing to think of himself as a Protestant, his abandonment of theological liberalism; his identification with the faith of the early Church; his loss of confidence in the Church of England as successor to that Church, and the shedding of his anti-Roman Catholic prejudices. The first four steps were completed before his Mediterranean holiday with the Froudes of 1832–3, during which he suffered the second serious illness of his life (it was most likely typhoid fever). He nearly died and on recovering, reflected on his spiritual condition. 'I have not sinned against the light,' he said, again and again. He drew two conclusions. Firstly, that the illness had been a punishment for his wilfulness in a row he had had with Edward Hawkins over the role and responsibility of college tutors; and secondly, that his life had been spared because God had work for him to do. This latter conviction meant that he returned home with a clear sense of being a man with a destiny.

Newman's Grand Tour, from 8 December 1832 to 8 July 1833, had taken in Gibraltar, Tangiers (where he refused even to look on the French tricolour), Malta, Corfu, Sicily, Naples, and Rome. Rome was 'a wonderful place', but 'the great enemy of God'. The holiday confirmed Newman in his developing love for Catholic Christianity, though not for the Roman version of it. Anglicanism he saw as the purest kind of Catholicism, a Catholicism reformed from anti-Christian superstitions and other corruptions which were even more obvious in Naples than in Rome or Sicily.

On 14 July 1833, five days after Newman landed in England, Keble preached his Assize Sermon at St Mary's with the title, *National Apostasy*. Newman had now found a cause that would awaken the theologian and journalist in him and call forth unsuspected powers of leadership. The issue Keble had raised was the effect on the Established Church of the *Irish Church Temporalities Bill*, for which the clergy had not even been consulted. They must be roused and a movement organised. The Church was under threat from the government. Newman knew that he was the man for the hour, though indirectly, for he fought and led by his pen. His belief in Christian self-effacement was in direct conflict with his love of controversy. *Thoughts on the Ministerial Commission* was the result of his stand against a secularising government. It was the first of the *Tracts for The Times* and a forerunner of modern mass lobbying. Newman saw clearly the task that lay ahead: he and his friends must save the Church, launch a second Reformation, bring the Church back to Catholic Christianity, and combat liberalism. Newman had always had an interest in military matters, and the crisis he and his friends discerned gave him an opportunity to display a flair for tactical thinking and strategic planning. His strength and integrity of character, combined with the clarity of his convictions, resulted in him becoming what would nowadays be termed a 'guru'. As such, he began to exert a powerful hold over the minds of the young. The result was that for twelve years Anglican Oxford was preoccupied with theological conflict and Church politics. Not surprisingly, then, Newman has been charged with arresting for a generation the intellectual development of the University. Such was his dominance between 1833 and 1845 that while much of England was beginning to struggle with the issues posed for the Christian faith by critical scholarship and scientific discovery, Newman was guiding the minds of his contemporaries back to the past. In other words, the real battles of the nineteenth century were being fought elsewhere than in Oxford. There is a great deal of truth in this charge, though in identifying the conflict between faith and reason, liberalism versus revelation, as the real issue, Newman was perceptive: the dilemma is still far from resolved well over a century later. Newman, in his *Essay on Development*, was well in advance of his time in the way in which he interpreted the past. Christianity was a reality that grew organically. Faith was not a static concept. Newman often changed his opinions, though he always did so within a conservative framework.

Before 1833, Newman had published nothing, but that soon changed. He was a man with a mission. *Arians of the Fourth Century* was published in January 1834 and the first volume of *Parochial and Plain Sermons* followed later that year. Nine more volumes followed in the next ten years. In those sermons Newman said very little directly about the great struggle of the Church against the evils of sceptical thinking. Instead, he guided his congregation gently but certainly towards lives of Christian holiness. To that extent the sermons are timeless and are classics of non-heroic Anglican spirituality. Outside the pulpit, however, Newman thrived on controversy and dated the 'beginning of hostilities' to his attack, in 1836, on R.D. Hampden in *Elucidations of Dr Hampden's Theological Statements*. His poems, most of which were written on his Mediterranean holiday, were published in November 1836 as *Lyra Apostolica*. Then, in 1837, came his *Lectures on the Prophetical Offices of the Church viewed relatively to Romanism and Popular Protestantism*. This was followed in 1838 by his *Lectures on Justification. The Tamworth Reading Room* followed in 1841. This was a wonderfully satirical defence of the Christian basis of education against what he believed was a rationalist misuse of science.

A number of factors converged to make Newman a powerful writer.

To begin with, there was his gift of advocacy. He would have made a great barrister. When his writing is not a meditation, it is an argument. As an author he is always making points or arguing a case. It was the same in the pulpit. Then there is his literary style. Newman's is the theology of insight in the prose of a nineteenth-century Christian gentleman. His sentences are long, jargon free, elegantly phrased and teem with psychological under-standing. It is a style with emotional and intellectual power, designed not to overwhelm, but to persuade and guide to a shared conviction. It was a style that held the attention of readers and hearers and it was at the service of a movement that intended to save the Church from its enemies. For Newman, the key issue was the integrity and survival of the Church of England. Intent on reforming it along rationalist lines, a Whig Parliament had unleashed a secularising onslaught against the Church. Newman began to fight the war that all generals dread: a war on two fronts – against Protestantism on the one hand and Rome on the other, with the Church of England holding the ground of truth between them. For Newman, Anglicanism was the true faith for the English people. It was the Middle Way, the *Via Media* between Geneva and Rome, exemplified in the Oxford that Newman knew and loved, the living alternative to the presumptuous claims of the Church of Rome, which he saw as a Church corrupted by power and superstition, a Church of foreigners, and the Church all true Englishmen hated as the sponsor of attempted invasions from the Armada to the Jacobite Rebellion, which, in Newman's child-hood, was still within living memory.

'In the spring of 1839, my position in the Anglican Church was at its height,' Newman wrote later. It was a position soon to be assailed; in fact it was badly shaken during the long vacation later that year, when he was studying the ancient heresy of the Monophysites. It came to him that he also was 'a Monophysite, that the Church of the *Via Media* was in the posi-tion of the Oriental communion, Rome was where she is now; and the Protestants were Eutychians'. He worried too, that the Movement he had helped found was raising 'longings and tastes which we are not allowed to supply'. A week later came a second blow. He had read an article in the *Dublin Review*, by Nicholas Wiseman, which challenged the Anglican claim to Catholicity. The damage to his confidence had been caused by St Augustine's phrase, '*Securis judicat orbis terrarum*', (the judgement of the whole world is secure). The words seemed to apply to all secessions from Rome as 'from the centre of unity', including that of the Church of England. From 1839 to 1841, Newman continued to wrestle with rela-tions between the two churches. The final crisis came with the publication of Tract 90, in February 1841. Newman was the author. No one had ever read the Thirty-Nine Articles of the Church of England in the way he was now proposing: it was universally understood that they were 'Protestant' in their theology. Now, it was being claimed they could also be read in a very 'Catholic' way and for many, this was too much; Newman's arguments were forced and specious, and opened the door to the Council of Trent. Newman realised he was 'in a mess'; he was 'clean dished', as he wrote to his sister. The denunciation was general and it was cumulative. The Tract was condemned publicly by the University and his Bishop imposed silence on him. There would be no more tracts. His conviction that the Church of England was the church closest in belief and practice to the early Church was under increasing threat. In the summer of 1841 he began translating St Athanasius. 'I saw clearly,' he wrote, 'that in the history of Arianism, the pure Arians were Protestants, the semi-Arians were the Anglicans, and that Rome now was what it was then. The truth lay not with the 'Via Media', but with what was called 'the extreme party'. Then, in the autumn, Tract 90 was condemned by the Bishops. It was as if his Church was rejecting him.

The event which 'finally shattered' his faith in the Church of England was the proposal to install a Bishop in Jerusalem, jointly with the Prussian State Church. To Newman the Church of England was 'in the way to fraternise with Protestants of all sorts, Monophysites, half-converted-Jews and even Druses'. It was a plan by which the Via Media would serve the interests of the State and subvert its own Catholicity.

Theologically, Newman had painted himself into a corner. He felt rejected by the two institutions which had given him his Christian identity and which he loved more than anything else, apart from God, his Church and his University. He was emotionally, spiritually and intellectually now quite homeless. Yet, for all that, he still could not bring himself to leave the Anglican Church or Oxford for the Church of Rome. Though he admired her Catholicity, he despised her superstition. Her ethos was totally foreign to him. It was not a church for an English gentleman. The hold of Anglican Oxford penetrated to his deepest sense of selfhood. In the 1830s and 1840s, the university was a bastion of Anglican privilege. Even the thought of admitting 'Dissenters' was abhorrent. How could a college tutor 'speak familiarly with those who have been baptised by strangers, and perhaps hold some deadly heresy?' His contempt for Rome was even greater. To convert would mean cutting himself off from everything he admired and embracing so much he held in contempt. Yet at Littlemore, the conviction grew that although Rome was a greatly corrupted Church, she might nevertheless still be the authentic successor to the primitive Church. As his attitude towards her softened, so he began to prepare a public retraction of his anti-Roman Catholic statements. It was published in January 1843 and produced little reaction. He wrote to Keble of his 'most dreadful suffering'. 'I am very far more sure that England is in schism, than that the Roman additions to the Primitive Creed may not be development, arising out of a vivid realising of the Divine Depositum of faith.'

As a Christian thinker, Newman had struggled to hold in balance head and heart, faith and reason. With regard to Rome, he resolved that he would be moved by reason, not feeling; and so he began to write what would become a classic of western theology: his *Essay on the Development of Christian Doctrine*. In it, he proposed that the Church's teachings changed over time by a process of organic development. The task of theology was to distinguish authentic from inauthentic development.

In July 1843, the University forbade Edward Pusey to preach for two years. Oxford was in turmoil and the fortunes of the Oxford movement were clearly at low ebb. In considerable anguish of spirit, Newman resigned his living at St Mary's. His sermon at Littlemore, on 25 September, *The Parting of Friends,* was the last he preached as an Anglican. By 1844, everyone who knew him was certain he would 'go over to Rome'. 1845 was spent in an agony of waiting. On 3 October, he resigned from Oriel College and from the University. The *Essay* was not quite finished but he could wait no longer. His logic had left him nowhere else to go. On 8 October, Newman began to make his confession to Father Barberi. It was completed the next day, and he was received into the Roman Catholic Church. Though his conversion was expected, it nevertheless caused an outcry sufficiently strong for Gladstone to be seriously concerned for the survival of the Church of England.

Yet, for all the controversy it occasioned Newman's conversion was, with hindsight, something of a marginal event in the life of both churches. It can be argued that the key struggle for Christians in the nineteenth century was the conflict Newman avoided: that of religious tradition with critical scholarship and scientific discovery. The liberal tide he fought so hard to stem, and which in resisting he was nudged ever nearer to Rome, in the end won out. The Anglican hold over Oxford was broken in the following generation. Newman had helped make it inevitable. For the remainder of his life, as the Vatican became more and more of an anti-liberal and anti-modern ghetto, Newman was safe from the liberal threat he had grown to dread. The irony, however, was that at the Second Vatican Council, after resisting them for over a hundred years, the Roman Catholic Church was eventually able to accommodate liberal and modernist insights to its theology, largely on the basis of Newman's work on doctrinal development. Newman had dealt with the liberal threat by refusing to deal with it. It simplified his struggle and made his conversion inevitable. Today, neither church can ignore the challenge as he did.

Had Newman got what it takes to be an Anglican? At one time, this was a favourite essay question in some Anglican theological colleges. The suggestion was that his mind, which could only work with black and white concepts and was unable to deal with shades of grey, unresolved dilemmas, contradictions, blurred definition, and the perpetual either/or of open issues, could only be happy in a communion which had no room for uncertainty at all. But since 1890, thanks partly to Newman, the gap between the churches has closed considerably; most Anglicans have little difficulty with their Catholic heritage, while Roman Catholics are beginning to come to terms with, and adapt to, an inescapable modernity derived from liberal values. That said, the problem Newman avoided is still far from solved. The world's major faiths are increasingly polarised between the conservative strategy for survival and the liberal. Newman chose the former strategy. What saved him from being a fundamentalist in his adopted Church were those very aspects of Anglicanism which he could never renounce, and happily was not required to shed – a faith which would not become an ideology and whose evidence was an undiminished humanity.

On 10 August 1890, Cardinal Newman, who was by now universally admired and respected, fell ill with pneumonia. He died the next day, mourned universally and ecumenically as one whose struggles had embodied those of the age. On his coffin, the pall carried his Cardinal's motto, *cor ad cor loquitur*, 'Heart speaks to heart'. There could be no finer summary of his preaching or writing. His memorial at Rednal, where he was buried, bore the epitaph he had chosen himself, *Ex umbris et imaginibus in veritatem*, 'out of shadows and images into reality'. (Unreality was the enemy Newman dreaded most.) Together with the quotations from Scott, they offer the most adequate summary of his faith and thought.

Most Anglicans have long since forgiven Newman for his defection to a sister church. His greatness is not in doubt and in a more ecumenical age an appreciation of that greatness, especially of his ability to transcend his fears and limitations, serves to bring the two Communions closer together.

The following selection from Newman's pre-1845 writings represents no more than a per cent or two of the millions of words that came from his pen during his Anglican years. Inevitably, the choice of passages has been to some extent a subjective one, but a serious attempt has been made to illustrate both his public life and the inner pilgrimage on which his life was based. In selecting and compressing the sermons, letters, lectures and other key works, the intention has been to give as much of an overview as is feasible while still retaining the argument – for Newman always wrote to persuade. His long sentences, which are packed like answers in an examination, with a point a line, convey the essence of the age, the place, the cause and the man. Although it could be argued that they are now of interest mainly to historians, they remain among the treasures of English literature. In an age that shares with Newman a love of plainness and fact, and yet has style everywhere but in its prose, it is important that his writings are remembered, even by liberals.

Chapter One: Newman as a Correspondent[1]

'The true life of a man is in his letters'

Like most public figures of his time, Newman was a prolific letter-writer, to family and friends especially – and, because they were valued, his letters were preserved. This enabled Newman later to recount the history of his conversion in his Apologia Pro Vita Sua. *It also made it possible for Anne Mozley, his sister Jemima's sister-in-law, to publish her two-volume collection of his correspondence as an Anglican.*

To W. Mayers [January 1817]

... I have not yet finished reading Bishop Beveridge, but it seems to me, as far as I have read it, an excellent work; and indeed I know it must be so, else you would not have given it me.

There is one passage in the first chapter of the second part that I do not quite comprehend: it is on the Sacrament of Baptism. I had, before I read it, debated with myself how it could be that baptised infants dying in their infancy could be saved unless the spirit of God was given them: which seems to contradict the opinion that baptism is not accompanied by the Holy Spirit. Dr Beveridge's opinion seems to be that the seeds of grace are sown in baptism, though they often do not spring up. That baptism is the means whereby we receive the Holy Spirit, although not the only means; that infants when baptised receive the inward and spiritual grace, without the requisite repentance and faith: if this be his opinion, the sermon Mr Milman preached on grace last year was exactly consonant with his sentiments ... [I:23].[2]

---

1 The letters quoted are all from Anne Mozley's two-volume collection, *Letters and Correspondence* (1891).
2 These figures refer to each letter's placing in Anne Mozley's book. The first figure gives the volume number; the second gives the page number.

To his brother Frank [August 1820]

Here at Oxford I am most comfortable. The quiet and stillness of every-thing around me tends to calm and lull those emotions which the near prospect of my grand examination, and a heart too solicitous about fame and too fearful of failure, are continually striving to excite. I read very much, certainly, but God enables me to praise Him with joyful lips when I rise, and when I lie down, and when I wake in the night. For the calm happiness I enjoy I cannot feel thankful as I ought. How in my future life, if I do live, shall I look back with a sad smile at these days! It is my daily, and I hope heartfelt, prayer that I may not get any honours here if they are to be the least cause of sin to me. As the time approaches and I have laboured more at my books, the trial is greater. [I:43].

To his father [3 June 1824]

[…] In the autumn of 1801 the parish of St Clement's contained about 400 inhabitants; in 1821 about 800. Since that time Oxford has become more commercial than before, owing to the new canals, &c., all which has tended to increase the population. But the increase of this particular period has been also owing to the improvements in the body of the town. Old houses which contained, perhaps, several families, have been pulled down to make way for collegiate buildings, to widen streets, to improve views. This has made building a very profitable speculation on the outskirts of the place, and the poor families once unpacked, have not been induced to dwell as thickly as before. The parish in which I am interested I find consists at present of 2,000, and it is still increasing. The living, I am told, is worth about £80; I do not suppose the curacy will be more than £40 or £50. […] [I:85].

To his mother [28 July 1824]

[…] About ten days ago I began my *visitation* of the whole parish, going from house to house, asking the names, numbers, trades, where they went to church, &c. I have got through, as yet, about a third (and the most respectable third) of the population. In general they have been very civil; often expressed gratification that a clergyman should visit them; hoped to see me again, &c. &c. If in the habit of attending the dissenting meeting, they generally excused themselves on the plea of the rector being old, and they could not hear him; or the church being too small, &c.; but expressed no unwillingness to come back. I rather dread the two-thirds of the parish which are to come; but trust (and do not doubt) I shall be carried through it well, and as I could wish. It will be a great thing done; I shall know my parishioners and be known by them. I have taken care always to speak kindly of Mr Hinton, the dissenting minister, expressed a wish to know him, &c.; said I thought he had done good – which he had – in the place. [...] [I:86].

To his mother [March 1826]

I feel pleased you like my sermons. I am sure I need not caution you against taking anything I say on trust. Do not be run away with any opinion of mine. I have seen cause to change my mind in some respects, and I may change again. I see I know very little about anything, though I often think I know a great deal.

I have a great undertaking before me in the tutorship here. I trust God may give me grace to undertake it in a proper spirit, and to keep steadily in view that I have set myself apart for His service for ever. There is always the danger of the love of literary pursuits assuming too prominent a place in the thoughts of a college tutor, or his viewing his situation merely as a secular office – a means of future provision when he leaves college. [I:130].

To his sister Harriett [1 May 1826]

You could not have proposed a more difficult question than in asking me to give you 'something to do'. I will write down a few suggestions as they occur to me; but whether they are rich or barren, difficult or easy, agreeable or disagreeable, I will not pretend to determine:

Compare St Paul's speeches in the Acts with any of his Epistles, with a view of finding if they have any common features.

Make a summary of the doctrines conveyed in Christ's teaching, and then set down over against them what St Paul added to them, what St Peter, what St John, and whether St Paul differs from the other three in any points; whether of silence or omission, or whether they all have peculiar doctrines, &c. &c. [...] [I:132].

To John Keble[3] [1 September 1826]

I have been commencing Hebrew in this retreat, an object I have long

---

3 John Keble [1792–1866]. Tractarian leader and poet. His *The Christian Year* was published the following year and in 1831 he was elected Professor of Poetry at Oxford.

had in view and had begun to despair of accomplishing, and just finishing Genesis, though I had hoped to have made further progress. The interest attending it has far surpassed all my anticipations, high as they were, and, though I clearly see I could never be a *scholar* without understanding Chaldee, Syriac and Arabic, yet I think I may get insight enough into the language at least to judge of the soundness of the criticisms of scholars, and to detect the superficial learning of some who only pretend to be scholars. Is it not very difficult to draw a line in these studies? There seems no *natural* limit before the languages above mentioned are mastered. And is it not very tantalising to stop short of them? I should like to know whether those languages *are* so formidable as is sometimes said; in Greek we have a variety of dialects, and works in every diversity of style; can the Semitic tongues all together contain one hundredth part of the difficulty of Greek? Considering, too (as I suppose is the case with them all), their greater simplicity of structure? I wish we began learning Hebrew ten years sooner. [...] [I:136].

To Richard Whately [14 November 1826]

Whately became a Fellow of Oriel in 1811 and Principal of St Alban Hall in 1825. In his Preface to his Elements of Logic, *he had written: 'I cannot avoid particularising the Rev. J. Newman, Fellow of Oriel College, who actually composed a considerable portion of the work as it now stands, from manuscript not designed for publication, and who is the original author of several pages.' Newman responded as follows:*

I cannot tell you the surprise I felt on seeing you had thought it worth while to mention my name as having contributed to the arrangement of the material. Whatever I then wrote I am conscious was of little value, &c. &c. ... Yet I cannot regret that you have introduced my name in some sort of connection with your own. There are few things which I wish more sincerely than to be known as a friend of yours, and though I may be on the verge of propriety in the earnestness with which I am expressing myself, yet you must let me give way to feelings which never want much excitement to draw them out, and now will not be restrained. Much as I owe to Oriel in the way of mental improvement, to none, as I think, do I owe so much as to you. I know who it was that first gave me heart to look about me after my election, and taught me to think correctly, and (strange office for an instructor) to rely upon myself. [I:107].

To his sister Harriett [19 March 1827]

As to Mr W.'s absurd question about my opinion on the Catholic question, tell him that I am old enough to see that I am not old enough to know anything about it. It seems to me a question of history. I am not skilled in the political and parliamentary history of Elizabeth, the Stuarts, and Hanoverians. How *can* I decide it by means of mere argument – theoretical argument, declamations about liberty, the antecedent speculative probability of their doing no harm? In my mind he is no wise man who attempts, without a knowledge of history, to talk about it. If it were a religious question I might think it necessary to form a judgement; as it is not, it would be a waste of time. What would be thought of a man giving an opinion about the propriety of this or that agrarian law in Rome who was unacquainted with Roman history? At the same time I must express my belief that NOTHING will satisfy the Roman Catholics. [...] [I:162].

To his mother [1 March 1829]

We have achieved a glorious victory.[4] It is the first public event I have been concerned in, and I thank God from my heart both for my cause and its success. We have proved the independence of the Church and of Oxford. So rarely is either of the two in opposition to government, that not once in fifty years can independent principle be shown. Yet, in these times, when its existence has been generally doubted, the moral power we shall gain by it cannot be over-estimated. We had the influence of government in unrelenting activity against us – the 'talent' so called of the University, the town lawyers, who care little for our credit, the distance off and the slender means of our voters – yet we have beaten them by a majority of 146 votes, 755 to 609. The 'rank and talent' of London came down superciliously to remove any impediment to the quiet passing of the great Duke's bill; confessing at the same time that *of course* the University would lose credit by turning out, whatever the Government might gain by it. They would make use of their suffrage, as members of the University, to degrade the University. No wonder that such as I, who have not, and others who have, definite opinions in favour of Catholic Emancipation, should feel we have a much nearer and holier interest than the pacification of Ireland, and should, with all our might, resist the attempt to put us under the feet of the Duke and Mr Brougham.

---

4 Newman is referring to Sir Robert Peel's failure to be re-elected to Parliament for the University of Oxford. The issue was Catholic emancipation.

Their insolence has been intolerable; not that we have done more than laugh at it. They have everywhere styled themselves the 'talent' of the University; that they have rank and station on their side I know; and that we have the inferior colleges and the humbler men of style. But as to talent, Whately, with perhaps Hawkins, is the only man of talent among them; as to the rest, any one of us in the Oriel Common-Room will fight a dozen of them apiece – and Keble is a host; Balliol too gives us a tough set, and we have all the practical talent, for they have shown they are mere sucking pigs in their canvass and their calculations. Several days since, their London chairman wrote to Mr Peel assuring him of complete and certain success. They strutted about (peacocks!) telling our men who passed through London that they should beat by eight to one, and they wondered we should bring the matter to a poll. We endured all this, scarcely hoping for success, but determining, as good Churchmen and true, to fight for the *principle*, not consenting to our own degradation. I am sure I would have opposed Mr Peel had there been only just enough with me to take off the appearance of egotism and ostentation; and we seriously contemplated about ten days since, when we seemed to have too slight hopes of victory to put men to the expense of coming up, we resident seventy, simply and solemnly to vote against Mr Peel, though the majority against us might be many hundreds. How much of the Church's credit depended on us residents! and how inexcusable we should have been, if by drawing back we had deprived our country friends of the opportunity of voting, and had thus in some sort betrayed them.

Well, the poor defenceless Church has borne the brunt of it, and I see in it the strength and unity of Churchmen. An hostile account in one of the papers says, 'High and Low Church have joined, being set on rejecting Mr Peel.'

I am glad to say I have seen no ill-humour anywhere. We have been merry all through it. [I:202].

To his mother [13 March 1829]

What a scribbler I am become! But the fact is my mind is so full of ideas in consequence of this important event, and my views have so much enlarged and expanded, that in justice to myself I ought to write a volume.

We live in a novel era – one in which there is an advance towards universal education. Men have hitherto depended on others, and especially on the clergy, for religious truth; now each man attempts to judge for himself. Now, without meaning of course that Christianity is in itself opposed to free enquiry, still I think it *in fact* at the present time opposed to the particular form which that liberty of thought has now assumed. Christianity is of faith, modesty, lowliness, subordination; but the spirit at work against it is one of latitudinarianism, indifferentism, and schism, a spirit which tends to overthrow doctrine, as if the fruit of bigotry and discipline – as if the instrument of priestcraft. All parties seem to acknowledge that the stream of opinion is setting against the Church. I do believe it will ultimately be separated from the State, and at this prospect I look with apprehension – (1) because all revolutions are awful things, and the effect of this revolution is unknown; (2) because the upper classes will be left almost religionless; (3) because there will not be that security for sound doctrine without change, which is given by Act of Parliament; (4) because the clergy will be thrown on their congregations for voluntary contributions.

It is no reply to say that the majesty of truth will triumph, for man's nature is corrupt; also, even should it triumph, still this will only be ultimately, and the meanwhile may last for centuries. Yet I do still think there is promise of preservation to the Church; and in its Sacraments, preceding and attending religious education, there are such means of Heavenly grace, that I do not doubt it will live on in the most irreligious and atheistical times.

Its enemies at present are (1) the uneducated or partially educated mass in towns, whose organs are Wooler's, Carlisle's publications, &c. They are almost professedly deistical or worse. (2) The Utilitarians, political economists, useful knowledge people – their organs the *Westminster Review*, the *London University*, &c. (3) The Schismatics in and out of the Church, whose organs are the *Eclectic Review*, the *Christian Guardian*, &c. (4) The Baptists, whose system is consistent Calvinism – for, as far as I can see, Thomas Scott, &c are inconsistent, and such inconsistent men would, in times of commotion, split, and go over to this side or that. (5) The high circles in London. (6) I might add the political indifferentists, but I do not know enough to speak, like men who join Roman Catholics on one hand and Socinians on the other. Now you must not understand me as speaking harshly of individuals; I am speaking of bodies and principles.

And now I come to another phenomenon: the talent of the day is against the Church. The Church party (visibly at least, for there may be latent talent, and great times give birth to great men) is poor in mental endowments. It has not activity, shrewdness, dexterity, eloquence, practical power. On what then does it depend? On prejudice and bigotry.

This is hardly an exaggeration; yet I have good meaning and one honourable to the Church. Listen to my theory. As each individual has certain instincts of right and wrong antecedently to reasoning, on which he acts – and rightly so – which perverse reasoning may supplant, which then can hardly be regained, but, if regained, will be regained from a different source – from reasoning, not from nature – so, I think, has the world of men collectively. God gave them truths in His miraculous revelations, and other truths in the unsophisticated infancy of nations, scarcely less necessary and divine. These are transmitted as 'the wisdom of our ancestors', through men – many of whom cannot enter into them, or receive them themselves – still on, on, from age to age, not the less truths because many of the generations through which they are transmitted are unable to prove them, but hold them, either from pious and honest feeling (it may be), or from bigotry or from prejudice. That they are truths it is most difficult to prove, for great men alone can prove great ideas or grasp them. Such a mind was Hooker's, such Butler's; and, as moral evil triumphs over good men on a small field of action, so in the argument of an hour or the compass of a volume would men like Brougham, or, again, Wesley, show to far greater advantage than Hooker or Butler. Moral truth is gained by patient study, by calm reflection, silently as the dew falls – unless miraculously given – and when gained it is transmitted by faith and by 'prejudice'. Keble's book is full of such truths, which any Cambridge man might refute with the greatest ease. [I:204].

To his sister Harriett [16 March 1829]

I am continuing in fact my letter to my mother. Well, then, taking the state of parties in the country as it is, I look upon the granting of the Catholic claims not so much in itself as in the principle and sentiments of which it is an indication. It is carried by indifference, and by hostility to the Church. I do not see how this can be denied. Not that it is not a momentous measure in itself; it is certainly an alteration in our Constitution, and, though I am used to think the country has not much to dread from Romanist opinions (the danger seeming to be on the side of infidelity), yet there is a general impression, which Blanco White's book confirms, that infidelity and Romanism are compatible, or rather connected with each other. Moreover, it is agreed on all hands that the Emancipation will endanger the Irish Protestant Church; some even say it must ultimately fall.

All these things being considered, I am clearly in *principle* an anti-Catholic; and, if I do not oppose the Emancipation, it is only because I do not think it expedient, perhaps possible, so to do. I do not look for the settlement of difficulties by the measure; they are rather begun by it, and will be settled by the downfall of the Established Church. If, then, I am for Emancipation, it is only that I may make my stand against the foes of the Church on better ground, instead of fighting at a disadvantage.

That Emancipation is necessary now I think pretty clear, because the intelligence of the country will have it. Almost all who have weight by their talent or station prefer, of the alternatives left to us, concession, to an Irish war. But that the anti-Catholic party, who have by far the majority of number, should have been betrayed by its friends suddenly, craftily, and that the Government should have been bullied by Mr O'Connell into concessions, is most deplorable. Perhaps there are circumstances in the background of which we know nothing. I have thought, perhaps, the Duke wants to have the energies of the country free and ready for a Russian war.

I do not reckon Pusey or Denison among our opponents, because they were strong for concession beforehand; and Pusey, I know, thought most highly of Mr Peel's integrity and generosity. [I:206].

To R.H. Froude [15 August 1829]

[...] Mozley[5] just now made his appearance in my rooms, having arrived for a few weeks' hermitage here [...] Dornford was, on the whole, I think, pleased with what he saw in Ireland, but did not see much, and was disappointed in the Irish character (its wit, I believe). I like what he says as far as it goes. He met some very clever Irish lads (Roman Catholics) who knew a great deal about their own tenets, and argued well. He seems to think a reformation to Protestantism quite chimerical, and likes the idea of a gradual improvement in the Roman Catholic system itself. This is Arnold's system too, bigot! And why it is not a good one I do not know. [...] [I:211].

To J.W. Bowden [13 March 1831]

I fully agree with you about the seriousness of the prospect we have before us, yet do not see what is to be done. The nation (*i.e.* numerically the πλῆθος) is for revolution ... They certainly have the physical power, and it is the sophism of the day to put religious considerations out of sight, and, forgetting there is any power above man's, to think that what man can do he may do with impunity.

I fear that petitions against Reform would but show the weakness of the Conservative party by the small number which could be got together. At all events, I believe the University has never come forward on ques-

---

5 This was Thomas Mozley, elected a Fellow of Oriel, April 1829.

tions purely political, or at least before others. Besides, the Church has for a long time lost its influence as a body – *Excoriatur*! Nor do I think it is in a humour to exert it on this occasion, if it had any. It is partly cowed and partly offended. Two years back the State deserted it. I do not see when, in consequence of that treachery, the State has got itself into difficulties, that the Church is bound to expose itself in its service.

Not that the Church should be unforgiving; but, if others think with me, *what* great interest has it that things should remain as they are? I much fear that society is rotten, to say a strong thing. Doubtless there are many specimens of excellence in the higher walks of life, but I am tempted to put it to you whether the persons you meet generally are – I do not say consistently religious; we never can expect that in this world – but believers in Christianity in any true sense of the word. No, they are Liberals, and in saying this I conceive I am saying almost as bad of them as can be said of anyone. What will be the case if things remain as they are? Shall we not have men placed in the higher stations of the Church who are anything but real Churchmen? The Whigs have before now designed Parr for a Bishop; we shall have such as him. I would rather have the Church severed from its temporalities and scattered to the four winds, than such a dese-cration of holy things. I dread above all things the pollution of such men as Lord Brougham, affecting to lay a friendly hand upon it ... [...] [I:236].

To his mother [25 October 1831]

I have today received a very valuable present of books from many of my new friends and pupils, consisting of thirty-six volumes of the Fathers; among these are the works of Austin, Origen, Basil, Ambrose, and Irenaeus. They are so fine in their outsides as to put my former ones to shame, and the editions are the best. Altogether, I am now set up in the patristical line, should I be blessed with health and ability to make use of them. [I:251].

To Thomas Mozley [13 May 1832]

[...] I hear you are thinking of duty, else I should not have mentioned it, considering your late illness. It has been very unfortunate that you were obliged to give up your engagement with Round, but all is for the best. I am truly rejoiced to find your desire for parochial employment has not diminished, and your opinion of your own health not such as to deter you. For myself, since I heard your symptoms, I have not been alarmed, but some persons have been very anxious about you. I trust you are to be preserved for many good services in the best of causes. I am sure you have that in you which will come to good, if you cherish and improve it. You may think I am saying a strange thing, perhaps an impertinent and misplaced, and perhaps founded on a misconception, yet let me say it, and blame me if it be harsh – namely, that had it pleased God to have visited you with an illness as serious as the Colchester people thought it, it would almost have seemed a rebuke for past waste of time. I believe that God often cuts off those He loves, and who are really His, as a judgement, not interfering with their ultimate safety, but as passing them by, as if unworthy of being made instruments of His purpose. It was an idea which was strong upon the mind of my brother, during his illnesses of the last year, while he did not doubt that his future interests were essentially secure. I doubt not at all that you have all along your illness had thoughts about it, far better than I can suggest; and I reflect with thankfulness that the very cause of it was an endeavour on your part to be actively employed; to the notion of which you still cling; yet I cannot but sorrowfully confess to myself (how much so ever I wish to hide the past from my own mind) that you have lost much time in the last four or five years. I say I wish to hide it from myself, because in simple truth, in it I perceive a humiliation to myself. I have expected a good deal from you, and have said I expected it. Hitherto I have been disappointed, and it is a mortification to me. I do expect it still, but in the meanwhile time is lost, as well as hope delayed. Now you must not think it unkind in me noticing this now, of all times of the year. I notice it, not as if you needed the remark most now, rather less, but because you have more time to think about it now. It is one especial use of times of illness to reflect about ourselves. Should you, however, really acquit yourself in your own mind, thinking that the course you have pursued, of letting your mind take its own way, was best for yourself, I am quite satisfied, and will believe you, yet shall not blame myself for leading you to the question, since no one can be too suspicious about himself. Doubtless you have a charge on you for which you must give account. You have various gifts, and you have good principles. For the credit of those principles, for the sake of the Church, and for the sake of your friends, who expect it of you, see that they bring forth fruit. I have often had – nay have – continually anxious thoughts about you, but it is unpleasant to obtrude them, and now I have hesitated much before I got myself to say what I have said, lest I should only be making a fuss; yet believe me to speak with very much affection towards you. Two men you know best, G. and C., appear to me to consider you not at all improved in your particular weak points. I differ from them. Perhaps I am exaggerating their opinion, and men speak generally and largely when they would readily, on consideration, make exceptions, &c. But if this be in any measure true, think what it implies? What are we placed here for, except to overcome the Ἐυπερίστατος ἁμαρτία,[6] whatever it be in our own case? [...] [I:258].

To F. Rogers [25 July 1832]

[...] After you went, we had a fatal case of cholera at Littlemore. It was not in my parish, but it made us very busy, being so very near. Between a fortnight and three weeks having passed without a second case, we consider we are as safe as any other part of the neighbourhood: though, I have heard, on my return, that the obstinate blockheads have actually first, not burnt, but buried, and now again actually dug up, the bed furniture of the poor patient they were ordered to destroy. Is not this the very spirit of Whiggery: opposition for its own sake, striving against the truth, because it happens to be commanded us; as if wisdom is less wise because it is powerful? and can we wonder at the brutishness of the Israelites in the desert, with such specimens before our eyes? As to the cholera, it is not yet formidable here, I am thankful to say, or I should not have gone away. (I have wandered – I meant to say, that perhaps it might come on and keep me here, and prevent my ramblings.) We have had altogether about forty cases – confined, I believe, to St Ebbe's, St Aldate's, the Jail, &c, though we cannot, of course, boast, were it but for the bad luck of it: For myself in these things it is as well to be a fatalist; I am practically so. Whether imagination would get the better, did I actually *see* a case, I cannot tell, but at present I am unable to realise the danger. Surely one's time is come, or it is not; the event is out of our power. David's meaning is evident to me in a way I never understood it before. When he speaks of falling into hands higher than human, he means to say that the pestilence is beyond the physicians; but famine is not beyond the chief butlers and bakers of Israel. The difficulty is to unite resignation *with* activity. Here we are only called to be resigned, which is comparatively easy. Then, again, when one argues about oneself, there is on one's own mind the strong impression (I know it is not a good argument, but fear is but an impression, and this works by a counter-imagination) that one is destined for some work, which is yet undone in my case. Surely my time is not yet come. So much for the cholera. [...] [I:268].

---

6   The reference is to Hebrews 12:1: 'the sin which doth so easily beset us'. [Authorised Version.]

To R.H. Froude [13 September 1832]

As to your proposal for me to accompany you, it is very tempting. It quite unsettled me, and I have had a disturbed night with the thought of it. Indeed, it makes me quite sad to think what an evidence it has given me of the little real stability of mind I have yet attained. I cannot make out why I was so little, or rather not at all, excited by the coming of the cholera, and so much by this silly prospect which you have put before me. It is very inconsistent, except, perhaps, that the present novelty has come upon me suddenly. But enough of philosophising.

I am much tempted by your proposal, for several reasons, yet there is so much of impediment in the way of my accepting it. I cannot divest myself of the feeling that I may be intruding upon your father; but, supposing this away, I see much in favour of the scheme. Probably I never shall have such an opportunity again. I mean that of going with a man I know so well as yourself. And going with a person older than myself, as your father, is to me a great temptation. I am indolently distrustful of my own judgement in little matters, and like to be under orders. ...

Then what a name the Mediterranean is! And the time of the year, for I think summer would be too hot for me; and the opportunity of getting there without touching Gallic earth (for I suppose you go by water), which is an abomination. And if I ever am to travel, is not this the time when I am most at liberty for it? My engagements being slighter now than they have been these many years, and than they are likely to be hereafter. And I feel the need of it; I am suspicious of becoming narrow-minded, and at least I wish to experience the feeling and the trial of expansiveness of views, if it were but to be able to *say* I had, and to know how to meet it in the case of others. And then I think I may fairly say my health requires it. Not that I ever expect to be regularly well as long as I live. It is a thing not to think of; but still I may be set up enough for years of work, for which, at present, I may be unequal.

But you must tell me (1) as to time. I could not allow myself to be absent from England beyond Easter (say the beginning of April). Would it not be possible for me to part company with you? (2) As to expense, which, I apprehend, will be a serious subject ... (3) As to my health. It is quite enough that *you* should be an invalid; but it would be an ungracious πάρεργον for me to fall sick also. Now I cannot answer for my health. If all of a sudden I fell ill? [...] [I:273].

To the Rev. E. B. Pusey [10 November 1832]

Pusey had written to say that his daughter, baptised by Newman, had died.

I trust the change of place and the retirement of the country have been a blessing to you and Mrs Pusey, as I am sure they have. It only requires to be alone for receiving the comfort which almost necessarily attends any dispensation from Above. Of course, only parents can tell the sorrow of the loss of a child. But all persons can see the nature of the comfort contained in it – the comfort of knowing that you have given an immortal spirit to Heaven, and of being released from all responsibility of teaching her right from wrong, and from the uncertainties of her final destiny. You have done what her age allowed. She has been dedicated to God, and he has received the offering. For me, I have had a great privilege in being the means of her dedication. It is the only service which we are given to perform with a rejoicing conscience and a secure mind. And, on recollection, it becomes doubly precious, and a festival work, when, in the case of your dear little one, we see the certainty of its having been accepted. [I:278].

To his mother [5 December 1832]

Newman writes from Falmouth. His Mediterranean holiday is about to begin. His letters from abroad extend from 11 December 1832 – July 1833.

[…] A night journey through Devonshire and Cornwall is very striking for its mysteriousness; and it was a beautiful night, clear, frosty, and bright with full moon. Mere richness of vegetation is lost by night, but bold features remain. As I came along, I had the whole train of pictures so vividly upon my mind, that I could have written a most interesting account of it in the most picturesque style of modern composition, but it is all gone from me by this time, like a dream.

The night was enlivened by what Herodotus calls a night engagement with a man, called by courtesy a gentleman, on the box. The first act ended by his calling me a d— fool, the second by his insisting on two most hearty shakes of the hand, with the protest that he certainly did think me very injudicious and ill-timed. I had opened by telling him he was talking great nonsense to a silly goose of a maid-servant stuck atop of the coach; so I had no reason to complain of his choosing to give me the retort uncourteous … He assured me he reverenced my cloth … It is so odd, he thought I had attacked him under personal feeling. I am quite ashamed of this scrawl, yet since I have a few minutes to spare I do not like to be otherwise employed than in writing. [I:283].

To his mother [11 December 1832]

Written on board the Hermes.

I wish you to receive the first letter I write home from foreign parts.

Today has been the most pleasurable day – as far as externals go – I have ever had that I can recollect; and now, in the evening, I am sleepy and tired with the excitement. We are now off Cape Finisterre. Lights were just now visible from farmhouses on shore which is, may be, fifteen miles off. This morning early we saw the high mountains of Spain – the first foreign land I ever saw, having finished most prosperously our passage across the formidable bay of Biscay. The land first discovered was Cape Ortegal and its neighbourhood, magnificent in its outline; and, as we neared it, marked out with three lines of mountains; in some places very precipitous. At first we were about fifty miles off them, then twenty-five perhaps. At the same time the day cleared, and the sea, which even hitherto had been very fine, now became of a rich indigo colour; and, the wind freshening, was tipped with white edges, which, breaking into foam, turned into momentary rainbows. The sea-gulls, quite at home, were sailing about; and the vessel rocked to and fro with a motion which, unpleasant as it might have been, had the wind been from the south-west, was as delightful as being from shore. [...]

The Captain is a very pleasant man. There are three midshipmen, and one above them, who may or may not be called lieutenant; for steam vessels are anomalies (they are all of the navy, as is the case with all packets now). There are, besides, a purser and a doctor. They are all of them, young men from twenty to twenty-five; have seen a great deal of all parts of the world, have much interesting information, and are very gentlemanlike. It amuses me to scrutinise them. One so clever, the others hardly so. They have (most of them) made very few inductions, and are not in the habit of investigating causes – the very reverse of philosophers. [...] [I:284].

To his mother [28 February 1833]

We leave Naples for Rome tomorrow morning. [...] I left Jemima without an account of the conditions of the lower classes in Sicily. I will now give you a traveller's description, which is proverbially superficial. The mixture of grandeur and dirt in the towns is indescribable, and to an Englishman incomprehensible. There, at Naples and at Palermo and Messina, the beggars are fearful, both in their appearance and their importunity. One fellow at Messina stuck by us for two hours. At Palermo they have beats; here at Naples their horribleness has most struck me: at Palermo their dirt and squalidness. Oh, the miserable creatures we saw in Sicily! I never knew what human suffering was before. Children and youths who looked as if they did not know what fresh air was, though they must have had it in plenty – well, what water was – with features sunk, contracted with perpetual dirt, as if dirt was their food. The towns of Partenico and Alcamo are masses of filth; the street is a pool; but Calatafirmi, where we slept! – I dare not mention facts. Suffice it to say, we found the poor children of the house slept in holes dug into the wall, which smelt not like a dog kennel, but like a wild beast's cage, almost overpowering us in the room upstairs. I have no sleep all night from insects of prey; but this was a slight evil. The misery is increased from the custom of having the stable on the ground floor and the kitchen on the first. The dwelling is on the second floor. Yet it is pleasing to discern a better seeming class amid the misery; even at Alcamo there was tidy clean-looking women, and outside the towns much washing was going on. A great number of the Sicilians and Calabrians we have seen are a striking and bright-looking race – regular features and very intelligent. Sparkling eyes, brownish skins, and red healthy-looking cheeks. At Amalfi yesterday we were quite delighted with them.

The state of the Church is deplorable. It seems as if Satan was let out of prison to range the whole earth again. As far as our little experience goes, everything seems to confirm the notion received among ourselves of the priesthood, while on the other hand the Church is stripped of its temporalities and reduced to distress. The churches at Messina and Palermo are superb, and there is a fine church at Monreale, which is the see of the primate (there are perhaps, ten sees in the island). It is worth £10,000 a year, but the present Bishop compounds with the government for £2,000. I think I heard that originally the Sicilian Church was expected to support the poor, but that the Bishops compounded for this by giving a certain sum to Government, which is now spent in paying Government pensions. We have just heard of the Irish Church Reform Bill. Well done! my blind Premier, confiscate and rob, till, like Samson, you pull down the Political Structure on your own head! At Naples the poverty of the church is deplorable. All its property, we are told, is lost. The grandfather of the present King, the Lazzaroni king, began the confiscation; the French completed it. Thus these countries have the evils of Protestantism without its advantages – that is Anglican Protestantism; for there are no advantages here whether in schism like Dissent, or Socinianism such as Geneva's. But here, too, they have infidelity and profaneness, as if the whole world (Western) were tending towards some dreadful crisis. I begin to hope that England after all is to be the 'Land of Saints' in this dark hour, and her

Church the salt of the earth. We met in the steamer an American who was a pompous man, and yet we contracted a kind of affection for him. He was an Episcopalian, and had better principles far than one commonly meets with in England, and a docile mind. We are quite sorry to have lost sight of him. Is the American Church to serve any purpose in the Divine scheme? I begin to enquire whether the Revelations do not relate to the European world only, or Roman Empire, so that as ages of time[7] may be summed up in the first verses of Genesis, and the history commences only with the creation of man, so the prophecy may end with the history of Christianity in the Roman empire, and its fortunes in America or China may be summed up obscurely in a few concluding sentences; if so one would almost expect some fresh prophecy to be given when the end of the European period comes. I should add we afterwards found out that our good friend belonged to the Wesleyan Episcopalians. To return, doubtless there are God's saints here, and perhaps brighter ones than with us. We heard of one man – at Messina, I think – who, while bearing his witness against the profligacy of the priesthood, rigidly attends Mass, and, on being asked why, answered that the altar is above the priest, and that God can bless his own ordinances, in spite of the instruments being base. This seems very fine, but the majority of the laity who think, run into infidelity. The priests have lost influence exceedingly since the peace. The French Revolution and empire seem to have generated a plague, which is slowly working its way everywhere. At Malta, we heard the same, and at Corfu. [I:351].

To J.F. Christie [7 March 1833]

[…] It seems quite a hopeless task to civilise the Morea – otherwise *i.e.* than by exterminating vast numbers of the inhabitants. We were told by travellers who had lately travelled through it that there is certainly a better sort of persons, and that the present anarchy is rather owing to the ascendancy of the worst spirits than to the character of the people. But even allowing this, how can you alter the inveterate habit which the better class have got of *succumbing* to the most violent? Nothing but great craft or great tyranny will be able to manage them. It is curious that with all their brutality these fellows observe most strictly the fast of the Church, which may be

---

7   The new sciences of Geology and Palaeontology were already rendering obsolete a literal interpretation of the first chapters of Genesis. Newman may have considered himself to be doctrinally 'anti-liberal' but clearly this did not necessarily mean he was theologically conservative.

called the distinguishing feature of the Greek Communion, as Masses &c., are of the Latin, and they both answer the same purpose, and are a substitute apparently for moral obedience and an opiate to the conscience. [...] [I:368].

[...] Well then, again, after this, you have to view Rome as a place of religion; and here what mingled feelings come upon one – you are in the place of martyrdom and burial of apostles and saints; you have about you the buildings and the sights they saw, and you are in a city to which England owes the blessing of the Gospel. But then, on the other hand, the superstitions, or rather, what is far worse, the solemn reception of them as an essential part of Christianity. But then, again, the extreme beauty and costliness of the churches; and then, on the contrary, the knowledge that the most famous was built (in part) on the sale of indulgences. Really this is a cruel place. There is more to be seen and thought of daily. It is a mine of all sorts of excellences. [...] [I:370].

To his sister Harriett [9 March 1833]

[...] Rome grows more wonderful every day. The first thought one has of the place is awful – that you see the great enemy of God – the Fourth Monarchy, the Beast dreadful and terrible. We need no Tower of Babel; the immense extent of the ruins; the purpose to which, when in their glory, they were dedicated; the arena where Ignatius suffered; the Jewish candlestick on the Arch of Titus; the columns, with the proud heathen inscriptions still visible, brand the place as the vile tool of God's wrath and Satan's malice.

Next, when you enter the museums, galleries and libraries, a fresh world is opened to you – that of imagination and taste. You find there collected the various creations of Greek genius. The rooms are interminable; and the marbles and mosaics astonishing for their costliness. The Apollo is quite unlike his casts. I never was moved by them at all, but at the first sight of the real statue I was subdued at once. I was not prepared for this at all. I had only been anxious to see it, and the celebrated pictures of Raphael. They are beyond praise: such expression! What struck me most was the strange simplicity of look which he has the gift to bestow on the faces.

As to the third view of Rome, here pain and pleasure go together, as is obvious. It is strange to be standing in the city of the Apostles, and among the tombs of the martyrs and saints. We have visited St Gregory's (the Great) Church. It is built on the site of his house; and an inscription at the entrance records the names of some of our early Bishops, including the monk Augustine, as proceeding from the convent attached to it. The

Roman clergy are said to be a decorous, orderly body, and certainly most things are very different from Naples. There are no trumpery ornaments or absurd inscriptions in the streets, profaning the most sacred subjects, and the look of the priests is superior. But there are (seemingly) timidity, indolence, and that secular spirit which creeps on established religion everywhere. It is said they got Mr Spencer quickly out of Rome because his fastings shames them,[8] and that no one thinks of fasting here – a curious contrast with the Greeks. The schools are neat and pleasant looking. One I saw yesterday, of orphan girls, was very interesting; but the choristers at St Peter's are as irreverent as at St Paul's. [...] [I:359].

To his sister Jemima [20 March 1833]

[...] We saw the Pope at St Peter's last Friday.

We are in good spirits about the prospects of the Church. We find Keble is at length roused, and if (at once up) he will prove a second St Ambrose; and others too are moving. So that wicked spoliation bill is already doing service; no thanks to it. We have encouraging accounts about Prussia from Mr Bunsen, who has received us very kindly. There is every reason for expecting that the Prussian Communion will be applying to us for ordination in no long time. We hear, also, much about Germany, in the way of painters! which leads us to hope that a high reverential spirit is stirring among them. And the Wilberforces tell us that the recently rejected ministers of Geneva are applying to England for Episcopal ordination. Further, our friend the Yankee, whom we fell in with again here, gave us so promising an account of the state of things in America, that we mean, when turned out of St Mary's, to go preaching through the churches of the United States!

As to poor Italy, it is mournful to think about it. Doubtless there are seven thousand in Israel. There are great appearances of piety in the churches, still, as a system, the corrupt religion – and it is very corrupt – must receive severe inflictions; and I fear I must look upon Rome as a city still under a curse, which will one day break out in more dreadful judgements than heretofore. Yet, doubtless, the Church will thereby be let loose from thraldom.

As to Greece, it does not teach Purgatory and the Mass – two chief practical delusions of Romanism. Its worst error is its Saint-worship, which is demoralising in the same sense Polytheism was; but this is not the Church's

---

8 When the letters were published, Newman added in brackets at this point: 'This is nonsense.'

act (though it sanctions it in fact), but the people's corruption of what is good – the honour due to Saints; whereas the doctrines of the Mass and Purgatory are not perversions, but inventions. [...] [I:376].

To his mother [5 April 1833]

[...] As to the *Roman* Catholic system, I have ever detested it so much that I cannot detest it more by seeing it; but to the Catholic system I am more attached than ever, and quite love the little monks[9] of Rome; they look so innocent and bright, poor boys! and we have fallen in, more or less, with a number of interesting Irish and English priests. I regret that we could form no intimate acquaintance with them. I fear there are very grave and far-spreading scandals among the Italian priesthood, and there is mummery in abundance; yet there is a deep substratum of true Christianity; and I think they may be as near truth at the least as that Mr B., whom I like less and less every day. [I:378].

To F. Rogers [5 June 1833]

[...] From my return to Catania I sickened. When the idea of illness first came upon me I do not know, but I was obliged on 1 May to lie down for some time when I had got half through my day's journey; and the next morning I could not proceed. This was at Leonforte, above one hundred miles from Palermo. Three days I remained at the inn there with the fever increasing, and no medical aid. On the night of the third day I had a strange (but providential) notion that I was quite well. So on the next morning I ordered the mules, and set off towards Girgenti, my destination. I had not gone far when a distressing choking feeling (constriction?) of the throat and chest came on; and at the end of seven miles I lay down exhausted in a cabin near the road. Here, as I lay on the ground, after a time, I felt a hand at my pulse; it was a medical man who by chance was at hand, and he prescribed for me, and enabled me by evening to get to Castro Giovanni (the ancient Enna). At first I had difficulty in getting a lodging – had it been known I had the fever I suppose it would have been impossible, for numbers were dying of it there, at Girgenti, and, I believe, everywhere. However, at last I got most comfortably housed. I did not know then what was the matter with me, I believe, but at Leonforte I had thought myself so bad that I gave my servant directions how to convey news of my death (should it be so) to England, at the same time expressing to him a clear and

---

9   The seminarians.

confident conviction that I should *not* die. The reason I gave was that I thought God had work for me. I do not think there was anything wrong in this, on consideration. [...] [I:407].

To Rev. J. Keble [5 August 1833]

[...] Froude wishes to break with Rose, which must not be, I think. Let us wait the course of events. Rose is hoping for a reaction: till we clearly see it to be impossible, there is no reason we should talk of the repeal of the *Praemunire* – to say nothing of people not being prepared for it – and yet we may protest against measures we think unchristian. Rose has a notion of a Synod, lay and clerical, and to get it as an exchange for the Church rate being put on us, which he thinks inevitable. Is it lawful to compound in this way?

Do you think we should act in concert, as nearly in the way of a Society as possible? *i.e.* to take measure for the circulation of tracts, pamphlets, &c., and to write systematically to stir up our friends? Would it be acceptable to the Archbishop to know the feelings of people as to his speech on the second reading? Do you not think we could get many signatures under the heading of, 'We, the undersigned members of the University of Oxford'? [...]

Do you know enough of the ecclesiastical law to decide what the clergy of Waterford should do? If you can show that they ought not to obey a Bishop of Cashel, ought we not to do our part in stirring them up, or in stirring up the Bishops to consecrate a Bishop of Waterford?

[...] As to your proposal about the Discipline question, unless it turns out to be very formidable, I should like to do it. I do not know Bishop Jebb's arguments, but it seems so open to common sense that a Church must have discipline (else, might a figure exist without outline) that it seems as if our business was rather to accustom the *imagination* of men to the notion than to convince their reason.

I fear they did not get on very well at Hadleigh. Froude wants you to give your friend Arthur Perceval a bit of advice, which I think Froude himself partly requires. We shall lose all our influence when times are worse, if we are prematurely violent. I heartily wish things may keep quiet for a year or two, that we may ascertain our position, get up precedents, and know our duty. Palmer thinks both Froude and Perceval very deficient in learning, and therefore rash.

I do not think we have yet made as much as we ought of our situation at Oxford, and of the deference paid to it through the country. Are not many eyes looking towards us everywhere, not as 'masters and scholars', but as residents, so that all our acts, as coming from the University, might have the authority of a vote of Convocation almost, in such cases as when Convocation cannot be expected to speak out? Now no party is likely to be active in Oxford but ourselves, so the field is before us. Do let us agree on some plan as to writing letters to our friends, just as if we were canvassing. Now, if I could say that other persons agreed with me in thinking it desirable to say and do all in our power to stir up the Church, and if I knew the points of agreement – *i.e.* if we were to settle on some uniform plan of talking as to principles, &c., – then I would not mind writing, as in an election, canvassing, to men I knew very little of. Pray think of this, and send me a sketch of principles – e.g. that by the Irish Bill the Church's liberties are invaded, &c. And should we not aim as getting up petitions next year to the King? [...] What do you think of preaching about the state of things? Of course no one should do so who is not conscious to himself that he is free from excitement, nay sick of all the nasty bustle [...]. If we leave our flocks in ignorance [...] will they not be surprised at a call to follow us *from* the Establishment, should it come to that? [I:439].

To J.W. Bowden [31 August 1833]

[...] As to the state of the Church, I suppose it was in a far worse condition in Arian times, except in the one point you mention – that there was the *possibility* of true minded-men becoming Bishops, which is now almost out of the question. If we had *one* Athanasius or Basil, we could bear with twenty Eusebius's, though Eusebius was not at all the worst of the bad. The scandals of Arian times are far worse than any now. I wish the Archbishop had somewhat of the boldness of the old Catholic prelates; no one can doubt he is a man of the highest principle, and would willingly die a martyr, but if he had but the little finger of Athanasius, he would do us all the good in the world. Things have come to a pretty pass when one must not speak as a Christian minister, for fear of pulling down the house over our heads. [...]

[...] We do not like our names to be known, but we hope the plan will succeed. We have already got assistants in five or six counties. Our objects are 'to arouse the clergy, to inculcate the Apostolical Succession, and to defend the Liturgy'. We hope to publish tracts &c.

[...] But one gains nothing by sitting still. I am sure the Apostles did not sit still: and agitation is the order of the day. I do not at all fear for the result, were we thrown on the people, though for a while many of us would be distressed *in re pecunaria* – not that I would advocate a separation of Church and State unless the nation does more tyrannical things against us; but I do feel I should be glad if it were done and over, much as the nation would lose by it; for I fear the Church is being corrupted by the union. [I:448].

To J. Keble [November 1833]

I have heard so much criticism on my Tracts that it is comfortable to have heard one or two things of a more pleasant kind: [...] The principle thing I fear is their being neglected, but if Bishops prick up their ears and D.D.s and poetry professors encourage, I care for nothing more. As to my anxiety for many tracts, it is simply on this account, because there are various classes to be addressed. We have scarcely any for the poor, and not many for the clergy, or (again) the middle classes.

Besides, *one improves by writing*: one hits off the thing better, and, at least, one offers a selection of styles to the reader, and tastes differ so that this is no slight advantage. [...]

It must be recollected, too, that it is quite necessary to go into more detail; our present Tracts are vague and general, and too much in the way of *hints*, as you yourself observed. We have heard, on good authority from London, that the Marriage Service is to be altered to please Dissenters. What this means I know not, but it is quite certain *you* must forthwith write a tract on that subject. [I:474].

To R.H. Froude [7 November 1833]

I miss you very much. You will be glad to hear that your article on *Praemunire*,[10] &c., has done much good. Palmer brought word from town that you had effectually stopped the probability of certain promotions; in fact, that the Archbishop would be *afraid* to consecrate obnoxious persons; and at least you have given him a good pretence for refusing, as it was *known* that there was a party in the Church, 'and they not weak in talent',[11] &c., who would go all lengths rather than submit to State tyranny. [...] [I:476].

---

10 The Statutes of Praemunire of 1353, 1365 and 1393 were designed to safeguard the rights of the crown against encroachment by the Pope. Henry VIII, Elizabeth I and James I used the penalties prescribed by the Statutes to cower the clergy. The Statutes were repealed by the Criminal Law Act of 1967.
11 Newman is quoting a phrase of Rose's in the *British Magazine*.

To F. Rogers [19 December 1833]

Newman was about to publish the first volume of his sermons.

[...] As to Mssrs. Rivington and your diplomacy, to which I return, on consideration I think I return to the octavo form; the duodecimo form is used, I believe, for the sake of reading in the pulpit. Now I have no wish to be spouted over the kingdom. That 1,000 (octavo) is equivalent to buying the copyright, antecedently speaking, I grant; but so with these very sermons, perhaps, in the first edition 12mo. I suspect no volume of sermons (generally speaking) goes beyond the first edition. If they used to do, yet Tyler's series have created a glut in the market now. I do not expect mine will, and therefore think it more respectable, as it is also more lucrative, to publish in octavo. If unexpectedly my sermons take, as something out of the way, then there would be a second edition, whether of octavo or duodecimo. [...] I may not have expressed my meaning clearly, yet I think I have a meaning. ... [II:9].

To J.W. Bowden [4 January 1834]

There is a *chance* of my being elected Professor of Moral Philosophy. I have no special wish for it. It would oblige me to take up a line of reading somewhat out of my present course; yet it might be the means of giving me influence with the undergraduate, and there is no situation which combines respectability with lightness of responsibility and labour so happily as the office of a professor. [...] [II:16].

To J.W. Bowden [14 March 1834]

I am floored as to the professorship. I heard of no other candidate till the day before, *i.e.* this day week, when the Principal of St Mary Hall[12] was named, and has succeeded. [...]

The Duke has begun his campaign by advising us strenuously to resist the London University granting degrees in arts and divinity, and there is to be a convocation next week about it. Indeed, it does seem a little too bad that the Dissenters are *to take our titles*. Why should they call themselves M.A. except to seem like us? Why not call themselves Licentiates,

---

12 Namely, Renn Dickson Hampden (1793–1868), a 'Broad Churchman'. His 1832 Bampton Lectures reduced the dogmatic factor in Christian theology and angered Newman. In 1836, the Tractarians attempted unsuccessfully to prevent his becoming Regius Professor of Divinity. In 1847, he became Bishop of Hereford.

&c.? And what is to hinder the Bishops being bullied into putting up with a London M.A.? Certainly they would soon. [...] [II:28].

To Rev. R.F. Wilson. [15 June 1834].

That Newman was a sensitive pastor is clear from the following letter.

You must not be at all surprised or put out at feeling the difficulties you describe. It is the lot of all men who are by themselves, on first engaging on parochial duty, especially of those who are of an anxious turn of mind. I felt so much of it on starting that I should compassionate you very much unless I recollected that after a while the prospect before me cleared, as doubtless it will with you, through God's mercy. It certainly is very distressing to have to trust one's own judgement on such important matters, and the despondency resulting is made still more painful by the number of little, unimportant matters which must be decided one way or other, though without any good reason to guide the decision, and which in consequence are very fidgetting. You will not get over all this at once; yet in time all will be easy, in spite of whatever you may have to urge about your own disposition.

So much then generally, though you tell me not to speak in that way. Then as to your coldness which you complain of, I am sorry I can give no *recipe* here. I can only say that I have much to lament in that way myself; that I am continually very cold and unimpressed, and very painful it is, but what can be done? Would we could so command our minds as to make them feel as they ought! But it is their very disease that they are not suitably affected according to the intrinsic value of the objects presented to them; that they are excited by objects of this world, not by the realities of death and judgement, and the mercies of the Gospel. Meanwhile, it is our plain *duty* to speak, to explain and to pray, even while we find ourselves cold, and, please God, while we thus do what is a plain duty, perchance He may visit us and impress us with the realities of the subjects we are speaking upon. Certain it is (looking at things merely humanly) the oftener you go to a sick person, the more you are likely at last to get interested in him. How can you expect to feel anything the first or second time, when you as yet know nothing of his state? Interest will grow upon you, as you ascertain his state of mind. It is an irrational despondency and an impatience to complain because nothing comes of your first visit. Be sure also that what he is to get from you is not communicated all at once – nay, not in words. What he will first gain will be the sight of your earnestness ... and will thence be impressed with the reality of that which makes you earnest, your coming day by day to him, sacrificing your own ease &c. ... [II:45].

To R.H. Froude [15 June 1834].

[...] I could tell you much, only it is renewing sorrows and nothing else, of the plague the Tracts have been to us, and how we have removed them to Rivington's. That the said Tracts have been of essential benefit it is impossible to doubt. Pamphlets, sermons, &c., on the Apostolic Succession are appearing in every part of the kingdom; and every other Sunday we have a University sermon on the subject ...

H. Wilberfore engaged to marry Miss S. last December – was afraid to tell me, and left Oxford without; spread abroad I had cut R. for marrying. Yet he has not ratted, and will not (so be it). Marriage, when a crime, is a crime which it is criminal to repent of. [...] [II:47].

To R.H. Froude [21 June 1834]

[...] Meanwhile let *us* read, and prepare ourselves for better things. I am sitting in the Bodleian, collating manuscripts of Dionysius, &c., and intend to be happy. I reflect with some pleasure that some of our most learned men lived and acted in most troublous times, as Usher, Hammond, Taylor, and in primitive times Clement of Alexandria, Dionysius, and Origen. Surely our intervals of repose (so be it) will be many, and give room for reading and thinking. [...]

The Bishop of Lincoln has, in a letter to Rose, criticised my account of the *Disciplina Arcani*; and he thinks lightly of my learning, which truly *is* little enough, but yet, I think, enough for my purpose, and far more than he thinks. Because I have given conclusions without noticing objections, and their answers, he thinks me ignorant of the existence of the objections. [...]

It is now a year since I have been anxious to begin a weekly celebration of the Lord's Supper, but as yet I have not moved a step. I think I shall begin with Saints' days first. What I *have* done is to have a Wednesday evening's service, beginning in April with the long days, which is followed by a lecture extempore on the Creed. Next year I may take some lives – Hooker, Ridley, Bull, &c. I am quite fluent, although I never shall be eloquent. I at first drew above a hundred, chiefly University men, though they fell off. Further, I think I mean on St Peter's day, *i.e.* next Sunday, to announce my intention of reading the morning service daily in the chancel while and whenever I am in Oxford, *according* to the injunctions of the Church, whether people attend or not. I shall have a desk put up near the altar, facing south, from which I shall read the Psalms and Lessons, keeling, however, towards the east. It seems to me that the absurdity, as it appears to many, of Tom Keble's daily plan is, his praying to *empty benches.*

Put yourself near the altar and you may be solitary. I see that this agrees with a notion of yours. [...] [II:48].

To his mother [8 July 1834]

You will like to hear what I have to say.[13] Till the last hour[14] I have felt to be one man against a multitude. No one, apparently, to encourage me, and so many black averted faces, that unless from my youth I had been schooled to fall back upon myself, I should have been quite out of heart. I went and sat twenty minutes with Mrs Small[15] by way of consolation. [...] [II:55].

To J.W. Bowden [13 July 1834]

Perhaps you have seen in the papers the Jubber affair. The only thing that annoyed me was that I was represented to have spoken rudely, which was not the case. As to refusing marriage to unbaptised persons, we must make a stand *somewhere*. Things are rolling downhill so gradually that, wherever one makes a stand, it will be said to be a harsh measure. But I am determined (please God) that, as far as I am concerned, the Church shall not crumble away without my doing in my place what I can to hinder it. I had had a long conversation with this man before on the subject of his daughter's baptism; I did not *seek out* the case, and it was a new one at St Mary's. I had no time to refer to the Bishop. I never can be sorry for what I have done; nothing can make me sorry, though existing Church authorities should declare against me. [...] [II:56.]

To A.P. Perceval [20 July 1834]

As to the Tracts, everyone has his own taste. You object to some things, another to others. If we altered to please every one the effect would be spoiled. They were not intended as symbols *ex cathedra*, but as expressions of *individual* minds, and individuals feeling strongly; while, on the one hand, they are incidentally faulty in mode or language, on the other they are still peculiarly effective. No great work was ever done by a system, whereas systems arise out of individual exertions. Luther was an individual.

---

13 The reference is to the 'Jubber Matter'. Newman, always decisive and consistent on matters of principle, had refused to marry a couple because the woman concerned, a Dissenter, had not been baptised.
14 The post had brought supporting letters from Pusey and Keble.
15 Mrs Small was the old schoolmistress at the Littlemore Dame School.

The very faults of an individual excite attention; he loses, but his cause, if good, and he powerful-minded, gains. This is the way of things; we promote truth by self-sacrifice. [...] [II:57].

To S. Rickards [30 July 1834]

Thank you for a sight of Lady W.'s letter. Since you have let me see her opinion of me, I suppose the best return I can make is to let you know my opinion of her. And I am led first of all to express my thanks at her benevolent intention of having me shown up in some Review or other, which is not the less benevolent because it is impracticable in *the way* she wishes. I mean it would be easy to get some party or professedly eclectic Review to lash me, but that would not answer her purpose. On the other hand, a Church Review, such as the 'British Critic', though it might not agree with me, would know enough of Church theology to find it was a very difficult thing to convict me of running counter to the great stream of our divines. [...]

She knows (apparently) nothing of the Church of England *as such*. She jumbles *us* with what she calls 'Protestants', and thinks it sufficient to prove that so-and-so is not the 'Protestant' doctrine. Now I should frighten good people if I were to say I disown the word 'Protestant', yet in the sense she uses it I do disown it. I protest as much against Calvin as against the Council of Trent, whereas Protestant in her sense is a crooked stick, bent on one side. The word Protestant does not, as far as I know, occur in our formularies. It is an uncomfortable, perplexing word, intended to connect us – and actually connecting us – with the Protestants abroad. We are a 'Reformed' Church, not a 'Protestant'. I care not a whit for the Diet of Augsburg. Calvin is no guide to me, not even as an authority, and as for Bucer I wish he had never crossed the sea. [...] [II:58].

To his sister Jemima [2 October 1834]

I dined with the Dean yesterday, who is a kind unassuming man ... He has no *views*, and in consequence is like a ship without a rudder. Since I have been away I have read Butler's *Book of the Roman Catholic Church*, Marsh's *Comparative View*, and Faber's *Romanism* almost, and have more of a view. To *become* a Romanist seems more and more impossible; to unite with Rome (if she would let us) not impossible; but she would not, without ceasing to be Rome. Somehow my own confidence in my views seems to grow. I am aware I have not yet fully developed them to myself. There are opinions as yet unknown to me, which must be brought out and received; inconsistencies, too, perhaps to be set right; but, on the whole, I seem to have a grasp of a system, very comprehensive. I could go on a great way with Rome, and a great way with the Evangelicals; nay, I should not despair of religious Dissenters. [...] [II:66].

To Archbishop Whately [28 October 1834]

Whately, who had become Archbishop of Dublin, had written to ask if there was any truth in the rumour that Newman had absented himself from chapel 'on purpose to avoid receiving the communion along with me'.

My dear Lord, – My absence from the Sacrament [...] was occasioned solely and altogether by my having it on that day in St Mary's; and I am pretty sure, if I may trust my memory, that I did not know of your Grace's presence there till after the service. Most certainly such knowledge would not have affected my attendance. I need not say, that this being the case, that the report of my having made any statement on the subject is quite unfounded; indeed, your letter of this morning is the first information I have had in any shape of the existence of the report.

I am happy in being thus able to afford an explanation as satisfactory to you as the kind feelings which you have ever entertained towards me could desire; yet on honest reflection I cannot conceal from myself that it was generally a relief[16] to me to see so little of your Grace when you were in Oxford, and it is a greater relief now to have an opportunity of saying so to yourself. I have ever wished to observe the rule, never to make a public charge against another behind his back; and though in the course of conversation and the urgency of accidental occurrence it is sometimes difficult to keep it, yet I trust I have not broken it, especially in your case, *i.e.* though my most intimate friends know how deeply I deplore the line of ecclesiastical policy adopted under your archiepiscopal sanction, and though in society I may have clearly shown that I have an opinion one way rather than the other, yet I have never in my intention – never, as I believe, at all spoken of your Grace in a serious way before strangers; indeed mixing little in general society and not over-apt to open myself in it, I have little temptation to do so. Least of all should I so forget myself as to take undergraduates into my confidence in such a matter.

I wish I could convey to your Grace the mixed and very painful feelings which the late history of the Irish Church has raised in me – the union

---

16 Here and in the next letter Newman exhibits something of his gift for irony and acerbic surprise. It was part of his struggle for holiness to keep his capacity for a cruel wit strictly under control.

of her members with men of heterodox views, and the extinction (without ecclesiastical sanction) of half her candlesticks[17] [...] I willingly own that, both in my secret judgement and my mode of speaking concerning you to my friends, I have had great alternations and changes of feeling – defending, then blaming, your policy, next praising yourself and protesting against your measures, according as the affectionate remembrances which I had of you, rose against my utter aversion of the secular and unbelieving policy in which I consider the Irish Church to be implicated. [...]

May I be suffered to add that your name is ever mentioned in my prayers, and to subscribe myself, your Grace's very sincere friend and servant, [II:69].

To Dr Hampden [28 November 1834]

Newman wrote: 'This letter was the beginning of hostilities in the University.' The pamphlet in question was Hampden's application of his Bampton Lectures to the question of Subscription[18] in Oxford.

The kindness which has led to your presenting me with your pamphlet encourages me to hope that you will forgive me, if I take the opportunity it affords to express to you my very sincere and deep regret that it has been published. [...]

While I respect the tone of piety in which the pamphlet is written, I feel an aversion to the principles it professes, as (in my opinion) legitimately tending to formal Socinianism.[19]

And I also lament that, by its appearance, the first step has been taken towards an interruption of that peace and mutual good understanding which has prevailed so long in this place; and which, if ever seriously disturbed, will be succeeded by dissensions the more intractable, because justified in the minds of those who resist innovations, by a feeling of imperative duty. [II:77].

To R.H. Froude [22 June 1835]

I want your view of the extent of power which may be given to the laity in the Church system, e.g. the maintenance of the Faith is their clear

---

17 The image (from Revelation 2:5) refers to the abolition of two Archdioceses and a reduction in Bishoprics from 18 to 10, by the passing of the Irish Church Temporalities Act passed on August 14, 1833.
18 Before they could matriculate, Oxford undergraduates were obliged to subscribe to the Thirty-Nine Articles of the Church of England.
19 Socinianism is what would nowadays be known as Unitarianism.

prerogative. Qu: What power may they have in Synods? Judicially? In legislation? &c. I have heard from Acland (11 June), and he wants to know whether Churchmen might not admit (what the Liberals are bent on) a subsidiary system of education to the Church system for Dissenters. To answer abstractly, I think they might; but I doubt not irreconcilable differences would arise in the detail. The Church must not reconcile itself to it, yet must claim to have control over it.

Think of this, please, and answer me; and do not say 'the whole system is rotten', and so dismiss the subject. We must take things as they are, and make the most of them. Acland wants to be allowed to acknowledge a system 'inferior, secondary, partial, local, temporary; the State saying that education *ought* to be based on Religion, and Religion on the Church; that this is what alone it considers to be National Education; but that it is willing to give some assistance to a secondary system in the hope of giving it *a good direction.*' And then follows the question which has especially led me to mention the subject to you. Would you attempt a sort of Scripture School, which, without actively opposing the Church, should endeavour to teach children on the foundation of the Bible without inculcating the peculiarities of the Church, as it is distinguished from those bodies which do not on the one hand deny its creeds (the Socinians) or deny that it is a Church at all (the Romanists), e.g. Kildare Street?

I was taken with the influenza and could not finish this. On second thoughts I gave up all Acland's plan as a mare's nest, and wrote him word so. At the same time I should like your opinion whether there is any way in which, under colour of giving a pure Scripture education, we might yet inculcate our notions. The difficulty is this – *are* our notions so on the surface of Scripture that a plain person ought to see them there, at least when suggested to him? Or, again, *how far* is the unpopularity of our notions among readers of Scripture, to be traced to Protestant blindness and prejudice? [II:110].

To his mother [31 July 1835]

[...] yesterday a person made his appearance as an avant-courier of Dr Wiseman of Rome, who is to be here for some weeks. He is a Mr Maguire, a Roman Catholic priest. He dined with us and had a good deal of conversation.

[...] I shall have above fifteen candidates for Confirmation, some very interesting ones. When I am employed in that sort of work, I always feel how I should like a parish with nothing but pastoral duties. One great advantage of a large parish is that *one can do nothing else.* Nothing is so hampering to the mind as *two* occupations; this is what I have found both at St Clement's and when I was Tutor at Oriel. As it is, my parish is not enough to employ me, so I necessarily make to myself two occupations – which, though necessary, is to me distracting. Some people can work better for a division of duties. Some persons cannot attend to one thing for more than two hours without a headache. I confess for myself I never do anything so well as when I have nothing else to do. I would joyfully give myself to read or again to a parish. However, as to a large parish, there seems to me in the present state of things two special drawbacks: one, the amount of mere secular business laid on a clergyman, attendance at vestries, &c.; the other, that really at the present day we are all so ignorant of our duties, that I should be actually afraid myself, without a great deal more learning, to undertake an extensive charge. I find daily from reading the Fathers how ignorant we are in matters of practice. E.g. I mean the kind of mistakes, though not so flagrant, of the poor fellow who re-baptised a whole set of Dissenters. Hooker does a great deal for one, but even to master Hooker is no slight work. I do really fear that, for the want of knowing what is right and what is wrong, the best intentioned people are making the most serious and mischievous mistakes. [...] [II:118].

To F. Rogers [30 August 1835]

[...] We are expecting Dr Wiseman now, as his avant-courier said he would come when September began. The said courier was a Mr Maguire, a Roman Catholic priest of the College of St Edmund's, near Ware ... He would not allow that Dr Wiseman was desirous Sir R. Peel should remain in power, which is what some one told me. [...] I can fancy we shall be honoured with the peculiar hatred of these people, if we are ever in a condition to show fight. I see in him the very same spirit I saw in Dr Wiseman, the spirit of the cruel Church. I believe he would willingly anni-hilate the English Church. [...] [II:131].

To his sister Harriett [10 October 1835]

[...] Rationalism is the attempt to know *how* things are about which you can know nothing. When we give reasons for alleged facts and reduce them into dependence on each other, we feel a satisfaction which is wanting when we receive them as isolated and unaccountable, *i.e.* a satis-faction of the *reason*. On the other hand, when they stand unaccounted for, they impart a satisfaction of their own kind – namely, of the *imagina-tion*. When we ask for reasons when we should not, we *rationalise*. When we detach and isolate things which we should connect, we are superstitious. [II:137].

To J.W. Bowden [10 October 1835]

I am quite decided that I cannot be editor of the Tracts if they come out once a month, nor would I recommend any one else to be. It is the way to make them mere trash. One is pressed for time, and writes for the occasion stopgaps. I am conscious that there are some stopgaps in the Tracts already ... We shall be losing credit and influence if we so go on. As I was strongly for short tracts on beginning, so am I for longer now. We must have much more treatises than sketches. As to how often [...] I have no view at present; but I foretell ruin to the cause if the Tracts go on by monthly driblets ... [II:137].

To his sister Jemima [21 February 1836]

[...] Thank also my mother and Harriett for their congratulations upon this day.[20] They will be deserved if God gives me grace to fulfil the purpose for which He has led me on hitherto in a wonderful way. I think I am conscious to myself that, whatever are my faults, I wish to live and die to His glory – to surrender wholly to Him as His instrument, to whatever work and at whatever personal sacrifice, though I cannot duly realise my own words when I say so. He is teaching me, it would seem, to depend on Him only; for, as perhaps Rogers told you, I am soon to lose dear Froude – which, looking forward to the next twenty-five years of my life, and its probable occupations, is the greatest loss I could have. I shall be truly widowed, yet I hope to bear it lightly. [II:170].

To J.W. Bowden [2 March 1836][21]

Yesterday morning brought me news of Froude's death; and if I could collect my thoughts at this moment, I would say something to you about

---

20 It was Newman's thirty-fifth birthday.
21 Later, Newman wrote, 'March 1836 is a cardinal point of time. It gathers about it, more or less closely, the following events: 1. Froude's death. 2. My mother's death [17 May] and my sister's marriage [28 April to John Mozley]. 3. My knowing and using the Breviary. 4. First connection with the *British Critic*. 5. The tracts become treatises. 6. Start of the "Library of the Fathers". 7. Theological Society. 8. My writing against the Church of Rome. 9. Littlemore Chapel.'

him, but I scarcely can. He has been so very dear to me, that it is an effort to me to reflect on my own thoughts about him. I can never have a greater loss, looking on for the whole of my life; for he was to me, and he was likely to be ever, in the same degree of continual familiarity which I enjoyed with yourself in our Undergraduate days; so much so that I was from time to time confusing him with you, and only calling him by his right name and recollecting what belonged to him, and what to you, by an act of memory.

[…] It is very mysterious that anyone so remarkably and variously gifted, and with talents so fitted for these times, should be removed. I never on the whole, fell in with so gifted a person. In variety and perfection of gifts I think he far exceeded even Keble. For myself, I cannot describe what I owe to him as regards the intellectual principles of religion and morals. It is useless to go on to speak of him, yet it has pleased God to take him, in mercy to him, but by a very heavy visitation to all who were intimate with him. Yet everything was so bright and beautiful about him, that to think of him must always be a comfort. The sad feeling I have is, that one cannot retain in one's memory all one wishes to keep there, and that, as year passes after year, the image of him will be fainter and fainter. [II:174].

To J. Keble [18 April 1836]

[…] I hope you will not forget your promise of a volume of sermons. I put it on this simple ground. *We are raising a demand for a certain article, and we must furnish a supply.* Men are curious after Apostolic principles, and we must not let the season slip. The seizing opportunities [*sic*] is the beginning, middle, and end of success; or rather (to put it higher) it is the way in which we co-operate with the providential course of things. […] [II:191].

To Mrs John Mozley [19 January 1837]

[…] Tell Miss M. that I must decline the place in her poetical collection. I never can write except in a season of idleness. When I have been doing nothing awhile, poems spring us as weeds in fallow fields.

I have been reading *Emma*. Everything Miss Austen writes is clever, but I desiderate something. There is a want of *body* to the story. The action is frittered away in over-little things. There are some beautiful things in it. Emma herself is the most interesting to me of all her heroines. I feel kind to her whenever I think of her. But Miss Austen has no romance – none at all. What vile creatures her parsons are! She has not a dream of the high

Catholic ἦθος. That other woman, Fairfax is a dolt – but I like Emma.

I have nearly finished Southey's *Wesley* which is a very superficial concern indeed: interesting of course. He does not treat it historically in its connection with the age, and he cannot treat it theologically, if he would [...]. I do not like Wesley – putting aside his exceeding self-confidence, he seems to me to have a very black self-will, a bitterness of religious passion, which is very unamiable. Whitfield seems far better. [II:223].

To Mrs Thomas Mozley [3 May 1837]

I began weekly communion at Easter, and have found the church very well attended. I have it at seven in the morning. Last Sunday I had thirty-six communicants. [...] [II:231].

To F. Rogers [1 June 1837]

[...] If it is to turn out as you forbode, it is only a fresh instance of what I suppose one must make up one's mind to think, that those who are early taken away are the fittest to be taken, and that it is a privilege so to be taken, and they are in their proper place when taken. Surely God would not separate us from such, except it were best both for them and for us, and that those who are taken away are such as are most acceptable to Him seems proved by what we see; for scarcely do you hear of some special instance of religious excellence, but you have also cause of apprehension how long such a one is to continue here. I suppose one ought to take it as the rule. We pray daily 'Thy kingdom come' – if we understand our words, we mean it as a privilege to leave the world, and we must not wonder that God grants the privilege to some of those who pray for it. It would be rather wonderful if He did not. When we use the Lord's prayer, we pray not only for our eventual regathering, but our dispersion in the interval. The more we live in the world that is not seen, the more shall we feel that the removal of friends into that unseen world is a bringing them near to us, not a separation. I really do not think this fancifulness. I think it attainable – just as our Saviour's going brought Him nearer, though invisibly, in the Spirit. [...] [II:232].

To J. Keble [27 August 1837]

Thank you for wishing me at the consecration, and I should have much liked it. I think I am very cold and reserved to people, but I cannot ever realise to myself that anyone loves me. I believe that is partly the reason, or I *dare* not realise it. [II:242].

To Mrs John Mozley [29 January 1838]

[...] My book on Justification has taken incredible time. I am quite worn out with the correcting. I do really think that every correction I make is for the better, and that I am not wasting time in an over-fastidious way, or even making it worse than it was; but I can only say this – openings for correction are inexhaustible.

I write, I write again: I write a third time in the course of six months. Then I take the third: I literally fill the paper with corrections, so that another person could not read it. I then write it out fair for the printer. I put it by; I take it up; I begin to correct again: it will not do. Alterations multiply, pages are rewritten, little lines sneak in and crawl about. The whole page is disfigured; I write again; I cannot count how many times this process is repeated. [...] [II:250].

To J.B. Mozley [2 August 1838]

As to your preaching distinctly, the art consists in not *dropping your words*, which is very difficult. I have not attained to it from want of strength. You must not glibly run over bits of sentences, but enunciate and enucleate every word.[22] [II:255].

To J. Keble [14 August 1838]

I am just come away from hearing the Bishop's Charge, and certainly I am disappointed in the part in which he spoke of us.

He said he must allude to a remarkable development, both in matters of discipline and of doctrine, in one part of his Diocese; that he had had many anonymous letters, charging us with Romanism; that he had made enquiries; that, as far as discipline went, he found nothing to find fault with – one addition of a clerical vestment there had been, but that had been discontinued; but this he would say, that in choice of alternatives, he would rather go back to what is obsolete, in order to enforce the Rubric, than break it in order to follow the motley fashions now prevailing. Next, as to doctrine, he had found many most excellent things in the *Tracts for the Times* (this was the only book he referred to), and most opportune and serviceable; but for some words and expressions he was sorry, as likely to lead *others* into error; he feared more for the disciples than for the masters,

---

22 This advice derives from the trouble Newman took in attempting to overcome the faults of his own delivery.

and he conjured those who were concerned in them to beware, lest, &c.

Now does it not seem rather hard that he should publicly attack things in the Tracts without speaking to me about them privately? Again, what good does it do to fling an indefinite suspicion over them, when in the main they be orthodox? Then again, it seems hard that those who work, and who while working necessarily commit mistakes, instead of being thanked for that work, which others do *not* do, are blamed. It is very comfortable to do nothing and to criticise. [II:257].

To J.W. Bowden [17 August 1838]

I delayed writing in order to give you an account of our Bishop's Charge, which an ear-witness told me was favourable by name to the *Tracts for the Times*. [...]

This is too strong a way of putting it, but my impression of it is this: it has *acted towards* our *objects* and at the same time given *us* a slap; which, by-the-bye, is what I have always predicted would be our fate. What he said was very slight indeed, but a Bishop's lightest word, *ex cathdra*, is heavy. The whole effect, too, was cold towards us, in this way: that he had had anonymous letters saying we were going into Romanism, that he had made enquiries of our way of conducting the service, &c., and *found* nothing. Thus it was negation: there was no praise. Then, as to the Tracts, he said that we were sincere, and that certain objects recommended in them, such as keeping Fast and Festival, were highly desirable; but [...]

Now here, as far as the Cause goes, is abundant gain. He spoke strongly in favour of observing the Rubric, of recurring to Antiquity, of Saints' days; and by implication he allowed of turning to the East, the πρόθεσις, &c.: but what has he done to *us*? Why we stand thus. [*sic*] How many times in a century is a book, and that principally the writing of a person in a Bishop's diocese, noticed in a Bishop's Charge? it is not usual. Next it is said by him to contain exceptionable expressions. Is it possible of any work in the world, of four thick volumes, should not? Certainly not. The *truth*, then, of the remark is not enough to account for what a Bishop says, unless it is *important* to say it. Nothing but important truths will enter into a Bishop's Charge; and since he has not said *what* the exceptionable things are, he has thrown a general suspicion over all the volumes.

Under these circumstances I felt that it was impossible for me to continue the Tracts, and wrote to Keble on the subject. He, without knowing my opinion, quite took the same view, stating it very strongly; and I feel, whatever the difference of opinion there may be about it, I cannot do otherwise. It would be against my feelings. Pusey is at

Weymouth, and knows nothing yet of what has happened; nor does anyone else; so do not talk of it to anyone. Accordingly I have written to the Archdeacon, not as archdeacon, but as a friend, to say that I propose to stop the Tracts and withdraw the existing ones from circulation; that this is very unpleasant to me; that the only way I can see to hinder it is, if I could learn privately from the Bishop any particular Tract he disapproves, which I would at once suppress [...]. Well, my dear Bowden, has not this come suddenly and taken away your breath? It nearly has mine. But I do not think I can be wrong, and I think good may come of it. It will be a considerable loss of money, I fear; and the fifth volume is nearly ready for publication, but I think the precedent will be very good; and it will make people see we are sincere and not ambitious. [...] [II:259].

To J. Keble [22 August 1838]

[...] The Archdeacon answered me that he had not seen the Charge before he heard it, that the Bishop had not consulted him, and he thought I had better think nothing of himself, and address the Bishop [...] I then wrote to the Bishop [...].

I received his answer yesterday morning. He begins by saying that he had been pained ever since he received my letter, not with me, because I had perfectly satisfied him in my own demeanour, &c., but at the idea of having pained me; and he entreated me to wait at least till the Charge was printed; that to withdraw the Tracts, at least at once, would be unfair to him, as making him seem to say more than he meant; that he had been forced to give judgement on account of anonymous letters and of other Bishops having spoken; that he had in his Charge approved very much of what we had done, censured nothing, only warned; that he considered that the opposite party had rather cause to complain he had gone so far; that my impression was not the general one; [...] Nothing could be kinder or more sympathetic than his letter.

It seems to me plain from it that he thought a great deal in the Tracts very good but would not commit himself in any way to them.[...] that he has not read them; that he goes by what he hears said; has seen extravagant persons &c., and (not thinking of our feelings at all, any more than if we were the very paper Tracts themselves) he propitiates the popular cry against us with a vague disapprobation, just as men revile Popery in order to say strong Catholic things. Of course this is *entre nous*, and I have expressed myself much more strongly than would be right, were I not putting you in possession of my thoughts with reference to forming a judgement. [...] I think he has not considered that a Bishop's word is an act, that I am under his jurisdiction, that he cannot criticise, but commands only.

I answered him last night that I would certainly wait till his Charge came out, that I had ever studied to please him in word and deed, and that no two persons agree on minor matters, in expediency, in opinion, or in expressions; that his ordinary silence as regards his clergy had been interpreted by me to mean that in such matters, whichever way his own judgement lay, he allowed such differences, but that I had ever felt that he could withdraw his permission, and that, when he spoke, his word was my rule; and that, as to the Tracts, they were a large work, and but a human production, and doubtless full of imperfections. I knew this anyhow, but his formal noticing the faults made them *important* [...]. [II:261].

To J. Keble [28 August 1838]

The Bishop, you will be glad to know, is very much pleased with my letter, and wishes that nothing should appear in his Charge[23] which may give any pain. [...] This is a great comfort, since [...] both Pusey and Bowden are annoyed. [...] Your quotation from Virgil brought tears into my eyes. No one has encouraged me but you. Pusey was so cast down when he heard it, that he himself needed comfort. I have no cough, thank you; it is always voluntary, proceeding not from my lungs but from weakness in my muscles of utterance. [II:265].

To J.W. Bowden [4 September 1838]

... To suffer my Bishop to breathe a word against me would be to put myself in a false position. Depend upon it our strength [...] is *consistency*. If we show we are not afraid of carrying out our principles [...] nothing can hurt us, and it seems the most likely way of obtaining a blessing. [...] I do not think I am out of the wood yet; for I do not see how the Bishop can materially alter his Charge or how I can bear any blow whatever. However, I am sanguine it will end well. [...] [II:265].

To F. Rogers [12 July 1839]

[...] Two things are very remarkable at Chalcedon – the great power of the Pope (as great as he claims now almost), and the marvellous inter-

---

23 Newman had heard confidentially that the Bishop wished to make 'any alterations in his Charge which may relieve me'.

ference of the civil power, as great almost as in our kings. Hence when Romanists accuse our Church of Erastianising, one can appeal to the Council, and when our own Erastians appeal to it, one can bring down on them a counter-appeal to prove the pope's power, as a *reductio ad absurdum* [...]. [II:284].

To F. Rogers [15 September 1839]

Your account of your priest is amusing. *Can* the R.C.s have any tender feelings towards Anglicanism? Who among us ever showed them any kindness? Are we not the pets of a State which has made it felony to celebrate Mass even (I believe) in private, a law which (Ward declares) remained in existence until 1780. [...]

You see, if things were to come to the worst, I should turn Brother of Charity in London – an object which, *quite* independently of any such perplexities, is growing on me, and, peradventure, will some day be accomplished, if other things do not impede me. [...] [II:285].

To F. Rogers [22 September 1839]

Since I wrote to you, I have had the first real hit from Romanism which has happened to me. R.W., who has been passing through, directed my attention to Dr Wiseman's article in the new *Dublin*. I must confess it has given me a stomach-ache. You see the whole history of the Monophysites has been a sort of alterative.[24] And now comes this dose at the end of it. It certainly does come upon one that we are not at the bottom of things. At this moment we have sprung a leak; and the worst of it is that those sharp fellows, Ward, Stanley, and Co. will not let one go to sleep upon it. [...] I have not said much to anyone.

I seriously think this is a most uncomfortable article [...] I think I shall get Keble to answer it. As to Pusey, I am curious to see how it works with him.

[...] It is no laughing matter. I will not blink the question, so be it; but you don't suppose I'm a madcap to take up notions suddenly – only there is an uncomfortable vista opened which was closed before. I am writing upon my first feelings. [II:286].

---

24 A medical term: something used as a cure, or to alleviate symptoms.

To F. Rogers [3 October 1839]

[...] Well then, once more: as those who sin after baptism cannot at once return to their full privileges, yet are not without hope, so a Church which has broken away from the centre of unity is not at liberty at once to return, yet is not nothing. May she not put herself into a state of penance? Are not her children best fulfilling their duty to her – not by leaving her, but by promoting her return, and not thinking they have a *right* to rush into such a higher state as communion with the centre might give them. If the Church Catholic, indeed, has actually commanded their return to her at once, that is another matter; but this she cannot have done without pronouncing their present Church good-for-nothing, which I do not suppose Rome has done of us.

In all this, which I did not mean to have inflicted on you, I assume, on the one hand, that Rome is right; on the other that we are not bound by uncatholic subscriptions. [II:288].

To F. Rogers [8 January 1840]

Newman gives an account of a visit by Mr Spencer, a Roman Catholic priest.

[...] He is a gentlemanlike, mild, pleasing man, but sadly smooth. I wonder whether it is their habit of internal discipline, the necessity of confession, &c., which makes them so. He did not come to controvert – his sole point was to get English people to pray for the R.C.s. He said he had been instrumental in setting on foot the practice in France towards England, that it was spreading in Germany, and that we should be soon agreed if we really loved one another; that such prayers would change the face of things. [...] [II:295]

To Mrs J. Mozley [25 February 1840]

[...] Everything is miserable. I expect a great attack upon the Bible – indeed, I have long expected it. At the present moment indications of what is coming gather. Those wretched Socialists on the one hand, then Carlyle on the other – a man of first rate ability, I suppose, and quite fascinating as a writer. His book on the 'French Revolution' is most taking (to me). I had hoped he might have come round right, for it was easy to see that he was not a believer; but they say he has settled the wrong way. His view is that Christianity has good in it, or is good *as far as it goes*, which, when applied to Scripture, is of course, a picking and choosing of its contents. Then, again, you have Arnold's school, such as it is ... Then you have all your political economists, who *cannot* accept ... the Scripture rules about almsgiving, renunciation of wealth, self-denial, &c., and then your geologists giving up parts of the Old Testament [...]

But this is not all. I begin to have serious apprehensions lest any religious body is strong enough to withstand the league of evil but the Roman Church [...] [II:300].

To F. Rogers [25 November 1840]

[...] I wrote to Keble some time since telling him at full my difficulties about St Mary's, and resolving to go by his judgement. I had three heads: (1) my inability to get on with my parish; (2) my exercising an influence on undergraduates to which I was not called; (3) the tendency of my opinions to create Roman *sympathies*. The third was the only ground he thought much of, and he gave me full leave to resign, if I could do it without creating scandal. At the same time he said he wished me to remain, and did not think it a reason *necessitating* resignation. Upon this I felt I ought to remain; because what I wanted to get from him was *leave* to do so. I mean, there are so many reasons making it a duty to remain, so soon as one comes to the conclusion that it is not a duty to go. Three considerations have gone far to reconcile me to it since his decision: (1) That we don't know yet what the English Church will bear of infused Catholic truth. We are, as it were, proving cannon. I know that there is a danger of bursting; but still, one has no right to assume that our Church will not stand the test. (2) If I fear the tendency of what I teach towards Rome, it is no more than I see in Hooker or Taylor. [...] We all create a sympathy towards Rome so far as our system does not realise what is realised in Rome. (3) For what we know, Liberalism, Rationalism, is the foe at our doors. [...] I am more certain that Protestantism leads to infidelity than that my own views lead to Rome. [...] My only solicitude has been to have an answer in *controversy* why an *individual* is not bound to leave the English Church. That we are suffering dreadfully (so are the Romans), and that we are wrong in our separation, I do not doubt. I think Rome the *centre* of unity, and yet not to say that she is infallible, when she is by herself. [...] The upshot is, whether I continue so or not, that I am much more comfortable than I have been. I do not fear at all any number of persons as likely to go to Rome, if I am secure about myself. If I can trust myself, I can trust others. We have so many things on our side, that a good conscience is all that one wants. [II:318].

To J.W. Bowden [13 March 1841]

[…] I expect the very worst – that is, that a condemnation will be passed in Convocation upon the Tracts as a whole, by the non-resident Establishment men, Liberals and Peculiars.

[…] That it will turn to good, I doubt not; but we have been too prosperous. I am only sorry that my friends should suffer through me. [II:327].

To Mrs Thomas Mozley [15 March 1841]

I just hear the Heads of Houses have printed a very strong resolution, viz. that my explanation of the Articles is *evasive*. I assure you it is a *great* relief to me that it affirms no doctrine. […] [II:335].

To John Keble [25 March 1841]

I write to you in some anxiety. The Bishop wishes me, in a letter I am to write to him, to say that, 'at his *bidding*', I will suppress Tract 90.

I have no difficulty in saying and doing so if he tells me, but my difficulty is as to my *then* position. […]

… I think I am observing my duty to the Bishop by suppressing the Tract, and my duty to my principles by resigning my living. […] [II:338].

To the 'lady of excitable temperament' [April, 1841]

I am not surprised at anyone being drawn to the Roman Church under your feelings, wrong as I think it. And I lament as much as any one can our present state in the English, in which high aspirations have so little means of exercise. If you will allow me to add it, I think you were *hasty* in your resolve. So great a matter as a change of religion ought not to be thought of without years (I may say) of prayer and preparation. Nor do I think it God's way, generally speaking, for *individuals* to leave one religion for another – it is so much like an exercise of private judgement. […] [II:346].

To J.W. Bowden [12 October 1841]

So far from thinking lightly of the Jerusalem matter, I said something very strong about it in my 'Private Judgement' article, before most people suspected what was going on. It is hideous […]

The facts that strike me are the following: 'We have not,' says Mr Formby last week to me (who is just returned from Jerusalem) 'a single

Anglican there: so that we are sending a Bishop to *make* a communion, not to govern our own people.' Next, the *excuse* is that there are converted Anglican Jews there who require a Bishop. Mr Formby tells me that he does not think there are half-a-dozen. But for *them* the Bishop is sent out, and for them he is a Bishop of the *circumcision* against the Epistle to the Galatians pretty nearly. Thirdly, *for the sake of Prussia*, he is to take under him all the foreign Protestants who will come; and the political advantages will be so great from the influence of England that there is no doubt they will come. They are to sign the Confession of Augsburg, and there is nothing to show that they hold the doctrine of Baptismal Regeneration. Next, the Socinian-Mahomedan Druses have asked for an English Bishop, and it is supposed Bishop Alexander will develop in that direction. Lastly there is a notion of coalescing with the Monophysites.

The Bishop, who has no Church principles, *is not to be made under the jurisdiction of the English Bishops,* and thus you have an Episcopate set up to gather, literally, Jews, Turks, infidels and heretics from all quarters. And why? Because Russia being represented by the Greeks, and France by the Latins, it is very desirable that England should have a Church there as a means of political influence, a *resident* power in the country.

[...] the case is this: many persons are doubtful whether we have the Notes of the true Church upon us; every act of the Church, such as this of coalescing with heretics, *weakens* the proof. And in some cases it may be the last straw that breaks the horse's back.

As to myself, I shall do nothing whatever, unless, indeed, it were to give my signature to a protest [...] having been in a way silenced. [...] [II:353].

To J. Keble [31 October 1841]

[...] I have no hope at all at present that certain persons will remain in our Church twenty years, unless some accommodation takes place with Rome; but I see no sign at all of any *immediate* move. I think that men are far too dutiful; and in twenty years things must either get much better, or the poor Church must have got much worse or have broken to pieces; and then one's sorrow will be roused by greater events than the loss of one or two of its members. I don't know whether I am intelligible. [II:357].

To J.W. Bowden [28 February 1842]

[...] I am out of the way here[23] of seeing the papers, and so am no judge,

---

25 Newman was writing from Littlemore.

or I should say that the Tract ferment is lulling again. [...]

I have got my books[26] nearly all in their places,[27] and talk of insuring them. Not, one would trust, that there is much danger of fire, but I am somewhat given to fancy mischances, and when they *are* insured I shall be dwelling on the chance of their being destroyed, as Dr Priestley's, by a mob shouting 'No Popery', as in 1780 [...] [II:389].

To the Bishop of Oxford [14 April 1842]

I am very much obliged by your Lordship's kindness in allowing me to write to you on the subject of my house at Littlemore [...]

It is now a whole year since I have been the subject of incessant misrepresentations. A year since I submitted entirely to your Lordship's authority [...] I not only stopped the series of tracts on which I was engaged, but withdrew from all public discussion of Church matters [...] I turned myself at once to the preparation for the press of the translation of St Athanasius [...] and in the concerns of my own parish and in practical works.

[...] For many years, at least thirteen, I have wished to give myself to a life of greater religious regularity than I have hitherto led; but it is very unpleasant to confess such a wish even to my Bishop, because it seems arrogant, and because it is committing me to a profession which may come to nothing. What have I done that I am to be called to account by the world for my private actions in a way in which no one else is called? [...] I feel it very cruel, though the parties at fault do not know what they are doing, that very sacred matters between me and my conscience are made a matter of public talk. [...]

[...] As to my intentions, I purpose to live there myself a good deal, as I have a resident Curate in Oxford. In doing this I believe I am consulting for the good of my parish, as my population in Littlemore is at least equal to that of St Mary's in Oxford, and the *whole* of Littlemore is double of it. It has been very much neglected; and in providing a parsonage-house at Littlemore, as this will be, and will be called, I conceive I am doing a very great benefit to my people. At the same time it has appeared to me that a partial or temporary retirement from St Mary's Church might be expedient under the prevailing excitement.

---

26 In February 1841, Newman had written to Mrs John Mozley saying that he had bought 'a lot of books', as 'a good investment'. During 1841 he spent no less than £858 on books, a sum that would have provided for ten curates.
27 Newman had converted the barn at Littlemore into a library.

[...] your Lordship will perceive from what I have said that no 'monastery is in process of erection', there is 'no chapel', no 'refectory', hardly a dining-room or parlour. The 'cloisters' are my shed connecting the cottages. [...] 'I am not attempting a revival of the Monastic Orders in anything approaching to the Romanist sense of the term.' [II:392].

To J. Keble [20 December 1842]

As to reminding my people about Confession, it is the most dreary and dismal thought that I have about my parish, that I dare do so little, or rather nothing. I have long thought it would hinder me from ever taking another cure. Confession is the life of the Parochial charge; without it all is hollow, and yet I do not see my way to say that I should not do more harm than good by more than the most distant mention of it. Reading the First exhortation at the Communion is the only thing I do of a direct kind. I hope that that is of a nature to startle those who listen, though not enough perhaps to persuade them. [II:405].

To Miss H. [8 March 1843]

Religious truth is reached, not by reasoning but by an inward perception [...] only disciplined, educated, formed minds can perceive. Nothing, then, is more important to you than habits of self-command [...] You are overflowing with feeling and impulse; all these must be restrained, ruled, brought under, converted into principles and habits and elements of character. Consider that you have this great work to do, to change yourself; and you cannot doubt that, whatever be the imperfections of the English Church, and whatever the advantages of the Roman, there are gifts and aids in the former abundantly enough to carry you through this necessary work. [...] [II:410].

To J. Keble [25 August 1843]

I have just received a letter from Lockhart, one of my inmates, who has been away for three weeks, saying that he is on the point of joining the Church of Rome, and is in retreat under Dr Gentili of Loughborough. ... You may fancy how sick it makes me feel. [II:417].

To J.B. Mozley [1 September 1843]

[...] The truth is then I am not a good son enough of the Church of England to feel I can in conscience hold preferment under her. I love the

Church of Rome too well.

Now please *burn this*, there's a good fellow, for you sometimes let letters lie on your mantelpiece. […] [II:423].

To Mrs J. Mozley [22 September 1843]

[…] You cannot estimate what so many (alas!) feel at present, the strange effect produced on the mind when the conviction flashes, or rather pours, in upon it that Rome is the true Church. Of course it is a most revolutionary, and therefore a most exciting, tumultuous conviction. For this reason persons should not act under it, for it is impossible in such a state of emotion that they can tell whether their conviction is well founded or not. They cannot judge calmly […] [II:424].

To Mrs Thomas Mozley [29 September 1843]

I do so *despair* of the Church of England, and am so evidently cast off by her, and, on the other hand, I am so drawn to the Church of Rome, that I think it *safer*, as a matter of honesty, *not* to keep my living.

This is a very different thing from having any *intention* of joining the Church of Rome. […] People cannot understand a man being in a state of *doubt, of misgiving*, of being unequal to *responsibilities, &c*.; but they will conclude that he has clear views either one way or the other. All I know is, that I could not without hypocrisy profess myself any longer a *teacher* and a *champion* for our Church.

Very few persons know this – hardly one person, only one (I think) in Oxford, viz. James Mozley. I think it would be most cruel, most unkind, most unsettling to tell them.

My dear Harriett, you must learn patience, so must we all, and resignation to the will of God. [II:425].

To Rev. J.B. Mozley [24 November 1844]

[…] Last summer four years (1839) it came strongly upon me, from reading first the Monophysite controversy, and then turning to the Donatists, that we were external to the Catholic Church. I have never got over this. […] [II:430].

To Mrs J. Mozley [24 November 1844]

[…] I cannot make out that I have any motive but a sense of indefinite risk to my soul in remaining where I am. A clear conviction of the substantial identity of Christianity and the Roman system has now been on my mind for a full three years. It is more than five years since the conviction first came on me, though I struggled against it and overcame it. I believe all my feelings and wishes are against change. I have nothing to draw me elsewhere. I hardly ever was at a Roman service; even abroad I knew no Roman Catholics. I have no sympathies with them as a party. I am giving up everything. I am not conscious of any resentment, disgust, or the like, to repel me from my present position; and I have no dreams whatever – far from it indeed. I seem to be throwing myself away.

Unless something occurs which I cannot anticipate I have no intention of any early step even now. But I cannot but think – though I can no more realise it than being made Dean of Ch[rist]. Ch[urch] or Bishop of Durham – that some day it will be, and at a definite distance of time. As far as I can make out I am in the state of mind which divines call *indifferentia*, inculcating it as a duty to be set on nothing, but to be willing to take whatever Providence wills. How *can* I at my age and with my past trials be set upon anything? […]

[…] This is a most abrupt letter, but I have no time, and am tired and out of spirits. [II:445].

To Mrs J. Mozley [8 October 1845]

My dear Jemima, – I must tell you what will pain you greatly, but I will make it as short as you would wish me to do.

This night Father Dominic, the Passionist, sleeps here. He does not know of my intention, but I shall ask him to receive me into what I believe to be the One Fold of the Redeemer.

This will not go till all is over. [II:468].

Chapter Two: Newman as a Preacher[1]

'Holiness rather than Peace'

Newman's preaching was legendary. Before he arrived at St Mary's, afternoon congregations consisted of 'High Street shopkeepers and their housemaids'. That changed as his students followed him from Oriel. Others followed until the Sunday afternoon service was better attended than the University Sermons. Several descriptions of his preaching survive, of which the most famous is Matthew Arnold's: 'Who could resist the charm of that spiritual apparition, gliding in the dim afternoon light through the aisles of St Mary's, rising into the pulpit, and then, in the most entrancing of voices, breaking the silence with words and thoughts which were a religious music, – subtle, sweet, mournful.'[2]

Principal Shairp[3] wrote that:

The service was very simple – no pomp, no ritualism [...] the most remarkable thing was the beauty, the silver intonation, of Mr Newman's voice, as he read the Lessons. It seemed to bring new meaning out of familiar words [...]. When he began to preach, a stranger was not likely to be much struck, especially if he had been accustomed to pulpit oratory of the Boanerges sort. Here was no vehemence, no declamation, no show of elaborated argument, so that one who came prepared to hear a 'great intellectual effort' was most sure to go away disappointed. [...] The delivery had a peculiarity which it took a new hearer some time to get over. Each separate sentence, or at least each short paragraph, was spoken rapidly,

---

1   Newman seems first to have written sermons when he was sixteen. He based them on his reading of the Calvinist Bishop Beveridge, especially his *Private Thoughts*. Anne Mozley lists the titles of seven of them: [1] He that eateth and drinketh unworthily. [2] Great things doeth He which we cannot comprehend. [3] These shall go into everlasting punishment. [4] Man is like to vanity, his days are as a shadow. [5] Let no one despise thy youth. [6] Let not sin therefore reign in your mortal bodies. [7] Thou when thou fastest.

2   *John Henry Newman*, Ian Ker (Oxford, 1990), p.90.

3   *Oxford Apostles*, Geoffrey Faber (Pelican, 1954), p.187. (John Campbell Shairp (1819–85) was a poet and critic, educated at Glasgow and Oxford universities. In 1868, he was made Professor of Poetry at Oxford. The quote comes from his *Studies in Poetry and Philosophy*, published in 1868.)

but with great clearness of intonation; and then at its close there was a pause lasting for nearly half a minute; and then another rapidly but clearly spoken sentence, followed by another pause. It took some time to get over this, but, that once done, the wonderful charm began to dawn on you […] he laid his finger – how gently, yet how power-fully! – on some inner place in the hearer's heart, and told him things about himself he had never know till then. Subtlest truths, which it would have taken philosophers pages of circumlocution and big words to state, were dropt out by the way in a sentence or two of the most transparent Saxon. And the tone of voice in which they were spoken, once you grew accustomed to it, sounded like a fine strain of unearthly music. Through the silence of that high Gothic building the words fell on the ear like the measured drippings of water in some vast dim cave.

As an Anglican, Newman read his sermons, his eyes fixed on the text. He spoke softly, with little inflection, and did not use body language other than stillness. J.A. Froude described how such an unpromising technique worked its magic:

he paused [Newman was describing Christ's passion]. For a few moments there was a breathless silence. Then, in a low clear voice, of which the faintest vibration was audible in the farthest corners of St Mary's, he said, 'Now I bid you recollect that He to Whom these things were done was Almighty God.' It was as if an electric shock had gone through the church, as if every person present understood for the first time the meaning of what he had been saying. I suppose it was an epoch in the mental history of more than one of my Oxford contemporaries.

Elsewhere he wrote:

A tone, not of fear but of infinite pity, runs through them all, and along with it a resolution to look facts in the face; not to fly to evasive generalities about infinite mercy and benevolence, but to examine what revelation really has added to our knowledge, either of what we are or what lies before us… When I entered at Oxford, John Henry was beginning to be famous. The responsible authorities were watching him with anxiety; the clever men were looking with interest and curiosity on the apparition among them of one of those persons of undisputed genius who was likely to make a mark on his time. His appearance was striking. He was above the middle height, slight and spare. His head was large, his face remarkably like that of Julius Caesar.[…] 'I had never then seen so impressive a person … I

attended his church and heard him preach Sunday after Sunday; he
is supposed to have been insidious, to have led his disciples on to the
conclusions to which he designed to bring them, while his purpose
was carefully veiled. He was on the contrary, the most transparent
of men. He told us what he believed to be true. No one who heard
his sermons in those days can forget them. They were seldom directly
theological. We had theology enough and to spare from the select
preachers before the University. Newman taking some biblical char-
acter for a text, spoke to us about ourselves, our temptations and
experiences. His illustrations were inexhaustible. He seemed to be
addressing the most secret consciousness of each of us ... he never
exaggerated; he was never unreal. A sermon from him was a poem,
formed on a distinct idea, fascinating by its subtlety, welcome – how
welcome! – from its sincerity, interesting from its originality, even
to those who were careless of religion; and to others who wished to
be religious, but had found religion dry and wearisome, it was like
the springing of a fountain out of the rock.[4]

*Newman wrote his sermons out repeatedly before preaching them. Like those of
Latimer, Andrewes and John Donne, they stand as literature, even though they
lack the delight in language that we find in writers of the sixteenth and seventeenth
century. Not for nothing did Newman call them,* Parochial and Plain Sermons.
In addition, he also published Sermons on Subjects of the Day *and* Oxford
University Sermons.

  There are 191 sermons in the eight volumes of the Parochial and Plain
Sermons. *Their length varies considerably, but average between three and four thou-
sand words, which meant that he would normally have preached for thirty to forty
minutes. In keeping with custom, his published sermons had titles: 'The Religious
Use of Excited Feelings' [1:9], 'The Self-Wise Enquirer' [1:17], 'Obedience the
Remedy for Religious Perplexity' [1:18], 'Affliction, a School of Comfort' [5:21],
'The Difficulty of Realising Sacred Privileges' [6:8], 'The Subjection of the Reason
and Feelings to the Revealed Word' [6:18], 'Religion a Weariness to the Natural
Man' [7:2], 'Religion Pleasant to the Religious' [7:14], 'Curiosity a Temptation
to Sin' [8:5], 'Truth Hidden when not Sought After' [8:13]. Throughout all his
sermons, Newman has one chief aim: to assist his hearers in their pursuit of holi-
ness. Extracts from some of the sermons follow.*

---

4 [Letter III, *The Oxford Counter-Reformation* (Short Studies, 4th Series, J.A.
    Froude. Longmans, 1883.)]

Holiness Necessary For Future Blessedness[5]

Holiness without which no man shall see the Lord.

[Hebrews 12:14]

In this text it has seemed good to the Holy Spirit to convey a chief truth of religion in a few words. It is this circumstance which makes it especially impressive; for the truth itself is declared in one form or other in every part of Scripture. It is told us again and again, that to make sinful creatures holy was the great end which our Lord had in view in taking upon Him our nature, and thus none but the holy will be accepted for His sake at the last day. The whole history of redemption, the covenant of mercy in all its parts and provisions, attests the necessity of holiness in order to salvation [*sic*]; as indeed even our natural conscience bears witness also. But in the text what is elsewhere implied in history, and enjoined by precept, is stated doctrinally, as a momentous and necessary fact, the result of some awful irreversible law in the nature of things, and the inscrutable determination of the Divine Will.

Now, someone may ask, 'Why is it that holiness is a necessary qualification for our being received into heaven? why is it that the Bible enjoins upon us so strictly to love, fear, and obey God, to be just, honest, meek, pure in heart, forgiving, heavenly-minded, self-denying, humble and resigned? Man is confessedly weak and corrupt; *why* then is he enjoined to be so religious, so unearthly? *Why* is he required (in the strong language of Scripture) to become a "new creature"? Since he is by nature what he is, would it not be an act of greater mercy in God to save him altogether without this holiness, which it is so difficult, yet (as it appears) so necessary for him to possess?'

Now we have no right to ask this question. Surely it is quite enough for a sinner to know that a way has been opened through God's grace for his salvation, without being informed why that way, and not another way, was chosen by Divine Wisdom. Eternal life is 'the *gift* of God'. Undoubtedly He may prescribe the terms on which He will give it; and if he has determined holiness to be the way of life, it is enough; it is not for us to enquire why He has so determined.

Yet the question may be asked reverently, and with a view to enlarge our insight into our own condition and prospects; and in that case the attempt to answer it will be profitable, if it be made soberly. I proceed, therefore, to state one of the reasons, assigned in Scripture, why present holiness is necessary, as the text declares to us, for future happiness.

---

5   P&P 1:1. Preached August 1826.

To be holy, is, in our Church's words, to have 'the true circumcision of the Spirit'; that is, to be separate from sin, to hate the works of the world, the flesh and the devil; to take pleasure in keeping God's commandments; to do things as He would have us do them; to live habitually as in the sight of the world to come, as if we had broken the ties of this life, and were dead already. Why cannot we be saved without possessing such a frame and temper of mind?

I answer as follows: That even supposing a man of unholy life were suffered to enter heaven, *he would not be happy there;* so that it would be no mercy to permit him to enter. [...]

Heaven then is not like this world; I will say what it is much more like, – *a church.* For in a place of public worship no language of this world is heard; there are no schemes brought forward for temporal objects, great or small; no information how to strengthen our worldly interests, extend our influence, or establish our credit. These things indeed may be right in their way, so that we do not set our hearts upon them; still (I repeat), it is certain that we hear nothing of them in a church. Here we hear solely and entirely of *God.* We praise Him, worship Him, sing to Him, thank Him, confess to Him, give ourselves up to Him, and ask His blessing. And *therefore,* a church is like heaven; viz. because both in the one and the other, there is one single subject – religion – brought before us. [...]

Nay, I will venture to say more than this; – it is fearful, but it is right to say it; – that if we wished to imagine a punishment for an unholy, reprobate soul, we perhaps could not fancy a greater than to *summon it to heaven.* Heaven would be hell to an irreligious man. We know how unhappy we are apt to feel at present, when alone in the midst of strangers, or of men of different tastes and habits from ourselves. How miserable, for example, would it be to have to live in a foreign land, among a people whose faces we never saw before, and whose language we could not learn? And this is but a faint illustration of the loneliness of a man of earthly dispositions and tastes, thrust into the society of saints and angels. How forlorn would he wander through the courts of heaven! He would find no one like himself; he would see in every direction the marks of God's holiness, and these would make him shudder. He would feel himself always in his presence. He could no longer turn his thoughts another way, as he does now, when conscience reproaches him. He would know that the Eternal Eye was ever upon him; and that Eye of holiness, which is joy and life to holy creatures, would seem to him an Eye of wrath and punishment. God cannot change His nature. Holy He must ever be. But while He is holy, no unholy soul can be happy in heaven. Fire does not inflame iron, but it inflames straw. It would cease to be fire if it did not. And so heaven itself would be fire to those, who would fain escape across the great gulf from the torments of hell. The finger of Lazarus would but increase their thirst. The very 'heaven that is over their head' will be 'brass' to them. [...].

[...] To obtain the gift of holiness is the work of *a life*. No man will ever be perfect here, so sinful is our nature. Thus in putting off the day of repentance, these men are reserving for a few chance years, when strength and vigour are gone, that WORK for which a *whole* life would not be enough. [...]

Tolerance of Religious Error[6]

'He was a good man, full of the Holy Ghost and of faith'.

[Acts 11:24]

Faith for Newman was the beginning of the road to holiness. He returns to the topic again and again, especially in the rival ways it is interpreted in the Anglican, Protestant, and Roman Catholic traditions. In this sermon, however, he treats of its subversion by a contemporary liberal and latitudinarian virtue, that of tolerance.

[...] Now it is very plain what description of character, and what kind of lesson, is brought before us in the history of this Holy Apostle.[7] Holy he was, full of the Holy Ghost and of faith; still the characteristics and the infirmities of man remained in him, and thus he is 'unto us for an example', consistently with the reverence we feel towards him as one of the foundations of the Christian Church. He is an example and warning to us, not only as showing us what we ought to be, but as evidencing how the highest gifts and graces are corrupted in our sinful nature, if we are not diligent to walk step by step, according to the light of God's commandments. Be our mind as heavenly as it may be, most loving, most holy, most zealous, most energetic, most peaceful, yet if we look off from Him for a moment, and look towards ourselves, at once these excellent tempers fall into some extreme or mistake. Charity becomes over-easiness, holiness is tainted with spiritual pride, zeal degenerates into fierceness, activity eats up the spirit of prayer, hope is heightened into presumption. We cannot guide ourselves. God's revealed word is our sovereign rule of conduct; and therefore,

---

6 P&P 2:23. This second volume of *Parochial and Plain Sermons*, published 21 February 1835, was dedicated to Newman's fellow student at Trinity and life long friend, John William Bowden, 'In the Cheerful conviction that the English Church amid many defections still holds her influence over an attached and zealous laity.'

7 *i.e.* St Barnabas. It was preached on his Feast Day.

among other reasons, is faith so principal a grace, for it is the directing power which receives the commands of Christ, and applies them to the heart.

And there is a particular reason for dwelling upon the character of St Barnabas in this age, because he may be considered as the type of the better sort of men among us, and those who are most in esteem. The world itself indeed is what it ever has been, ungodly; but in every age it chooses some one or other peculiarity of the gospel as the badge of its particular fashion for the time being, and sets up as objects of admiration those who eminently possess it. […] There is a great deal of thoughtful kindness among us, of conceding in little matters, of scrupulous propriety of words, and a sort of code of liberal and honourable dealings in the conduct of society. There is a steady regard for the rights of individuals, nay, as one would fain hope in spite of misgivings, for the interest of the poorer classes, the stranger, the fatherless, and the widow. […] When we think of the commandments, we know Charity to be the first and greatest; and we are tempted to ask with the young ruler, 'What lack we yet?'

I ask, then, […] does not our kindness too often degenerate into weakness, and thus become not Christian Charity, but lack of Charity, as regards the objects of it? Are we sufficiently careful to do what is right and just, rather than what is pleasant? Do we clearly understand our professed principles, and do we keep to them under temptation?

The history of St Barnabas will help us to answer this question honestly. Now I fear we lack altogether, what he lacked in certain occurrences in it, firmness, manliness, godly severity. I fear it must be confessed that our kindness, instead of being directed and embraced by principle, too often becomes languid and unmeaning; that it is exerted on improper objects, and out of season, and thereby is uncharitable in two ways, indulging those who should be chastised, and preferring their comfort to those who are really deserving. We are over tender in dealing with sin and sinners. We are deficient in jealous custody of the revealed Truths which Christ has left us. We allow men to speak against the Church, its ordinances, or its teaching, without remonstrating with them. We do not separate from heretics, nay, we object to the word as if uncharitable; and when such texts are brought against us as St John's command, not to show hospitality towards them, we are not slow to answer that they do not apply to us. […]

[…] Liberality is always popular, whatever be the subject of it, and excites a glow of pleasure and self-approbation in the giver, even though it involves no sacrifice, nay, is exercised upon the property of others. Thus in the sacred province of religion, men are led on – without any bad principle – […] led on to give up Gospel Truths, to consent to open the Church

to the various denominations of error which abound among us, or to alter
our Services so as to please the scoffer, the lukewarm, or the vicious. To
be kind is their one principle of action; and when they find offence taken
at the Church's creed, they begin to think how they may modify or curtail
it. [...] Not understanding that their religious privileges are a trust to be
handed on to posterity, a sacred property entailed upon the Christian
family, and their own in enjoyment rather than in possession, they act the
spendthrift, and are lavish of the goods of others. Thus, for instance, they
speak against the Anathemas of the Athanasian Creed, or of the
Commination Service, or of certain of the Psalms, and wish to rid them-
selves of them.

Undoubtedly, even the best specimens of these men are deficient in due
appreciation of the Christian Mysteries, and of their own responsibility in
preserving and transmitting them; yet, some of them are such truly 'good'
men, so amiable and feeling, so benevolent to the poor, and of such repute
among all classes, in short, fulfil so excellently the office of shining like
lights in the world, and witnesses of Him 'who went about doing good',
that those who most deplore their failing will still be most desirous of
excusing them personally, while they feel it a duty to withstand them. [...]
Now if by the tolerance of our Church, it be meant that she does not coun-
tenance the use of fire and sword against those who separate from her, so
far she is truly called a tolerant Church; but she is not tolerant of error, as
those very formularies, which these men wish to remove, testify [...]

I wish I saw any prospect of this element of zeal and holy sternness
springing up among us, to temper and give character to the languid,
unmeaning benevolence which we misname Christian love. I have no
hope of my country till I see it. Many schools of Religion and Ethics are
to be found among us, and they all profess to magnify, in one shape or
other, what they consider the principle of love; but what they lack is, a
firm maintenance of that characteristic of the Divine Nature, which, in
accommodation to our infirmity, is named by St John and his brethren,
the wrath of God. Let this be well observed. There are men who are advo-
cates of Expedience; these, as far as they are religious at all, resolve
conscience into an instinct of mere benevolence, and refer all the dealings
of Providence with his Creatures to the same one attribute. Hence, they
consider all punishment to be remedial, a means to an end, deny that the
woe threatened against sinners is of eternal duration, and explain away the
doctrine of the Atonement. [...]

But those who think themselves and others in risk of an eternal curse,
dare not be thus indulgent. [...]

Regenerating Baptism[8]

By one Spirit are we all baptised into one Body.

[I Corinthians 12:13]

As an Evangelical and Calvinist, Newman believed that Christians were saved by faith alone, which was the agent of their spiritual regeneration. As an Anglo-Catholic he came to believe that baptism was more than just a sign of that transformation: it was instrumental in the making of Christians. The doctrine of baptismal regeneration was one that defined theological and party allegiance. The controversy centred on Infant Baptism which Anglicans practised, but which Baptists rejected in favour of 'Believers' Baptism'. Anglican Evangelicals found it difficult to accept that baptised infants, unable to exercise faith as believers, were nevertheless 'regenerate'.

As there is one Holy Ghost, so there is also one only visible Body of Christians which Almighty God 'knows by name', and one Baptism which admits men into it. […]

Now, this is much more than many men are willing to grant, their utmost concession being that the Church has the presence of the Holy Spirit in it, and therefore, to be in the Church is to be in that which has the presence of the Holy Spirit; that is, to be in the *way* of the Spirit (so to speak), which cannot but be a state of favour and privilege; but, that the Holy Spirit is given to infants, one by one, on their Baptism, this they will not admit. Yet, one would think words could not be plainer than the text in proof of it; however, they do not admit it.

This defective view of the Sacrament of Baptism, for so I must not shrink from calling it, shall now be considered, and considered in its connection with a popular argument for the Baptism of infants, which, most, true as it is in its proper place, yet is scarcely profitable for these times, as seeming to countenance the error in question. I mean the assumed parallel between Baptism and Circumcision.

It is undeniable that Circumcision in some important respects resembles Baptism, and may allowably, nay, usefully be referred to in illustration of it. Circumcision was the entrance into the Jewish Covenant, and it typified the renunciation of the flesh. […] But, though it resembles Baptism in some respects, it is unlike it in others more important. When, then, it is found to be the chief and especially approved argument in favour of

---

8   P&P 3:19. The third volume of Newman's *Parochial and Plain Sermons*, dated 'The Feast of the Conversion of St Paul [25 January] 1836', was dedicated to The Archdeacon of Totnes, The Venerable Robert Hurrell Froude, father of Newman's friend, Richard Hurrell.

Infant Baptism among Christians, there is reason for some anxiety, lest this circumstance should betoken, or introduce, insufficient views of a Christian Sacrament. This remark, I fear, is applicable in the present day.

We baptise infants, in the first place, because the Church has ever done so; [...] even though Scripture said not a word on the subject, [...] But, besides, we consider we do find, in our Saviour's words, a command to bring children to Him, for His blessing. Again, he said, they were to be members of His Kingdom; also that Baptism is the only entrance, the new birth into it. We administer, then, Baptism to children as a sure *benefit* to their souls.

But, when men refuse to admit the doctrine of Baptismal Regeneration, in the case of infants, then they look about how they may defend Infant Baptism, which, perhaps, from habit, good feeling, or other causes, they do not like to abandon. The ordinary and intelligible reason for the Baptism of infants, is the securing to them remission of sins, and the gift of the Holy Ghost – Regeneration; but if this sacred privilege is not given to them in Baptism, why, it may be asked, should Baptism be administered to them at all? Why not wait until they can understand the meaning of the rite, and can have faith and repentance themselves? Certainly it does seem a very intricate and unreasonable proceeding, first, to lay stress on the necessity of repentance and faith in persons to be baptised, and then to proceed to administer Baptism universally in such a way as to exclude the possibility of their having repentance and faith. I say, this would be strange and inconsistent, were not baptism in itself, so direct a blessing [...] Otherwise the objection holds [...]. Let us go counter to Tradition rather than to Scripture. This being the difficulty which comes upon those who deny the Regeneration, yet would retain the Baptism of infants, let us see next how they meet it.

[...] They avail themselves of the instance of Circumcision as a proof that a divinely-appointed ordinance need not convey grace, even while it admits into a state of grace; [...]

... And it would be perfectly satisfactory, as a view, were it Scriptural. [...] Christ and his Apostles do attach a grace to the ordinance of Baptism, such as is not attached in the Old Testament to Circumcision – which is exactly that difference which makes the latter a mere rite, the former a Sacrament; [...].

Newman's argument rests on the traditional Christian disparagement of the Old Covenant which, since the Holocaust, Jews have rightly challenged. The relationship between the Church and the Jewish people was redefined at

*Vatican II, but in Newman's day the old 'Theology of Contempt' was
unquestioned.*

[...] If Baptism then has no spiritual virtue in it, can it be intended for
us Christians? If it has no regenerating power, surely they only are consis-
tent who reject it altogether. I will boldly say it, we have nothing dead and
earthly under the Gospel, and we act like the Judaising Christians of old
time if we submit to any thing such; therefore they only are consistent,
who, denying the virtue of Baptism, also deny its authority as a permanent
ordinance of the Gospel. [...] either Baptism is an instrument of the Holy
Ghost, or it has no place in Christianity. [...]

The Greatness and Littleness of Human Life[9]

*'The days of the years of my pilgrimage are an hundred and thirty years;
few and evil have the days of the years of my life been; and have not
attained unto the days of the years of the life of my fathers, in the days of
their pilgrimage.'*

[Genesis 47:9]

[...] When life is past, it is all one whether it has lasted two hundred years
or fifty. And it is this characteristic, stamped on human life in the day of
its birth, viz. that it is mortal, which makes it under all circumstances and
in every form equally feeble and despicable. All the points in which men
differ, health and strength, high or low estate, happiness or misery, vanish
before this common lot, mortality. Pass a few years, and the longest-lived
will be gone; nor will what is past profit him then, except in its conse-
quences.

[...] This is what we all feel, though at first sight it seems a contradic-
tion, that even though the days as they go be slow, and be laden with many
events, or with sorrows or dreariness, lengthening them out and making
them tedious, yet the year passes quick though the hours tarry, and time
bygone is as a dream, though we thought it would never go while it was
going. And the reason seems to be this; that, when we contemplate human
life in itself, in however small a portion of it, we see implied in it the pres-
ence of a soul, the energy of a spiritual existence, of an unaccountable
being; consciousness tells us this concerning it every moment. But when
we look back on it in memory, we view it but externally, as a mere lapse

---

9   P&P 4:14. Newman's fourth volume of sermons, dated 19 November 1838 was
    dedicated to Hugh James Rose, 'Who when hearts were failing, bade us stir up
    the gift that was in us, and betake ourselves to our true mother.'

of time, a mere earthly history. And the longest duration of this external world is as dust and weighs nothing, against one moment's life of the world within. Thus we are ever expecting great things from life, from our internal consciousness every moment of our having souls; and we are ever being disappointed, on considering what we have gained from time past, and can hope from time to come. And life is ever promising and never fulfilling; and hence, however long it be, our days are few and evil. [...]

Our earthly life then gives promise of what it does not accomplish. It promises immortality, yet it is mortal; it contains life in death and eternity in time; and it attracts us by beginnings which faith alone brings to an end. [...]

[...] The very greatness of our powers makes this life look pitiful; the very pitifulness of this life forces on our thoughts to another; and the prospect of another gives a dignity and value to this life which promises it; and thus this life is at once great and little, and we rightly condemn it while we exalt its importance. [...]

Unreal Words[10]

Thine eyes shall see the King in His beauty:
they shall behold the land that is very far off.

[Isaiah 33:17]

The Prophet tells us, that under the Gospel covenant God's servants will have the privilege of seeing those heavenly sights which were but shadowed out in the Law. Before Christ came was the time of shadows; but when He came, He brought truth as well as grace; and as He who is the truth has come to us, so does He in return require that we should be true and sincere in our dealings with Him. [...].

We are no longer then in the region of shadows: we have the true Saviour set before us, the true reward, and the true means of spiritual renewal. [...]. The Pharisees might have this excuse in their hypocrisy, that the plain truth had not yet been revealed to them, we have not even this poor reason for insincerity. We have no opportunity of mistaking one thing for another; [...]. Our professions, our creeds, our prayers, our dealings, our conversation, our arguments, our teaching must henceforth be sincere, or, to use an expressive word, must be *real*. [...]

And yet it need scarcely to be said, nothing is so rare as honesty and

---

10 P&P 5:3. The sermon illustrates the epitaph that Newman devised as a summary of his life. *Ex umbris et imaginibus in veritatem.* (Out of unreality into Reality.)

singleness of mind; so much so, that a person who is really honest is already perfect. [...] And what is said of profession of *discipleship* applies undoubtedly in its degree to *all* profession. To make professions is to play with edged tools, unless we attend to what we are saying. Words have a meaning, whether we mean that meaning or not; and they are imputed to us in their real meaning, when our not meaning it is our own fault. He who takes God's name in vain is not counted guiltless because he means nothing by it, – he cannot frame a language for himself; and they who make professions, of whatever kind, are heard in the sense of those professions, and are not excused because they themselves attach no sense to them.

Now this consideration needs especially to be pressed upon Christians at this day; for this is especially a day of professions. You will answer in my own words, that all ages have been ages of profession. So they have been, in one way or another, but this day in its own especial sense; – because this is especially a day of individual profession. This is a day in which there is (rightly or wrongly) so much of private judgement, so much of separation and difference, so much of preaching and teaching, so much of authorship, that it involves individual profession, responsibility, and recompense in a way peculiarly its own. It will not then be out of place if, in connection with the text, we consider some of the many ways in which persons, whether in this age or in another, make unreal professions, or seeing see not, and hearing hear not, and speak without mastering, or trying to master, their words. [...] This I will attempt to do at some length and in matters of detail, which are not the less important because they are minute.

Of course, it is very common in all matters, not only in religion, to speak in an unreal way; viz., when we speak on a subject with which our minds are not familiar. [...]. His remarks would be theoretical and unreal.

Again, there cannot be a more apposite specimen of unreality than the way in which judgements are commonly formed upon important questions by the mass of the community. [...] This is a day in which all men are obliged to have opinions on all questions, political, social, and religious, because they have in some way or other an influence upon the decision; yet the multitude are for the most part absolutely without capacity to take their part in it. In saying this, I am far from meaning that this need be so, – I am far from denying that there is such a thing as plain good sense, or (what is better) religious sense, which will see its way through very intricate matters, or that this is in fact sometimes exerted in the community at large on certain great questions; but at the same time this practical sense is so far from existing as regards the vast mass of questions which in this day come before the public, that (as all persons who attempt to gain the people on their side know well) their opinions must be purchased by interesting their prejudices or fears in their favour; – not by presenting a question in its real and true substance, but by adroitly colouring it, or selecting out of it some particular point which may be exaggerated, and dressed up, and be made the means of working on popular feelings. And thus government and the art of government becomes, as much as popular religion, hollow and unsound.

And hence it is that the popular voice is so changeable. One man or measure is the idol of the people today, another tomorrow. They have never got beyond accepting shadows for things. [...]

What has been here noticed of individuals, takes place even in the case of whole Churches, at times when love has waxed cold and faith failed. [...] when the seductions of the world and the lusts of the flesh have eaten out this divine inward life, what is the outward Church but a hollowness and mockery [...].

And lastly, if this unreality may steal over the Church itself, which is in its very essence a practical institution, much more is it found in the philosophies and literature of men. Literature is almost in its essence unreal; for it is the exhibition of thought disjointed from practice. Its very home is supposed to be ease and retirement; and when it does more than speak or write, it is accused of transgressing its bounds. This indeed constitutes what is considered its true dignity and honour, viz. its abstraction from the actual affairs of life; its security from the world's currents and vicissitudes; its saying without doing. A man of literature is considered to preserve his dignity by doing nothing; and when he proceeds forward into action, he is thought to lose his position, as if he were degrading his calling by enthusiasm, and becoming a politician or a partisan. Hence mere literary men are able to say strong things against the opinions of their age, whether religious or political, without offence; because no one thinks they mean anything by them. [...]

Persons are culpably unreal in their way of speaking, not when they say more than they feel, but when they say things different from what they feel.

There are ten thousand ways of looking at this world, but only one right way. [...] it is the way in which God looks at the world. Aim at looking at it in God's way. [...]. All things that we see are but shadows to us and delusions, unless we enter into what they really mean.

Let us avoid talking, of whatever kind; whether mere empty talking, or censorious talking, or idle profession, or descanting upon Gospel doctrines, or the affectation of philosophy, or the pretence of eloquence. Let us guard against frivolity, love of display, love of being talked about, love of singularity, love of seeming original. Let us aim at meaning what we say, and saying what we mean; let us aim at knowing when we understand a truth, and when we do not. When we do not, let us take it on faith, and let us profess to do so. Let us receive the truth in reverence, and pray God to give us a good will, and divine light, and spiritual strength, that it may bear fruit with us.

The Subjection of Reason and Feelings to the Revealed Word[11]

'Bringing into captivity every thought to the obedience of Christ.'
[2 Corinthians 10:5]

The question may be asked, how is it possible to live as if the coming of Christ were not far off, when our reason tells us that it probably is distant? It may be objected that there are no grounds for expecting it now, more than for the last eighteen hundred years [...].

Now in considering this objection, which I shall do, I may have an opportunity of stating a great principle which obtains in Christian duty, the subjection[12] of the whole mind to the law of God.

I deny, then, that our feelings and likings are only moved according to the dictates of what we commonly mean by reason; so far from it, that nothing is more common, on the other hand, than to say, that reason goes one way, and our wishes go another. There is nothing impossible, then, in learning to look out for the day of Christ's coming more earnestly than according to its probability in the judgement of reason. As reason may be a right guide for our feelings and liking to go by up to a certain point, so there may be cases in which it is unable to guide us, from its weakness; and as it is not impossible for sinful and irreligious men to like what their reason tells them they should not like; therefore it is not impossible for religious men also to desire, expect and hope, what their reason is unequal to approve and accept. [...] Thus, if some dreadful occurrence has taken place, a fire, or a murder, or some horrible accident, persons become frightened, lest the same should happen to them; in a measure far exceeding what a mere calculation of probabilities warrants. [...] What Almighty God

---

11 P&P 6:18.
12 'Submission' and 'subjection' are key words in understanding the mind and spirituality of Newman. It was the lack of submission to revelation and moral authority that turned him against liberalism. When his Bishop seemed against Tract 90, Newman subjected himself to his authority. It was no accident therefore that his conversion to Rome was a very dramatic and emotional act of submission to Papal authority.

then requires of us is, to do that in one instance for His sake, which we do so commonly in indulgences of our own waywardness and weakness; to hope, fear, expect our Lord's coming, more than reason warrants, and in a way which his word alone warrants; that is to trust Him above our reason. [...] If He bids us, as a matter of duty, impress the prospect of His coming upon our imagination, He asks no hard thing; no hard thing, that is, to the willing mind; and what we can do we are bound to do.

This is what first suggests itself, but it opens the way to further thoughts. For only reflect, what is faith itself but an acceptance of things unseen, from the love of them, *beyond* the determination of calculation and experience? Faith outstrips argument. If there is only a fair chance that the Bible is true, that heaven is the reward of obedience, and hell of wilful sin, it is worth while, it is safe, to sacrifice this world to the next. [...] This then is what is meant by faith going against reason, that it cares not for the measure of probabilities; it does not ask whether a thing is more or less likely; but if there is a fair and clear likelihood what God's will is, it acts upon it. If Scripture were not true, we should in the next world be left where we were; we should, in the event, be no worse off than before; but if it be true, then we shall be infinitely worse off for not believing it than if we had believed it.[13] [...].

Here, then, I am led to make a further remark; that as it is our duty to bring some things before our minds, and contemplate them much more vividly than reason by itself would bid us, so, again, there are other things which it is a duty to put away from us, not to dwell upon, and not to realise, though they be brought before us.

[...] though religious men have gifts, and though they know it, yet they do not *realise* them. It is not necessary here to explain exactly what is mean by the word 'realising'; we all understand the word enough for my present purpose, and shall all confess that, at least, there is an abundance of matters which men do not realise, though they ought to do so. For instance; how loudly men talk of the shortness of this life, of its vanity and unprofitableness, and of the claims which the world to come has upon us! This is what we hear said daily; yet few act upon the truths they utter; and why? Because they do not *realise* what they are so ready to proclaim. They do not see Him who is invisible; and His eternal kingdom.

Well, then, what men omit to do when the doing is a duty, that they can surely omit to do in cases when omission is a duty. Serious men may know indeed, if it be so, what their excellences are, whether religious or moral, or any other, but they do not feel them in that vivid way which we

---

13 This is Newman's version of Pascal's Wager.

call realising. They do not open their hearts to the knowledge, so that it becomes fruitful. Barren knowledge is a wretched thing [...] but it is a good thing, when it would otherwise act merely as a temptation. ...

[...] you will find self-indulgent men unable to comprehend the real existence of sanctity and severity of mind in anyone. They think that all persons must be full of the same wretched thoughts and feelings which torment themselves [...] only that certain persons contrive to hide what goes on in their hearts [...]

[...] I might make the same remark also as regards the absence of resentment upon injury or insult, which characterises a really religious man. Often, indeed, such a one feels keenly what is done against him, though he represses the feeling as a matter of duty; but the higher state of mind is when he does not feel, that is when he does realise, that any injustice has been done to him; so that if he attempts to speak of it, it will be in the same sort of strange, unreal, and (as I may say) forced and unnatural way in which pretenders to religion speak of religious joy and spiritual comfort, for he is as little at home with anger and revenge as hypocrites are with thoughts of heaven.

[...] Here then are a number of cases, all in point, to illustrate one and the same truth, that the Christian's character is formed by a rule higher than that of calculation and reason, consisting in a Divine principle or life, which transcends the anticipations and criticism of ordinary men. Judging by mere worldly reason, the Christian ought to be self-conceited, for he is gifted; he ought to understand evil, because he sees and speaks of it [...] but not so; his mind and heart are formed on a different mould.

The Usurpation of Reason[14]

In 1831, Newman's thinking was being tugged in three directions. The pull of his Calvinist Evangelical past was still predominant, but the intellectual-ising, liberalising influence of Richard Whately was starting to tell, as was the Catholic bias of Froude, Pusey and Keble. The battleground for Christian truth and certainty was beginning to centre for Newman upon the rival claims of faith and reason and the relation between them.

[...] 'Wisdom is justified of her children.'[15] As if He said, 'There is no

---

14 Sermon 4 in the Oxford University Sermons. Preached 11 December 1831.
15 The text of the sermon was St Matthew 11:19. The meaning is not clear. A modern interpretation would be something like: 'The proof of wisdom is to be found in the consequences of an action.' Newman on the other hand understands Christians to be the 'Children of Wisdom'.

act on God's part, no truth of religion, to which a captious Reason may not find objections; and in truth the evidence and matter of Revelation are not addressed to the mere unstable Reason of man, nor can hope for any certain or adequate reception with it. Divine wisdom speaks, not to the world, but to her own children, or those who have been already under her teaching, and who, knowing her voice, understand her words, and are suitable judges of them. These justify her.'

In the text, then, a truth is expressed in the form of a proverb, which is implied all through Scripture as a basis on which its doctrine rests – viz. that there is no necessary connection between the intellectual and moral principles of our nature; that on religious subjects we may prove anything or overthrow anything, and can arrive at truth but accidentally, if we merely investigate by what is commonly called Reason, which is in such matters but the instrument at best, in the hands of the legitimate judge, spiritual discernment. When we consider how common it is in the world at large to consider the intellect as the characteristic part of our nature, the silence of Scripture in regard to it (not to mention its positive disparagement of it) is very striking. [...]

[...] No one can deny to the intellect its own excellence, nor deprive it of its due honours; the question is merely this, whether it be not limited in its turn, as regards its range, so as not without intrusion to exercise itself as an independent authority in the field of morals and religion.

[...] Were a being unacquainted with mankind to receive information concerning human nature from the Bible, would he ever conjecture its actual state, as developed in society, in all the various productions and exhibitions of what is called talent? And, next, viewing the world as it is, and the Bible in connection with it, what would he see in the actual history of Revelation, but the triumph of the moral powers of man over the intellectual, of holiness over ability, far more than of mind over brute force. [...]

[...] This opposition between Faith and Reason takes place in two ways, when either of the two encroaches upon the province of the other. It would be an absurdity to attempt to find out mathematical truths by the purity and acuteness of the moral sense. It is a form of this mistake which has led men to apply such Scripture communications as are intended for religious purposes to the determination of physical questions. This error is perfectly understood these days by all thinking men. This was the usurpation of the schools of theology in former ages, to issue their decrees to the subjects of the Senses and the Intellect. No wonder Reason and Faith were at variance. The other cause of disagreement takes place when reason is the aggressor, and encroaches on the province of Religion, attempting to judge of those truths which are subjected to another part of our nature, the moral sense. [...] the moral perception, though varying in the mass of men, is fixed in each individual, and is an original element within us. Hume, in his *Essay on Miracles*, has well propounded a doctrine, which at the same time he misapplies. He speaks of 'those dangerous friends or disguised enemies to the Christian Religion, who have undertaken to defend it by the principles of human Reason'. 'Our most holy Religion,' he proceeds, 'is founded on *Faith*, not on Reason.' This is said in irony; but it is true as far as every important question in Revelation is concerned, and to forget this is the error which is at present under consideration. [...]

[...] Why should we be surprised that one faculty of our compound nature should not be able to do that which is the work of another? [...] Our Reason assists the senses in various ways, directing the application of them, and arranging the evidence they supply; it makes use of the facts subjected to them, and to an unlimited extent deduces conclusions from them, foretells facts which are to be ascertained, and confirms doubtful ones; but the man who neglected experiments and trusted to the vigour of his talent, would be called a theorist; and the blind man who seriously professed to lecture on light and colours could scarcely hope to gain an audience.

[...] Such would be the fate of the officious Reason, busying itself without warrant in the province of sense. [...]

[...] In this day, then, we see a very extensive development of an usurpation which has been preparing, with more or less of open avowal, for some centuries, – the usurpation of Reason in morals and religion. [...]

The usurpation of the reason may be dated from the Reformation. Then, together with the tyranny, the legitimate authority of the ecclesiastical power was more or less overthrown; and in some places its ultimate basis also, the moral sense. One school of men resisted the Church; another went further, and rejected the supreme authority of the law of Conscience. Accordingly, Revealed Religion was in great measure stripped of its proof; for the existence of the Church had been its external evidence, and its internal had been supplied by the moral sense. Reason now undertook to repair the demolition it had made, and to render the proof of Christianity independent both of the Church and of the law of nature. From that time (if we take a general view of its operations) it has been engaged first in making difficulties by the mouth of unbelievers, and then claiming power in the Church as a reward for having, by the mouth of apologists, partially removed them.

[...] And now, what remains but to express a confidence, which cannot deceive itself, that, whatever be the destined course of the usurpation of

Reason in the scheme of Divine Providence, its fall must at last come, as that of other proud aspirants before it? [...] Our plain business, in the meantime, is to ascertain and hold fast our appointed station in the troubled scene, and then to rid ourselves of all dread of the future; to be careful, while we freely cultivate the Reason in all its noble functions, to keep it in its subordinate place in our nature: while we employ it industriously in the service of Religion, not to imagine that, in this service, we are doing any great things, or directly advancing its influence over the heart; and while we promote the education of others in all useful knowledge, to beware of admitting any principle of union, or standard of reward, which may practically disparage the supreme authority of the Christian fellowship. Our great danger is, lest we should not understand our own principles, and should weakly surrender customs and institutions, which go far to constitute the Church [*sic*] what she is, the pillar and ground of moral truth, – lest, from a wish to make religion acceptable to the world in general, more free from objections than any moral system can be made, more immediately and visibly beneficial to the temporal interests of the community than God's comprehensive appointments condescend to be, we betray to its enemies; lest we rashly take the Scriptures from the Church's custody, then commit them to the world, that is to what may be called public opinion; which men boast, indeed, will ever be right on the whole, but which, in fact, being the opinion of men, who as a body, have not cultivated the internal moral sense, and have externally no immutable rules to bind them, is, in religious questions, only by accident right, or only on very broad questions, and tomorrow will betray interests which today it affects to uphold. [...]

Wilfulness,[16] the Sin of Saul[17]

Newman's relationship to the regular congregations at St Mary's and the chapel at Littlemore, as well as to the University, was basically that of a spiritual director. He was concerned with Christian formation, especially with encouraging lives of Christian holiness. Of all the obstacles to spiritual maturity, 'wilfulness', the very opposite of faith, was perhaps the greatest in his

---

16 Newman preached this sermon on 2 December 1832, the day before he set out on his Mediterranean holiday, during which he wondered whether the fever from which he nearly died was a Divine punishment for his 'wilfulness'.

17 The ninth of the University Sermons upon the text 'It repenteth Me that I have set up Saul to be king; for he is turned back from following Me, and hath not performed My commandments'. [I Samuel 15:11]

view. He sought to root it out of himself and to discourage it in others.

The three chief religious patterns and divine instruments under the first Covenant, have each his complement in the Sacred History, that we may have a warning as well as an instruction. The distinguishing virtue, moral and political, of Abraham, Moses, and David, was their faith; by which I mean an implicit reliance in God's commands and promise, and a zeal for His honour; a surrender and devotion of themselves, and all they had, to Him. At His word they each relinquished the dearest wish of their hearts, Isaac, Canaan, and the Temple; the Temple was not to be built, the land of promise not to be entered, the child of promise not to be retained. All three were tried by the anxieties and discomforts of exile and wandering; all three, and especially Moses and David, were zealous for the Lord God of Hosts.

The faith of Abraham is illustrated in the luke-warmness of Lot, who, though a true servant of God, and a righteous man, chose for his dwelling place the fertile country of a guilty people. To Moses, who was faithful in all God's house, is confronted the untrue prophet Balaam, who, gifted from the same Divine master, and abounding in all self-knowledge and spiritual discernment, mistook words for works, and fell through love of lucre. The noble self-consuming zeal of David, who was at once ruler of the chosen people, and type of the Messiah, is contrasted with a still more conspicuous and hateful specimen of unbelief, as disclosed to us in the history of Saul. [...]

Saul's character is marked by much that is considered to be the highest moral excellence, – generosity, magnanimity, calmness, energy, and decision. [...]

The first announcement of his elevation came upon him suddenly, but apparently without unsettling him. [...]

The appointment was at first unpopular. 'The children of Belial said, How shall this man save us?' Here again his high-mindedness is discovered, and his remarkable force and energy of character. He showed no signs of resentment at the insult. [...] Soon the Ammonites invaded the country beyond Jordan, with the avowed intention of reducing its inhabitants to slavery. They, almost in despair, sent to Saul for relief; [...] a decisive victory over the enemy followed. Then the popular cry became, 'Who is he that said, Shall Saul reign over us? Bring the men that we may put them to death. And Saul said, There shall not a man be put to death this day; for today the Lord hath wrought salvation in Israel.'

We seem here to find noble traits of character; at the same time it must not be forgotten that sometimes such exhibitions are also the concomitants of a certain strangeness and eccentricity of mind, which are very perplexing to those that study it, and very unamiable. [...] It is probable, from the sequel of Saul's history, that the apparent nobleness of his first actions was connected with some such miserable principles and feelings, which then only existed in their seeds, but which afterwards sprang up and ripened to his destruction; and this in consequence of that one fatal defect of mind [...]

The world prevailed over the faith of Balaam; a more subtle, though not a rare temptation, overcame the faith of Saul; wilfulness, the unaccountable desire of acting short of simple obedience to God's will, a repugnance of unreserved self-surrender and submission to Him. [...]

Such was one distinguishing sin of the Israelites as a nation; and, as it proved the first cause of their rejection, so had it also ages before, corrupted the faith, and forfeited the privileges, of their first king. The signs of wilfulness run through his history from first to last. [...]

Two questions must be answered before we can apply the lessons of Saul's history to our own circumstances. It is common to contrast Christianity with Judaism, as if the latter were chiefly a system of positive commands, and the former addressed itself to the Reason and natural Conscience; and accordingly, it will perhaps be questioned whether Christians can be exposed to the temptation of wilfulness, that is, disobedience to the external word of God, in any way practically parallel to Saul's trial. And secondly, granting it possible, the warning against wilfulness, contained in his history and that of his nation, may be met by the objection that the Jews were a peculiarly carnal and gross-minded people, so that nothing can be argued concerning our danger at this day, from their being exposed and yielding to the temptation of perversity and presumption.

What follows is a quite remarkable paragraph which illustrates Newman's ability to rise above inherited religious and social prejudice of his day. From the days of the Church Fathers, Christian theology had a quite vicious and unexamined anti-Jewish[18] dimension. It was only at the Second Vatican Council that what Jules Isaac called the 'Theology of Contempt' was criticised and rejected. 'The events of the past year' to which Newman also refers were the widespread riots and disturbances that attended the passing of the 1832 Reform Bill, which had little support at Oxford. He shows a quite extraordinary sympathy towards the widely feared 'poorer classes'.

But such an assumption evidences a great want of fairness towards the

---

18 The term 'Anti-Semitic' was first used by Wilhelm Marr in 1879.

ancient people of God, in those who make it, and is evidently perilous in proportion as it is proved to be unfounded. All men, not the Jews only, have a strange propensity, such as Eve evidenced in the beginning, to do what they are told not to do. It is plainly visible in children, and in the common people; and in them we are able to judge what we all are, before education and habit lay restraints upon us. Need we even do more than appeal to the events of the past year, to the conduct of the lower classes when under that fearful visitation, from which we are now, as we trust, recovering, in order to detect the workings of that innate spirit of scepticism and obduracy which was the enemy of Jewish faith? Of course, all places did not afford the same evidence of it; but on the whole there were enough for my present allusion to it. A suspicion of the most benevolent exertions in their favour, a jealousy of the interference of those who knew more than themselves, a perverse rejection of their services, and a counteraction of their plans and advice, an unthankful credulity in receiving all the idle tales told in disparagement of their knowledge and prudence; these were admonitions before our eyes, not to trust those specious theories which are built on the supposition, that the actual condition of the human mind is better now than it was among the Jews. This is not said without regard to the difference of guilt in disobeying a Divine and a human command; nor, again, in complaint of the poorer classes, of whom we are especially bound to be tender, and who are not the worse merely because they are less disguised in the expression of their feelings; but as pointing out for our own instruction the present existence of a perversity in our common nature, like that which appears in the history of Israel. Nor, perhaps, can any one doubt, who examines himself, that he has within him an unaccountable and instinctive feeling to resist authority as such, which conscience or the sense of interest is alone able to overcome. [...]

With these principles fresh in the memory, a number of reflections crowd upon the mind in surveying the face of society, as at present constituted. The present open resistance to constituted power, and (what is more the purpose) the indulgent toleration of it, the irreverence towards Antiquity, the unscrupulous and wanton violation of the commands and usages of our forefathers, the undoing of their benefactions, the profanation of the Church, the bold transgression of the duty of Ecclesiastical Unity, the avowed disdain of what is called party religion (though Christ undeniably made a party the vehicle of His doctrine, and did not cast it at random on the world, as men would now have it), the growing indifference to the Catholic Creed, the sceptical objections to portions of its doctrine, the arguings and discussings and comparings and correctings and rejectings, and all the train of presumptuous exercises, to which its sacred articles are subjected, the numberless discordant criticisms on the Liturgy, which have shot up on all sides of us; the general irritable state of mind, which is everywhere to be witnessed, and cravings for change in all things; what do all these symptoms show, but that the spirit of Saul still lives? – that wilfulness, which is the antagonist principle to the zeal of David, the principle of cleaving and breaking down all divine ordinances, instead of building up. And with Saul's sin, Saul's portion awaits his followers, distraction, aberration; the hiding of God's countenance; imbecility, rashness, and changeableness in their counsels; judicial blindness, fear of the multitude; alienation from good men and faithful friends; subserviency to their worst foes, the kings of Amalek and the wizards of Endor. So was it with the Jews, who rejected their Messiah only to follow impostors; so it is with infidels, who become the slaves of superstition; and such is ever the righteous doom of those who trust their own wills more than God's word, in one way or other to be led eventually into a servile submission to usurped authority. As the Apostle says of the Roman Christians, they were but slaves of sin, while they were emancipated from righteousness. […]

These remarks may at first sight seem irrelevant in the case of those who, like ourselves, are bound by affection and express promises in the cause of Christ's Church; yet it should be recollected that very rarely have its members escaped the infection of the age in which they lived: and there certainly is the danger of our considering ourselves safe, merely because we do not go to the lengths of others, and protest against the extreme principles or measures to which they are committed.

The Parting of Friends

Preached on 25 September 1843 at Littlemore

This was Newman's last sermon. It was preached on the text, 'Man goeth forth to his work and to his labour until the evening,' [Psalm 104:23.][19] and was the last sermon in his Sermons on Subjects of the Day. *After recalling the parting of such Biblical figures as David, Jacob, Jesus, Naomi, Paul and others, Newman limits his own farewell to one short, final, deeply moving paragraph.*

[…] 'Scripture is a refuge in any trouble; only let us be on our guard against seeming to use it further than is fitting, or doing more than sheltering ourselves under its shadow. Let us use it according to our measure. It is far

---

19 This was the text of Newman's first sermon preached in 1824, and also of the first sermon in *Sermons on Subjects of the Day*, 'The Work of the Christian'.

higher and wider than our need; and its language veils our feelings while it gives expression to them. It is sacred and heavenly; and it restrains and purifies, while it sanctions them.

And now brethren, 'bless God, praise Him and magnify Him, and praise Him for the things which He hath done unto you in the sight of all that live. It is good to praise God, and exalt His Name, and honourably to show forth the works of God; and therefore be not slack to praise Him.' 'All the works of the Lord are good; and He will give every needful thing in due season; so that a man cannot say, This is worse than that; for in time they shall all be well approved. And therefore praise ye the Lord with the whole heart and mouth, and bless the Name of the Lord.'[20]

'Leave off from wrath, and let go displeasure; flee from evil, and do the thing that is good.' 'Do that which is good, and no evil shall touch you.' 'Go your way; eat your bread with joy, and drink your wine with a merry heart, for God now accepteth your works; let your garments always be white, and let your head lack no ointment.'[21] And, O my brethren, O kind and affectionate hearts, O loving friends, should you know anyone whose lot it has been, by writing or by word of mouth, in some degree to help you thus to act; if he has ever told you what you knew about yourselves, or what you did not know; has read to you your wants or feelings, and comforted you by the very reading; has made you feel that there was a higher life than this daily one, and a brighter world than that you see; or encouraged you, or sobered you, or opened a way to the enquiring, or soothed the perplexed; if what he has said or done has ever made you take an interest in him, and feel well inclined towards him; remember such a one in time to come, though you hear him not, and pray for him, that in all things he may know God's will, and at all times he may be ready to fulfil it.

---

20 [Tobit 12:6. Ecclesiasticus 39: 33–35] These quotations are from the Apocrypha. The sermon was addressed to a non-university congregation. It abounds with Biblical references and illustrations.

21 Psalm 37:8,27. Tobit 12:7. Ecclesiastes 9:7,8

Chapter Three: Newman as a Historian.
'The Arians of the Fourth Century'

In March 1831, Newman was invited to write a history of the ancient Councils of the Church. Instead, he wrote The Arians of the Fourth Century. *It was finished on 31 July 1832. Newman was not happy with it. Nor was his editor, who thought it too specialised and more Roman Catholic than Protestant. Though in places Newman's prose rivals that of Gibbon, it lacks Gibbon's acerbic irony. Newman was also uncritical of his sources, being happy to condense and restate them according to his own theological interest, which was to defend Christian orthodoxy from erosion by liberal academics. The result was one of the last great works of pre-modern historical scholarship. Its significance for Newman's own theological development was that it led to his identifying more with the Church of the fourth century than that of the nineteenth. It was the beginning, too, of his habit of understanding his own Church by seeing how it looked when projected back into earlier centuries – a practice which led him ultimately to Rome.*

Chapter 1 Schools and Parties in and about the Ante-Nicene Church, considered in their relation to the Arian Heresy

Section 2 The Schools of the Sophists

It is obvious, that in every contest, the assailant, as such, has the advantage of the party assailed; and that, not merely from the recommendations which novelty gives to his cause in the eyes of bystanders, but also from the greater facility in the nature of things, of finding, than of solving objections, whatever be the question in dispute. Accordingly, the skill of a disputant mainly consists in securing an offensive position, fastening on the weaker points of his adversary's case, and then not relaxing his hold till the latter sinks under his impetuosity, without having the opportunity to display the strength of his own cause, and to bring it to bear upon his opponent; or, to make use of a familiar illustration, in causing a sudden run upon his resources, which the circumstances of time and place do not allow him to meet. This was the artifice to which Arianism owed its first successes. It owed them to the circumstance of its being (in its original form) a sceptical rather than a dogmatic teaching; to its proposing to enquire into and reform the received creed, rather than to hazard one of its own. The heresies which preceded it, originating in less subtle and dextrous talent, took up a false position, professed a theory, and sunk under the obligations which it involved. The monstrous dogmas of the various Gnostic sects pass away from the scene of history as fast as they enter it. Sabellianism, which succeeded, also ventured on a creed; and vacillating between a similar wildness of doctrine, and a less imposing ambiguity, soon vanished in its turn. But the Antiochene School, as represented by Paulus of Samosata and Arius, took the ground of an assailant, attacked the Catholic doctrine, and drew the attention of men to its difficulties, without attempting to furnish a theory of less perplexity or clearer evidence. [...]

Arianism had in fact a close connection with the existing Aristotelic school. This might have been conjectured, even had there been no proof of the fact, adapted as that philosopher's logical system confessedly is to baffle an adversary, or at most detect error, rather than to establish truth. But we have actually reason, in the circumstances of its history, for considering it as the off-shoot of those schools of enquiry and debate which acknowledge Aristotle as their principal authority, and were conducted by teachers who went by the name of Sophists. It was in these schools that the leaders of the heretical body were educated for the part assigned them in the troubles of the Church. The oratory of Paul of Samosata is characterised by the distinguishing traits of the scholastic eloquence in the descriptive letter of the Council which condemned him; in which, moreover, he is stigmatised by the most disgraceful title[1] to which a Sophist was exposed by the degraded exercise of his profession. The skill of Arius in the art of disputation is well known. [...]. Aetius came from the School of an Aristotelian of Alexandria. Eunomius, his pupil, who re-constructed the Arian doctrine on its original basis, at the end of the reign of Constantius, is represented by Rufinius as 'Pre-eminent in dialectical power'. At a later period still, the like disputatious spirit and spurious originality are indirectly ascribed to the heterodox school, in the advice of Sisinnius to Nectarius of Constantinople, when the Emperor Theodosius required the latter to renew the controversy with a view to its final settlement. Well versed in theological learning, and aware that adroitness in debate was the very life and weapon of heresy, Sisinnius proposed to the Patriarch, to drop the use of dialectics, and merely challenge his opponents to utter a general anathema against all such Ante-Nicene Fathers as had taught what they themselves now denounced as false doctrine. On the experiment being tried, the heretics would neither consent to be tried by the opinions of the ancients, nor yet dared condemn those whom 'all the people counted as

---

1 [*sophistes kai goes*] *i.e.* a juggler.

prophets'. 'Upon this, say the historians who record the story, 'the Emperor perceived that they rested their cause on their dialectic skill and not on the testimony of the early Church.'[2] [...].

And while the science of argumentation provided the means, their practice of disputing for sake of exercise or amusement supplied the temptation, of assailing received opinions. This practice, which had long prevailed in the Schools, was early introduced into the Eastern Church. It was there employed as a means of preparing the Christian teacher for the controversy with unbelievers. The discussion sometimes proceeded in the form of a lecture delivered by the master of the school to his pupils; sometimes in that of an enquiry, to be submitted to the criticism of his hearers; sometimes by way of dialogue, in which opposite sides were taken for argument-sake. In some cases, it was taken down in notes by the bystanders, at the time; in others committed to writing by the parties engaged in it. Necessary as these exercises would be for the purpose designed, yet they were obviously open to abuse, though moderated by ever so orthodox and strictly scriptural a rule, in an age when no sufficient ecclesiastical symbol existed, as a guide to the memory and judgement of the eager disputant. It is evident too, how difficult it would be to secure opinions or arguments from publicity, which were but hazarded in the confidence of Christian friendship, and which when viewed apart from the circumstances of the case, lent a seemingly deliberate sanction to heterodox novelties. Athanasius implies, that in the theological works of Origen and Theognostus, while the orthodox faith was explicitly maintained, nevertheless heretical tenets were discussed, and in their place more or less defended, by way of exercise in argument. The countenance thus accidentally given to the cause of error is evidenced in his eagerness to give the explanation. But far greater was the evil, when men destitute of religious seriousness and earnestness engaged in the like theological discussions, not with any definite ecclesiastical object, but as a mere trial of skill, or as a literary recreation; regardless of the mischief thus done to the simplicity of Christian morals, and the evil encouragement given to fallacious reasonings and sceptical views. The error of the ancient Sophists had consisted in their indulging without restraint or discrimination of practical topics, whether religious or political, instead of selecting such as might

---

2 At the time he wrote this, Newman had not yet become famous (or infamous) for his own equally clever use of dialectic. The irony was that the publication of Tract 90 was to lead to just such accusations of Sophistry. Newman's way out of the dilemma posed by his own arguments was to appeal to the authority of the ancient Church, which as he saw it was still voiced through the papacy.

exercise, without demoralising, their minds. The rhetoricians of Christian times introduced the same error into their treatment of the highest and most sacred subjects of theology. We are told that Julian commenced his opposition to the true faith by defending the heathen side of religious questions, in disputing with his brother Gallus: and probably he would not have been able himself to assign the point of time at which he ceased merely to take a part, and became earnest in his unbelief. But it is unnecessary to have recourse to particular instances, in order to prove the consequences of a practice so evidently destructive of a reverential and sober spirit.[3]

Moreover, in these theological discussions, the disputants were in danger of being misled by the unsoundness of the positions which they assumed, as elementary truths or axioms in the argument. As logic and rhetoric made them expert in proof and refutation, so there was much in other sciences, which formed a liberal education, in geometry and arithmetic, to confine the mind to the contemplation of material objects, as if these could supply suitable tests and standards for examining those of a moral and spiritual nature; whereas there are truths foreign to the province of the most exercised intellect, some of them the peculiar discoveries of the improved moral sense (or what Scripture terms '*the Spirit*'), and others still less on a level with our reason, and received on the sole authority of Revelation. Then, however, as now, the minds of speculative men were impatient of ignorance, and loath to confess that the laws of truth and falsehood, which their experience of this world furnished, could not at once be applied to measure and determine the facts of another. Accordingly, nothing was left for those who would not believe the incomprehensibility of the Divine Essence, but to conceive of it by the analogy of sense; and using the figurative terms of theology in their literal meaning as if landmarks in their enquiries, to suppose that then, and only then, they steered in a safe course, when they avoided every contradiction of a mathematical and material nature. Hence, canons grounded on physics were made the basis of discussions about possibilities and impossibilities in a spiritual substance, as confidently and as fallaciously, as those which in modern times have been derived from the same false analogies against the existence of moral self-action or free-will. Thus the argument by which Paulus of Samosata baffled the Antiochene Council, was drawn from a sophistical use of the very word *substance*, which the orthodox had employed in expressing the scriptural notion of the unity subsisting between the Father and the Son. Such too was the mode of reasoning adopted at Rome by

---

3   This whole passage reflects Newman's own view of the liberal and German critical scholarship.

the Artemas or Artemon, already mentioned, and his followers, at the end of the second century. A contemporary writer, after saying that they supported their 'God-denying apostasy' by syllogistic forms of argument, proceeds, 'Abandoning the inspired writings, they devote themselves to geometry, as becomes those who are of the earth, and speak of the earth, and are ignorant of Him who is from above. [...] It is needless to declare that such perverters of the sciences of unbelievers to the purpose of their own heresy, such diluters of the simple Scripture faith with heathen subtleties, have no claim whatever to be called believers.' And such is Epiphanius's description of the Anomoeans, the genuine offspring of the original Arian stock. 'Aiming,' he says, 'to exhibit the Divine nature by means of Aristotelic syllogisms and geometrical data, they are thence led on to declare that Christ cannot be derived from God.'

Lastly, the absence of an adequate symbol of doctrine increased evils thus existing, by affording an excuse and sometimes a reason for investigations, the necessity of which had not yet been superseded by the authority of an ecclesiastical decision. The traditional system, received from the first age of the Church, had been as yet but partially set forth in authoritative forms; and by the time of the Nicene Council, the voices of the Apostles were but faintly heard throughout Christendom, and might be plausibly disregarded by those who were unwilling to hear. Even at the beginning of the third century, the disciples of Artemas boldly pronounced their heresy to be apostolical, and maintained that all the Bishops of Rome had held it till Victor inclusive, whose episcopate was but a few years before their own time. The progress of unbelief naturally led them to disparage, rather than to appeal to their predecessors; and to trust their cause to their own ingenuity, instead of defending an inconvenient fiction concerning the opinions of a former age. It ended in teaching them to regard the ecclesiastical authorities of former times as on a level with the uneducated and unenlightened of their own days. [...] it is one of the first accusations brought by Alexander against Arius and his party, that 'they put themselves above the ancients, and the teachers of our youth, and the prelates of the day; considering themselves alone to be wise, and to have discovered truths which had never been revealed to man before them.'

On the other hand, while the line of tradition, drawn out as it was to the distance of two centuries from the Apostles, had at length become of too frail a texture to resist the touch of subtle and ill-directed reason, the Church was naturally unwilling to have recourse to the novel, though necessary measure, of imposing an authoritative creed upon those whom it invested with the office of teaching. If I avow my belief, that freedom from symbols and articles is abstractly the highest state of Christian communion, and the peculiar privilege of the primitive Church, it is not from any tenderness towards that proud impatience of control in which many exult, as in a virtue: but first, because technicality and formalism are, in their degree, inevitable results of public confession of faith; and next, because when confessions do not exist, the mysteries of divine truth, instead of being exposed to the gaze of the profane and uninstructed, are kept hidden in the bosom of the Church, far more faithfully than is otherwise possible; and reserved by a private teaching, through the channel of her ministers, as rewards in due measure and season, for those who are prepared to profit by them; for those, that is, who are diligently passing through the successive stages of faith and obedience. And thus, while the Church is not committed to declarations, which, most true as they are, still are daily wrested by infidels to their ruin; on the other hand, much of that mischievous fanaticism is avoided, which at present abounds from the vanity of men, who think that they can explain the sublime doctrines and exuberant promises of the Gospel, before they have yet learned to know themselves and to discern the holiness of God, under the preparatory disciplines of the Law and Natural Religion. Influenced, as we may suppose, by these various considerations, from reverence for the free spirit of Christian faith, and still more for the sacred truths which are the objects of it, and again from tenderness both for the heathen and the neophyte, who were unequal to the reception of the strong meat of the full Gospel, the rulers of the Church were dilatory in applying a remedy, which nevertheless the circumstances of the times imperatively required. They were loath to confess, that the Church had grown too old to enjoy the free, unsuspicious teaching with which her childhood was blessed; and that her disciples must, for the future, calculate and reason before they spoke and acted. So much was this the case, that in the Council of Antioch (as has been said), on the objection of Paulus, they actually withdrew a test which was eventually adopted by the more experienced Fathers at Nicaea; and which, if then sanctioned, might, as far as the Church was concerned, have extinguished the heretical spirit in the very place of its birth. – Meanwhile, the adoption of Christianity, as the religion of the empire, augmented the evil consequences of this omission, excommunication becoming more difficult, while entrance into the Church was less restricted than before.

Section 3 The Church of Alexandria

Here, Newman introduces his readers to the 'Disciplina Arcana',[4] *which was to offend many Protestant readers. Though the idea did not originate with Newman, he embraced with enthusiasm the suggestion that in ancient Alexandria, Orthodox theologians communicated Christian truth with 'reserve' and 'economy', as potential converts were felt to be 'unequal to the reception of the strong meat of the full Gospel'. Catechumens were taught the most profound truths last of all; and, even then, Newman thought, because of the inadequacies of language and the human propensity to argue over words, these were expressed but minimally. Having cast off his own Evangelicalism, he now disapproved of the way in which many Protestants in their preaching exploited the emotional power of the atonement and so gave their hearers strong meat before they were ready for it. For Newman, Christian doctrine was a subtle thing. Unless prepared by the reserve of the Disciplina Arcana, it was all too easy for people to mistake 'words for things'. The resulting arguments were where so much heresy began. Attempts to heal any resulting schism often led to ambiguity in the re-statement of doctrine. While Anglicans saw this as a good thing, Newman eventually came to see it as the 'unreal' position of a 'paper' Church.*

Since Newman's time, scholars have dropped the notion of the Disciplina Arcana, which was no more than an academic conjecture to explain the silence of the Fathers on certain topics. Their silence is now thought to be best explained by the idea of doctrinal development, which Newman himself advanced, as well as by necessary prudence in times of persecution and an understandable wish to safeguard the sacred from the scorn of outsiders.

'Proselytism, then, in all its branches, the apologetic, the polemical, and the didactic, being the peculiar function of the Alexandrian Church, it is manifest that the writings of its theologians would partake largely of an esoteric character. I mean, that such men would write, not with the openness of Christian familiarity, but with the tenderness or the reserve with which we are accustomed to address those who do not sympathise with us, or whom we fear to mislead or to prejudice against the truth, by precipitate disclosures of details. The example of the inspired writer of the Epistle to the Hebrews was their authority for making a broad distinction between the doctrines suitable for the state of the weak and ignorant, and those which are the peculiar property of a baptised and regenerate Christian. The Apostle in that Epistle, when speaking of the most sacred Christian veri-

---

4 'Discipline of the Secret.' The term was coined by a seventeenth-century Calvinist, Jean Daillé who rejected the authority of the Church Fathers.

ties, as hidden under the allegories of the Old Testament, seems suddenly to check himself, from the apprehension that he was divulging mysteries beyond the understanding of his brethren; who, instead of being masters in Scripture doctrine, were not yet versed even in its elements, needed the nourishment of children rather than of grown men, nay, perchance, having quenched the illumination of baptism, had forfeited the capacity of comprehending even the first elements of the truth. In the same place, he enumerates these elements, or foundations of Christian teaching, in contrast with the esoteric doctrines which the 'long-exercised habit of moral discernment' can alone appropriate and enjoy, as follows: repentance, faith in God, the doctrinal meaning of the right of baptism, confirmation as the channel of miraculous gifts, the future resurrection, and the final separation of good and bad. His first Epistle to the Corinthians contains the same distinction between carnal or imperfect and the established Christian, which is laid down in that addressed to the Hebrews. [...] As before he speaks to the difference of doctrine suited respectively to neophytes and confirmed Christians, under the analogy of the difference of food proper for the old and young; a difference which lies, not in the arbitrary will of the dispenser, but in the necessity of the case, the more sublime truths of Revelation affording no nourishment to the souls of the unbelieving or unstable.

Accordingly, in the system of the early catechetical schools, the *perfect*, or men in Christ, were such as had deliberately taken upon them the profession of believers; had made the vows, and received the grace of baptism; and were admitted to all the privileges and revelations of which the Church had been constituted the dispenser. But before reception into this full discipleship, a previous season of preparation, from two to three years, was enjoined, in order to try their obedience, and instruct them in the principles of revealed truth. During this introductory discipline, they were called *Catechumens*, and the teaching itself, *Catechetical*, from the careful and systematic examination by which their grounding in the faith was effected. The matter of the instruction thus communicated to them, varied with the time of their discipleship, advancing from the most simple principle of Natural Religion to the peculiar doctrines of the Gospel, from moral truths to the Christian mysteries. On their first admission they were denominated *hearers*, from the leave granted them to attend the reading of the Scriptures and sermons in the Church. Afterwards, being allowed to stay during the prayers, and receiving the imposition of hands as the sign of their progress in spiritual knowledge, they were called *worshippers*. Lastly, some short time before their baptism, they were taught the Lord's Prayer (the peculiar privilege of the regenerate), were entrusted with the knowledge of the Creed, and, as destined for incorporation into the body of believers, received the title of *competent* or *elect*. Even to the last, they were granted nothing beyond a formal and general account of the articles of the Christian faith; the exact and fully developed doctrines of the Trinity and the Incarnation, and still more, the doctrine of the Atonement, as once made upon the cross, and commemorated and appropriated in the Eucharist, being the exclusive possession of the serious and practised Christian. On the other hand, the chief subjects of catechisings, as we learn from Cyril, were the doctrines of repentance and pardon, of the necessity of good works, of the nature and use of baptism, and the immortality of the soul; as the Apostle had determined them.

The esoteric teaching, thus observed in the Catechetical Schools, was still more appropriate, when the Christian teacher addressed himself, not to the instruction of willing hearers, but to controversy or public preaching. At the present day, there are many sincere Christians, who consider that the evangelical doctrines are the appointed instruments of conversion, and, as such, exclusively attended with the Divine blessing. In proof of this position, with an inconsistency remarkable in those who profess a jealous adherence to the inspired text, and are not slow to accuse others of ignorance of its contents, they appeal, not to Scripture, but to the stirring effects of this (so called) Gospel preaching, and to the inefficiency, on the other hand, of mere exhortations respecting the benevolence and mercy of God, the necessity of repentance, the rights of conscience, and the obligation of obedience. But it is scarcely the attribute of a generous faith, to be anxiously enquiring into the consequences of this or that system, with a view to decide its admissibility, instead of turning at once to the revealed word, and enquiring into the rule there exhibited to us. [...]

As to Scripture, I shall but observe, [...] that no one sanction can be adduced thence, whether of precept or example, in behalf of the practice of stimulating the affections, such as gratitude or remorse, by means of the doctrine of the Atonement, in order to the conversion of hearers; that, on the contrary, it is its uniform method to connect the Gospel with Natural Religion, and to mark out obedience to the moral law as the ordinary means of attaining to a Christian faith, the higher evangelical truths, as well as the Eucharist, which is the visible emblem of them, being received as the reward and confirmation of habitual piety; that, in the preaching of the Apostles and Evangelists in the Book of Acts, the sacred mysteries are revealed to individuals in proportion to their actual religious proficiency; that the first principles of righteousness, temperance, and judgement to come, are urged upon Felix; while the Elders of Ephesus are reminded of the divinity and vicarious sacrifice of Christ, and the presence and power of the Holy Spirit in the Church; lastly, that among those converts who were made the chief instruments of the first propagation of the Gospel, or who are honoured with special favour in Scripture, none are found who had not been faithful to the light already given them, and were not distinguished, previously to their conversion, by a strictly conscientious deportment. Such are the divine notices given to those who desire an apostolical rule for dispensing the word of life; and as such, the ancient Fathers received them. They received them as the fulfilment of our Lord's command, not to give that which is holy to dogs, nor to cast pearls before swine; a text cited by Clement and Tertullian among others, in justification of their cautious distribution of sacred truth. They also considered this caution as the result of the most truly charitable consideration for those whom they addressed, who were likely to be perplexed, not converted, by the sudden exhibition of the whole evangelical scheme. This is the doctrine of Theodoret, Chrysostom, and others, in their comments upon the passage in the Epistle to the Hebrews. 'Should a catechumen ask thee what the teachers have determined, (says Cyril of Jerusalem) tell nothing to one who is without. For we impart to thee a secret and a promise of the world to come. Keep safe the secret for Him who gives the reward. Listen not to one who asks, "What harm is there in my knowing also?" Even the sick ask for wine, which, unseasonably given, brings on delirium; and so there come two ills, the death of the patient and the disrepute of the physician.' [...]

The work of St Clement of Alexandria, called Stromateis, or Tapestry-work, from the variety of its contents, well illustrates the Primitive Church's method of instruction, as far as regards the educated portion of the community. It had the distinct object of interesting and conciliating the learned heathen who perused it; but it also exemplifies the peculiar caution then adopted by Christians in teaching the truth – their desire to rouse the moral power to internal voluntary action, and their dread of loading or formalising the mind. In the opening of his work, Clement speaks of his miscellaneous discussions as mingling truth with philosophy; 'or rather,' he continues, 'involving and concealing it, as the shell hides the edible fruit of the nut'. In another place he compares them, not to a fancy garden, but to some thickly-wooded mountain, where vegetation of every sort growing promiscuously, by its very abundance conceals from the plunderer the fruit trees which are intended for the rightful owner. 'We must hide,' he says, 'that wisdom, spoken in mystery, which the Son of God has taught us. Thus the Prophet Esaias has his tongue cleansed with fire, that he may be able to declare the vision; and our ears must be sanctified as well as our tongues if we aim at being recipients of the truth. This was a hindrance to my writing; and still I have anxiety, since Scripture says, "Cast not your pearls before swine"; for those pure and bright truths, which are so marvellous and full of God to goodly natures, do but provoke laughter, when spoken in the hearing of the many.' The Fathers considered that they had the pattern as well as recommendation of this pattern of teaching in Scripture itself.

Chapter Four: Newman as a Poet

Newman, who ranks only as a rather minor nineteenth-century poet, began writing poetry at school. His first published poetry appeared in 1833, in the British Magazine, *under the heading 'Lyra Apostolica'. As a poet, Newman shares in the general weakness of the poetry of the Oxford Movement, in that his poetry was invariably the vehicle for worthy theological and moral sentiments. When, in 1868, he published his 'Verses on Various Occasions', the earliest poem he included was 'Solitude'. Though its heroic couplets are classical in form, its thought and feeling places Newman among the romantics. His poems are often a good guide to his inner life. Even as a student, his mind needed the inwardness it cultivated in 'Solitude'.*

Solitude

There is in stillness oft a magic power
To calm the breast, when struggling passions lower;
Touch'd by its influence, in the soul arise
Diviner feelings, kindred with the skies.
By this the Arab's kindling thoughts expand,
When circling skies enclose the desert sand;
For this the hermit seeks the thickest grove,
To catch th'inspiring glow of heavenly love.
It is not solely in the freedom given
To purify and fix the heart on heaven;
There is a Spirit singing aye in air,
That lifts us high above all mortal care.
No mortal measure swells that mystic sound,
No mortal minstrel breathes such tones around,
The Angels' hymn, – the sovereign harmony
That guides the rolling orbs along the sky,
And hence perchance the tales of saints who view'd
And heard Angelic choirs in solitude.
By most unheard, because the earthly din
Of toil or mirth has charm their ears to win.
Alas for man! he knows not of the bliss,
The heaven that brightens such a life as this.

Oxford, Michaelmas Term 1818

1827 was a busy year for Newman. To accept a tutorship at Oriel he had given up his curacy at St Clement's. His religious views were in flux. The moral behaviour of his students troubled him, as did some aspects of his own thinking. Academic and family pressures weighed on him and he was heading for a breakdown.

The Trance of Time

Felix, qui potuit rerum cognoscere causas,
Atque metus omnes, et inexorabile fatum
Subjecit pedibus, strepitumque Acherontis avari!

In childhood, when with eager eyes
    The season-measured year I view'd
        All, garb'd in fairy guise,
            Pledged constancy of good.

Spring sang of heaven; the summer flowers
    Bade me gaze on, and did not fade;
        Even suns o'er autumn bowers
            Heard my strong wish, and stay'd.

They came and went, the short-lived four;
    Yet, as their varying dance they wove,
        To my young heart each bore
            Its own sure claim of love.

Far different now; the whirling year
    Vainly my dizzy eyes pursue;
        And its fair tints appear
            All blent in one dusk hue.

Why dwell on rich autumnal lights,
    Spring-time, or winter's social ring?
        Long days are fire-side nights,
            Brown autumn is fresh spring.

Then what this world to thee, my heart?
    Its gifts nor feed thee nor can bless.
        Thou hast no owner's part
            In all its fleetingness.

The flame, the storm, the quaking ground,
    Earth's joy, earth's terror, nought is thine;
        Thou must but hear the sound
            Of the still voice divine.

O priceless art! O princely state!
 E'en while by sense of change opprest,
  Within to antedate
   Heaven's Age of fearless rest.

Highwood, October 1827

*On 4 January 1828, Newman's youngest sister, Mary, died unexpectedly.
Her death made him feel more intensely than ever, 'the transitory nature of
this world', and the reality of the next. Horsepath was a village near Oxford.
His mother and sisters had rented a cottage there.*

A Voice From Afar

Weep not for me;
 Be blithe as won't, nor tinge with gloom
 The stream of love that circles home,
  Light hearts and free!
 Joy in the gifts Heaven's bounty lends;
  Nor miss my face, dear friends!

I still am near;
 Watching the smiles I prized on earth,
 Your converse mild, your blameless mirth;
  Now too I hear
 Of whisper'd sounds the tale complete,
  Low prayers, and musings sweet.

A sea before
 The Throne is spread; its pure still glass
 Pictures all earth-scenes as they pass.
  We, on its shore,
 Share, in the bosom of our rest,
  God's knowledge, and are blest.

Horsepath, 29 September 1829

Though a general Christian virtue, perseverance was particularly emphasised in Calvinism, some aspects of which stayed with Newman all his life. His first book, The Arians of the Fourth Century, *had cost him a great deal of effort. In this sonnet he searches his motives, draws a conclusion and makes a life-long resolve – not to 'sin against the light'.*

The Gift of Perseverance

Once, as I brooded o'er my guilty state,
   A fever seized me, duties to devise,
   To buy me interest in my Saviour's eyes;
Not that His love I would extenuate,
But scourge and penance, masterful self-hate,
   Or gift of cost, served by an artifice
   To quell my restless thoughts and envious sighs
And doubts, which fain heaven's peace would antedate.
Thus as I tossed, He said, – 'E'n holiest deeds
Shroud not the soul from God, nor soothe its needs;
Deny thee thine own fears, and wait the end.'
Stern lesson! Let me con it day by day,
And learn to kneel before the Omniscient Ray,
Nor shrink, when Truth's avenging shafts descend!
Oxford, 23 November 1832

From the Reformation onwards, the sign of the cross in the Church of England was used only in baptism. Newman's use of the sign privately probably derived from his reading of the Church Fathers.

The Sign of the Cross

Whene'er across this sinful flesh of mine
   I draw the Holy Sign,
All good thoughts stir within me, and renew
   Their slumbering strength divine;
Till there springs up a courage high and true
   To suffer and to do.

And who shall say, but hateful spirits around,
   For their brief hour unbound,
Shudder to see, and wail their overthrow?
   While on far heathen ground
Some lonely Saint hails the fresh odour, though
   Its source he cannot know.
Oxford, 25 November 1832

On 8 December 1832 Newman began his Mediterranean holiday with the
Froudes, Hurrell, a friend and fellow tutor at Oriel, and his father. Newman
did not return to England until July 1833. During this time he wrote some
eighty poems, about half of his life's output. The last line of 'Fair Words'
again articulates Newman's deepest spiritual fear, that he might 'sin against
the light'.

Fair Words

Thy words are good, and freely given,
 As though thou felt them true;
Friend, think thee well, to hell or heaven
 A serious heart is due.

It pains thee sore, man's will should swerve
 In his true path divine;
And yet thou ventur'st nought to serve
 Thy neighbour's weal nor thine.

Beware! Such words may once be said,
 Where shame and fear unite;
But, spoken twice, they mark instead
 A sin against the light.

Gibraltar, 17 December 1832

On 28 March Newman was in Rome. Three days earlier he had been scan-
dalised by the 'unedifying dumbshow' at High Mass in Santa Maria Sopra
Minerva, during which the Pope's foot had been kissed. Nevertheless, there
were aspects, not of Roman Catholicism, but of 'Catholicism' which appealed
to him. This could well be the 'temptation' to which he refers. In the second
verse, there are clearly aspects of the cult of the Virgin which he is beginning
to find attractive.

Temptation

O Holy Lord, who with the Children Three[1]
 Didst walk the piercing flame,
Help, in those trial-hours, which, save to Thee,
 I dare not name;
Nor let these quivering eyes and sickening heart
Crumble to dust beneath the Tempter's dart.

---

1 Daniel Chapter 3, Shadrach, Meshach and Abednego, in the fiery furnace.

Thou, who didst once Thy life from Mary's breast
    Renew from day to day,
Oh, might her smile, severely sweet, but rest
    On this frail clay!
Till I am Thine with my whole soul; and fear,
Not feel a secret joy, that Hell is near.

Frascati, 28 March 1833

Between 1823 and 1827, Newman, increasingly free from his Calvinist past, found himself pulled two ways: by the theological liberalism of Whately, and the Catholicism of Pusey. He wrote later, 'I was beginning to prefer intellectual excellence to moral; I was drifting in the direction of the liberalism of the day. I was rudely awakened from my dream at the end of 1827 by two great blows – illness and bereavement'. Newman feared that liberalism might leave him with no secure doctrinal ground under him, a possibility he could not face. Liberalism was not religious enough for his strongly religious nature. In the end, only Rome offered the religious certainty he craved.

Liberalism

*'Jehu destroyed Baal out of Israel. Howbeit from the sins
of Jeroboam Jehu departed not from after them, to wit,
the golden calves that were in Bethel, and that were in Dan.'*

Ye cannot halve the Gospel of God's grace;
    Men of presumptuous heart! I know you well.
    Ye are of those who plan that we should dwell,
Each in his tranquil home and holy place;
Seeing the Word refines all natures rude,
And tames the stirrings of the multitude.

And ye have caught some echoes of its lore,
    As heralded amid the joyous choirs;
    Ye mark'd it spoke of peace, chastised desires,
Good-will and mercy – and ye heard no more;
But, as for zeal and quick-eyed sanctity,
And the dread depths of grace, ye pass'd them by.

And so ye halve the Truth; for ye in heart,
    At best, are doubters whether it be true,
    The theme discarding, as unmeet for you,
Statesmen or Sages. O new-encompass'd art

Of the ancient Foe! – but what, if it extends
O'er our own camp, and rules amid our friends.

Palermo, 5 June 1833

On 13 June Newman set out for home. In this poem he contemplates the Roman Catholic Church as he had experienced it at first hand. The attraction is emotional, the repulsion intellectual.

The Good Samaritan

O that thy creed were sound!
For thou dost soothe the heart, thou Church of Rome,
By thy unwearied watch and varied round
Of service, in thy Saviour's holy home.
  I cannot walk the city's sultry streets,
  But the wide porch invites to still retreats,
Where passion's thirst is calm'd, and care's unthankful gloom.

  There, on a foreign shore,
The homesick solitary finds a friend:
Thoughts, prison'd long for lack of speech, outpour
Their tears, and doubts in resignation end.
  I almost fainted from the long delay
  That tangles me within this languid bay,
When comes a foe, my wounds with oil and wine to tend.

Palermo, 13 June 1833

The orange boat in which Newman was sailing to Marseilles was becalmed for a week in a fog bank in the Straits of Bonifacio, between Corsica and Sardinia. The landscape was obscured, as was his future. 'The Pillar of the Cloud',[2] is Newman's best poem. Its language universal. Newman mistakenly attributed its popularity as a hymn to John B. Dykes' tune 'Lux Benigna'.

The Pillar of the Cloud

  Lead, Kindly Light, amid the encircling gloom,
    Lead Thou me on!
  The night is dark, and I am far from home –
    Lead Thou me on!

---

2 The reference is to Exodus 13:21.

Keep Thou my feet; I do not ask to see
The distant scene – one step enough for me.

I was not ever thus, nor prayed that Thou
   Shouldst lead me on.
I loved to choose and see my path, but now
   Lead Thou me on!
I loved the garish day, and, spite of fears,
Pride ruled my will: remember not past years.

So long Thy power hath blest me, sure it still
   Will lead me on,
O'er moor and fen, o'er crag and torrent, till
   The night is gone;
And with the morn those angel faces smile
Which I have loved long since, and lost awhile.

16 June 1833

For Newman, Protestant liberalism and argumentative individualism were the Mark of Cain upon the Church.

The Religion of Cain

'Am I my brother's keeper?'

The time has been, it seem'd a precept plain
   Of the true faith, Christ's tokens to display;
And in life's commerce still the thought retain,
   That men have souls, and wait a judgement-day;
   Kings used their gifts as ministers of heaven,
Nor stripped their zeal for God, of means which God had given.

'Tis altered now – for Adam's eldest born
   Has train'd our practice in a selfish rule,
Each stands alone, Christ's bonds asunder torn;
   Each has his private thoughts, selects his school,
   Conceals his creed, and lives in closest tie
Of fellowship with those who count it blasphemy.

Brothers! spare reasoning; men have settled long
    That ye are out of date, and they are wise;
Use their own weapons; let your words be strong,
    Your cry is loud, till each scared boaster flies;
    Thus the Apostles tamed the pagan breast,
They argued not, but preach'd and conscience did the rest.

Off Sardinia, 19 June 1833

All his adult life Newman wrestled with the meaning of faith and its rela-tion to reason.

Vexations

Each trial has its weight; which, whoso bears
    Knows his own woe, and need of succouring grace;
    The martyr's hope half wipes away the trace
Of flowing blood; the while life's humblest cares
Smart more, because they hold in Holy Writ no place.

This be my comfort, in these days of grief,
    Which is not Christ's, nor forms heroic tale.
    Apart from Him, if not a sparrow fail,
May not He pitying view, and send relief
When foes or friends perplex, and peevish thoughts prevail?

Then keep good heart, nor take the niggard course
    Of Thomas, who must see ere he would trust.
    Faith will fill up God's word, not poorly just
To the bare letter, heedless of its force,
But walking by its light amid earth sun and dust.

Off Sardinia, 21 June 1833

When young, Newman struggled continually against a tendency to wilful-ness. It was the subject of his last sermon before leaving for the Mediterranean. Once, as a child, he failed to get his own way with his mother. 'You see,' John she said, 'you did not get your own way.' 'No,' he answered, 'but I tried very hard.'[3] In Sicily, Newman even considered the possibility that his illness had been a punishment for his wilfulness (see Introduction, p.xiv). His way of mastering the temptation had always been to defer to the wishes of

---

3 Moz. Vol 1. p.16.

others. Now as the desire to lead began to reassert itself, his conviction that God had a purpose for him meant that he need no longer interpret it as wilfulness. A month later, his growing self confidence found its opportunity. 'Pusillanimity' is the poem that marks what was perhaps the most significant step to date in his search for a realistic and mature Christian sanctity.

Pusillanimity

How didst thou start, Thou Holy Baptist, bid
    To pour repentance on the Sinless Brow!
Then all thy meekness, from thy hearer's hid
    Beneath the Ascetics' port and Preacher's fire,
Flow'd forth, and with a pang thou didst desire
    He might be chief, not thou.

And so on us at whiles it falls, to claim
    Powers that we dread, or dare some forward part;
Nor must we shrink as cravens from the blame
    Of pride, in common eyes, or purpose deep;
But with pure thoughts look up to God, and keep
    Our secret in our heart.

At sea, 22 June 1833

In this sonnet, Newman voices his conviction that, in Sicily, God had spared his life because he had some great work for him to do.

Semita Justorum

When I look back upon my former race,
    Seasons I see at which the Inward Ray
    More brightly burn'd, or guided some new way;
Truth, in its wealthier scene and nobler space
Given for my eye to range, and feet to trace.
    And next I mark, 'twas trial did convey,
    Of grief, or pain, or strange eventful day,
To my tormented soul such larger grace.
So now, whene'er, in journeying on, I feel
The shadow of the Providential Hand,
Deep breathless stirrings shoot across my breast,
Searching to know what He will now reveal,
What sin uncloak, what stricter rule command,
And girding me to work His full behest.

At sea, 25 June 1833

*In 'The Elements' Newman takes comfort in the 'thought that the sciences
can pose no real threat to his faith because the powers of the mind are limited'.*

The Elements

Man is permitted much
   To scan and learn
In Nature's frame;
Till he well-nigh can tame
Brute mischiefs and can touch
Invisible things, and turn
All warring ills to purposes of good.
   Thus, as a god below,
   He can control,
And harmonise, what seems amiss to flow
As sever'd from the whole
And dimly understood.

But o'er the elements
   One Hand alone
   One Hand has sway.
What influence day by day
In straiter belt prevents
The impious Ocean, thrown
Alternate o'er the ever-sounding shore?
   Or who has eye to trace
   How the plague came?
Forerun the doublings of the Tempest's race?
   Or the Air's weight and flame
   On a set scale explore?

   Thus God has will'd
That man, when fully skill'd,
Still gropes in twilight dim;
Encompass'd all his hours
   By fearfullest powers
   Inflexible to him.
That so he may discern
   His feebleness,
And e'en for earth's success,
   To Him in wisdom turn,
Who holds for us the keys of either home,
Earth and the world to come.

At sea, 25 June 1833

Newman had grown up during the Napoleonic Wars when France was the national enemy. Worse still, with the apostasy of the Revolution, she had become the enemy of the Christian faith. On 20 December 1832, he could not bring himself even to look at the tricolour of a French vessel in the port at Algiers. Newman was a man long defined by his religious hates and prejudices. It was one reason why his progress to Rome was so slow.

Apostasy

France! I will think of thee as what thou wast,
    When Poictiers[4] showed her zeal for the true creed;
Or in that age, when Holy Truth, though cast
    On a rank soil, yet was a thriving seed,
Thy schools within, from neighbouring countries chased;
    E'en of thy pagan day I bear to read,
Thy Martyrs sanctified the guilty host,
The sons of blessèd John, reared on a western coast.

I dare not think of thee as what thou art,
    Lest thoughts too deep for man should trouble me.
It is not safe to place the mind and heart
    On brink of evil, or its flames to see,
Lest they should dizzy, or some taint impart,
    Or to our sin a fascination be.
And so in silence I will now proclaim
Hate of thy present self, and scarce will sound thy name.

Off the French coast, 26 June 1833

As an Anglican priest, Newman was under an obligation to say the Prayer Book offices daily. Then, at some point in 1836, he began using his friend Hurrell Froude's[5] Roman Breviary for his personal devotions. At times he would say all the Breviary offices, an exercise which took three or four hours. From 1836 to 1838, Newman made a series of free translations. The following poem is from the Parisian Breviary.

---

4 Newman's reference is to St Hilary of Poitiers [c.315–367/8] who was known as the Athenasius of the West for his championship of the Nicaean Creed against the Arians.

5 Froude had died in February 1836. His death came as a tremendous blow to Newman.

Prime (From The Parisian Breviary)[6]

Jam lucis orto sidere.

Now that the day-star glimmers bright,
　　We suppliantly pray
That He, the uncreated Light,
　　May guide us on our way.

No sinful word, nor deed of wrong,
　　Nor thoughts that idly rove;
But simple truths be on our tongue,
　　And in our hearts be love.

And, while the hours in order flow,
　　O Christ, securely fence
Our gates, beleaguer'd by the foe –
　　The gate of every sense.

And grant that to Thine honour, Lord,
　　Our daily toil may tend;
That we begin it at Thy word,
　　And in Thy favour end.

And, lest the flesh in its excess
　　Should lord it o'er the soul,
Let taming abstinence repress
　　The rebel, and control.

To God the Father glory be,
　　And to His Only Son,
And to the Spirit, One and Three,
　　While endless ages run.

Littlemore, February 1842

6　'vide the Anglo-Norman History of Sir Francis Palgrave (Vol. III. p. 588), who
　did the Author the honour of asking him for a translation of this hymn.'

Chapter Five: Newman as a Controversialist

Newman's shyness meant that in matters that required public self-assertion he was something of a late developer. For example, his powers of leadership were not really evident until he was in his early thirties. His abilities as a controversialist, however, appeared a little earlier. When he heard of Thomas Arnold's proposals to broaden the Church of England and open up its parish churches, he wrote with some humour to his sister Jemima:

If I understand it right, all sects (the Church inclusive) are to hold their meetings in the Parish Church – though not at the same hour of course. He excludes Quakers and Roman Catholics – yet even with this exclusion surely there will be too many sects in some places for one day? … If I might propose an amendment, I should say, pass an Act to oblige some persuasions to *change* the Sunday – if you have two Sundays in a week, it is plain you could easily accommodate any probable number of sects […]. Nor would this interfere with the Jews' worship (which of course is to be in the Church) – they are too few to take up a whole day. Luckily the Mohammedan holiday is already on a Friday; so there will be no difficulty of arrangement in that quarter. (L&D, 3: p.257–8).

Tracts for the Times[1]

In England, there was a long radical tradition of religious and political pamphleteering going back to the sixteenth century. Tracts for the Times differed in that they were the work of men who were profoundly conservative in both religion and politics. The following 'Advertisement' by Newman to the collection issued on 1 November 1833, serves as a manifesto as well as an introduction.

---

1   Of the ninety Tracts published between 9 September 1833 and 25 January 1841, Newman contributed twenty-nine: numbers 1–3, 6–8, 10, 11, 15, 19, 20, 21, 31, 33, 34, 38, 41, 45, 47, 71, 73, 74, 75, 79, 82, 83, 85, 88 and 90. They began as short leaflets and developed into learned treatises. At first, they were given away. Circulation improved when they were sold, and later, when bound into volumes, they sold faster than they could be printed. Numerous reprints with alterations means that there is no standard edition.

'The following Tracts were published with the object of contributing something towards the practical revival of doctrines, which, although held by the great divines of our Church, at present have become obsolete with the majority of her members, and are withdrawn from public view even by the more learned and orthodox few who still adhere to them.

The Apostolic succession, the Holy Catholic Church, were principles of action in the minds of our predecessors of the seventeenth century; but in proportion as the maintenance of the Church has been secured by law, her ministers have been under the temptation of leaning on an arm of flesh instead of her own divinely-provided discipline, a temptation increased by political events and arrangements which need not here be more than alluded to. A lamentable increase of sectarianism has followed; being occasioned (in addition to other more obvious causes) first, by the cold aspect which the new Church doctrines have presented to the religious sensibilities of the mind, next to their meagreness in suggesting motives to restrain it from seeking out a more influential discipline. Doubtless obedience to the law of the land, and the careful maintenance of 'decency and order', (the topics in useage among us,) are plain duties of the Gospel, and a reasonable ground for keeping in communion with the Established Church; yet, if Providence has graciously provided for our weakness more interesting and constraining motives, it is a sin thanklessly to neglect them; just as it would be a mistake to rest the duties of temperance or justice on the mere law of natural religion, when they are mercifully sanctioned in the Gospel by the more winning authority of our Saviour Christ. Experience has shown the inefficacy of the mere injunctions of Church order, however, scripturally enforced, in restraining from schism the awakened and anxious sinner; who goes to a dissenting preacher 'because (as he expresses it) he gets good from him': and though he does not stand excused in God's sight for yielding to the temptation, surely the Ministers of the Church are not blameless if, by keeping back the more gracious and consoling truths provided for the little ones of Christ, they indirectly lead him into it. Had he been taught as a child that the Sacraments, not preaching, are the sources of Divine Grace; that the Apostolical ministry had a virtue in it which went out over the whole Church, when sought by the prayer of faith; that fellowship with it was a gift and privilege, as well as a duty, we could not have had so many wanderers from our fold, nor so many cold hearts within it.

This instance may suggest many others of the superior influence of an apostolical over a mere secular method of teaching. The awakened mind knows its wants, but cannot provide for them; and in its hunger will feed upon ashes, if it cannot obtain the pure milk of the word. Methodism and

Popery are in different ways the refuge of those whom the Church stints of the gift of grace; they are the foster-mothers of abandoned children. The neglect of the daily service, the desecration of festivals, the Eucharist scantily administered, insubordination permitted in all ranks of the Church, orders and offices imperfectly developed, the want of Societies for particular religious objects, and the like deficiencies, lead the feverish mind, desirous of a vent to its feelings, and a stricter rule of life, to the smaller religious Communities, to prayer and Bible meetings, and ill-advised institutions and societies, on the one hand – on the other, to the solemn and captivating services by which Popery gains its proselytes. Moreover, the multitude of men cannot teach or guide themselves; and an injunction given them to depend on their private judgement, cruel in itself, is doubly hurtful as throwing them on such teachers as speak daringly and promise largely, and not only aid but supersede individual exertion.

These remarks may serve as a clue, for those who care to pursue it, to the views which have led to the publication of the following Tracts. The Church of Christ was intended to cope with human nature in all its forms, and surely the gifts vouchsafed it are adequate for that gracious purpose. There are zealous sons and servants of her English branch, who see with sorrow that she is defrauded of her usefulness by particular principles and theories of the present age, which interfere with the execution of one portion of her commission; and while they consider that the revival of this portion of truth is especially adapted to break up existing parties in the Church, and to form instead a bond of union among all who love the Lord Jesus Christ in sincerity, they believe that nothing but these neglected doctrines, faithfully preached, will repress that extension of Popery, for which the ever multiplying divisions of the religious world are too clearly preparing the way.

Oxford, The Feast of All Saints, 1834

Tract 1: Thoughts on the Ministerial Commission Respectfully addressed to the Clergy

In 1833, Newman published no less than eight Tracts.[2]

I am but one of yourselves – a Presbyter; and therefore I conceal my name, lest I should take too much on myself by speaking in my own person. Yet speak I must; for the times are very evil, yet no one speaks against them.

Is this not so? Do not we 'look upon one another', yet perform nothing?

---

2 These were: numbers: 1–3 [September]; 7 & 8 [October]; 10 [November]; 15 & 20 [December].

Do we not all confess the peril into which the Church is come, yet sit still each in his own retirement, as if mountains and seas cut off brother from brother? Therefore suffer me, while I try to draw you forth from those pleasant retreats, which it has been our blessedness hitherto to enjoy, to contemplate the condition and prospects of our Holy mother in a practical way; so that one and all may unlearn that idle habit, which has grown upon us, of owning the state of things to be bad, yet do nothing to remedy it.

Consider a moment. Is it fair, is it dutiful, to suffer our Bishops to stand the brunt of the battle without doing our part to support them? Upon them comes 'the care of all the Churches'. This cannot be helped: indeed it is their glory. Not one of us would wish in the least to deprive them of the duties, the toils, the responsibilities of their high Office. And, black event as it would be for the country, yet, (as far as they are concerned) we could not wish them a more blessed termination of their course, than the spoiling of their goods, and martyrdom.

To them then we willingly and affectionately relinquish their high privileges and honours; we encroach not upon the rights of the SUCCESSORS OF THE APOSTLES; we touch not their sword and crosier. Yet surely we may be their shield bearers in the battle without offence; and by our voice and deeds be to them what Luke and Timothy were to St Paul.

Now then let me come at once to the subject which leads me to address you. Should the Government and Country so far forget their GOD as to cast off the Church, to deprive it of its temporal honours and substance, on what will you rest the claim of respect and attention which you make upon your flocks? Hitherto you have been upheld by your birth, your education, your wealth, your connections; should these secular advantages cease, on what must Christ's Ministers depend? Is not this a serious practical question? We know how miserable is the state of religions not supported by the State. Look at the Dissenters on all sides of you, and you will see at once that their Ministers, depending simply on the people, become the creatures of the people. Are you content that this should be your case? Alas! Can a greater evil befall Christians, than for their teachers to be guided by them, instead of guiding? How can we 'hold fast the form of sound words' and 'keep that which is committed to our trust', if our influence is to depend simply upon our popularity? Is it not our very office to *oppose* the world? Can we then allow ourselves to court it? to preach smooth things and prophecy deceits? To make the way of life easy to the rich and indolent, and to bribe the humbler classes by excitements and strong intoxicating doctrine? Surely it must not be so – and the question recurs, on what are we to rest our authority, when the State deserts us?

CHRIST has not left his Church without claim of its own upon the attention of men. Surely not. Hard master he cannot be, to bid us oppose the world, yet give us no credentials for so doing. There are some who rest their divine mission on their own unsupported assertion; others, who rest it upon their popularity; others, on their success; and others, who rest it upon their temporal distinctions. This last case has, perhaps, been too much our own; I fear we have neglected the real ground on which our authority is built – OUR APOSTOLICAL DESCENT.

We have been born, not of blood, nor of the will of the flesh, nor of the will of man, but of GOD. The LORD JESUS CHRIST gave his SPIRIT to His Apostles; they in turn laid hands on those who should succeed them; and these again on others; and so the sacred gift has been handed down to our Bishops, who have appointed us as their assistants, and in some sense representatives.

Now every one of us believes this. I know that some will at first deny they do; still they do believe it. Only, it is not sufficiently practically impressed on their minds. They do believe it; for it is the doctrine of the Ordination Service, which they have recognised as truth in the most solemn season of their lives. In order then, not to reprove, but to remind and impress, I entreat your attention to the words used when you were made Ministers of CHRIST's Church.

The office of deacon was thus committed to you: 'Take thou authority to execute the office of Deacon in the Church of God committed unto thee: In the name,' &c.

And the priesthood thus:

'receive the HOLY GHOST, for the office and work of a priest, in the Church of GOD, now committed unto thee by the imposition of our hands. Who sins thou dost forgive, they are forgiven; and whose sins thou dost retain, they are retained. And be thou a faithful dispenser of the Word of GOD, and of His Holy Sacraments: In the name,' &c.

These, I say, were words spoken to us, and received by us, when we were brought nearer to GOD than at any other time of our lives. I know the grace of ordination is contained in the laying-on of hands, not in any form of words – yet in our own case (as has ever been usual in the Church) words of blessing have accompanied the act. Thus we have confessed before GOD our belief, that through the Bishop who ordained us, we received the HOLY GHOST, the power to bind and loose, to administer the Sacraments, and to preach. Now *how* is he able to give these great gifts? *Whence* is his right? Are these words idle, (which would mean taking GOD's name in vain) or do they express merely a wish, (which surely is very far below their meaning) or do they not rather indicate that the Speaker is conveying a gift? Surely they can mean nothing short of this? But whence, I ask, his right to do so? Has he any right, except as having received the power from those who consecrated him to be a Bishop? He could not give what he had never received. It is plain then that he but *transmits*; and that the Christian ministry is a *succession*. And if we trace back the power of ordination from hand to hand, of course we shall come to the Apostles at last. We know we do, as a plain historical fact; and therefore all we, who have been ordained clergy, in the very form of our ordination acknowledge the doctrine of the APOSTOLICAL SUCCESSION.

And for the same reason, we must necessarily consider none to be really ordained who have not been thus ordained. For if ordination is a divine ordinance, it must be necessary; and if it is not a divine ordinance, how dare we use it? Therefore, all who use it, all of *us*, must consider it necessary. As well we might pretend the Sacraments are not necessary to Salvation, while we make use of the offices of the Liturgy; for when GOD appoints means of grace, they are *the* means.

I do not see how anyone can escape from this plain view of the subject, except (as I have already hinted) by declaring that the words do not mean all that they say. But only reflect what a most unseemly time for random words is that, in which Ministers are set apart for their office. Do we not adopt a Liturgy, *in order to* hinder inconsiderate idle language, and shall we, in the most sacred of all services, write down, subscribe and use again and again forms of speech which have not been weighed, and cannot be taken strictly? Therefore, my dear Brethren, act up to your professions. Let it not be said that you have neglected a gift; for if you have the Spirit of the Apostles on you, surely this *is* a great gift. 'Stir up the gift of GOD which is in you.' Make much of it. Show your value of it. Keep it before your minds as an honourable badge, far higher than that secular respectability, or cultivation, or polish, or learning, or rank, which gives you a hearing with the many. Tell *them* of your gift. The times will drive you to do this, if you mean to be still any thing. But wait not for the times. Do not be compelled by the world's forsaking you, to recur as if unwillingly to the high source of your authority. Speak out now, before you are forced, both as glorifying in your privilege, and to ensure your rightful honour from your people. A notion has gone abroad, that they can take away your power. They think they have given and can take it away. They think it lies in the Church property, and they know that they have politically the power to confiscate that property. They have been deluded into a notion that present palpable usefulness, producible results, acceptableness to your flocks, that these and such like are the test of your Divine commission. Enlighten them in this matter. Exalt our Holy fathers, the Bishops, as the

Representatives of the Apostles, and the Angels of the Church; and magnify your office, as being ordained by them to take part in their Ministry.

But, if you will not adopt my view of the subject, which I offer to you, not doubtingly, yet (I hope) respectfully, at all events, CHOOSE YOUR SIDE. To remain neuter much longer will be itself to take a part. *Choose* your side; since side you shortly must, with one or other party, even though you do nothing. Fear to be of those whose line is decided for them by chance circumstances, and who may perchance find themselves with the enemies of CHRIST, while they think but to remove themselves from worldly politics. Such abstinence is impossible in troublous times. HE THAT IS NOT WITH ME, IS AGAINST ME, AND HE THAT GATHERETH NOT WITH ME SCATTERETH ABROAD.

Tract 90: Remarks on Certain Passages in the Thirty-Nine Articles

Like Tract 1, Tract 90 was published anonymously, though it was obvious that Newman was the author. He was now struggling with his doubts about the catholicity of the Church of England. This was at a time when most Englishmen had no doubt at all that it was a Protestant Church and that the Thirty-Nine Articles helped constitute it as such. Tract 90 turned everything on its head, arguing that just as the Prayer Book was Catholic in origin, so too the articles were to be interpreted as Catholic in their theology. A tide of outrage swept Newman towards Rome.

The Tract was a long one, of some eighty pages and 30,000 words, though selective[3] in the articles it examines: Holy Scripture and the Authority of the Church; Justification by Faith only; Works before and after Justification; The Visible Church; General Councils; Purgatory, Pardons, Images, Relics, Invocation of Saints; The sacraments; Transubstantiation; Masses; Marriage of Clergy; The Homilies; The Bishop of Rome. Newman quotes extensively from seventeenth-century Anglican writers as well as from the Fathers of the Church. He had once thought of being a lawyer. In the eyes of most of his fellow churchmen, Newman's powers of advocacy, which were considerable, had finally subverted themselves in Tract 90, where the articles selected were made to mean what it was clearly intended they should not. The usual form of his argument was that the inclusion of 'A' does not necessarily mean the exclusion of 'B' even though to most readers that was exactly what was intended! Put another way, the assertions of the articles are fixed in what

---

3   Tract 90 deals with articles: 11, 12, 13, 19, 21, 22, 25, 28, 31, 32, 35, 37.

they affirm, but permissive in what they pass over in silence,[4] *as the following sample section on 'Masses' shows.*

#9. Masses: Article xxxi. 'The sacrifices (sacrificia) of Masses, in the which it was commonly said, that the priest did offer CHRIST for the quick and the dead, to have remission of pain or guilt, were blasphemous fables and dangerous deceits (pernicosae imposturae).'

Nothing can show more clearly than this passage that the Articles are not written against the creed of the Roman Church, but against actual existing errors in it, whether taken into its system or not. Here the sacrifice of the Mass is not spoken of, in which the special question of doctrine should be introduced; 'but the sacrifice of the *Masses*', certain observances, for the most part privately and solitary, which for the writers of the Articles knew to have been in force in time past, and saw before their own eyes, and which involved certain opinions and a certain teaching. Accordingly the passage proceeds, 'in which it was *commonly said*', which surely is a strictly historical mode of speaking […].[5]

These sacrifices are said to be 'blasphemous fables and pernicious impostures'. Now the 'blasphemous fable' is the teaching that there is a sacrifice for sin other than CHRIST's death, and that masses are that sacrifice. And the 'pernicious imposture' is the turning this belief into a means of filthy lucre.

That the 'blasphemous fable' is the teaching that masses are sacrifices for sin distinct from the sacrifice of CHRIST's death, is plain from the first sentence of the Article. 'The offering of CHRIST *once made*, is that perfect redemption, propitiation, and satisfaction for *all* the sins of the *whole world*, *both original and actual. And there is none other* satisfaction for sin, but *that alone. Wherefore* the sacrifices of masses, &c.' It is observable too that the heading of the Article runs, 'Of the one oblation of CHRIST finished upon the cross,' which interprets the *drift* of the statement contained in it about masses.

Our Communion Service shows it also, in which the prayer of conse-

---

4   Newman's own Bishop, Richard Bagot (1782–1854) said of Tract 90 that it was 'A system of interpretation which is so subtle that by it the Articles may be made to mean anything or nothing'. He asked Newman to publish no more tracts. Newman complied. Though in his Charge to the Clergy in 1842 he thought the Tractarians showed a 'lamentable want of judgement' he nevertheless stood by them.

5   Somewhat surprisingly Newman quotes the latitudinarian Whig Bishop, Gilbert Burnet (1643–1715), who had once proposed incorporating the Nonconformists into the Church of England.

cration commences pointedly with a declaration, which has the force of a protest, that CHRIST made on the cross, 'by His *one* oblation of Himself *once* offered, a *full perfect* and *sufficient* sacrifice, oblation, and *satisfaction* for the sins of the whole world.'

And again in the offering of the sacrifice: 'We entirely desire Thy fatherly goodness mercifully to accept our sacrifice of praise and thanksgiving, most humbly beseeching Thee to grant that *by the merits and death of Thy* SON JESUS CHRIST, and through faith in His blood, we and all Thy whole Church may obtain *remission of our sins and all other benefits* of His passion [...].[6]

But the popular charge, still urged against the Roman system, as introducing in the Mass a second or rather continually recurring atonement, is a sufficient illustration, without further quotation, of this part of the Article.

That the 'blasphemous and pernicious imposture' is the turning of the Mass into a gain, is plain from such passages as the following:

> [...].What dens of thieves the Churches of England have been made by the blasphemous *buying and selling the most precious body and blood of* CHRIST *in the Mass*, as the world was made to believe, at dirges, at months minds, at trentalls[7], in abbeys and chantries, besides other horrible abuses, (GOD's holy name be blessed for ever) which we now see and understand. All those abominations they that supply the room of CHRIST are cleansed and purged the Churches of England of, taking away all such fulsomeness and filthiness, as through blind devotion and ignorance hath crept into the Church these many hundred years.
>
> *On Repairing and Keeping Clean of Churches.*[8] p.230.

Newman also quotes supporting passages from the homilies: 'On the Time and Place of Prayer' and the 'Homily concerning the Sacrament'. There are further extracts to illustrate the same point from Bishop Bull's Sermons, Burnet on Article 22.

---

6 Newman here quotes the opening of the first of the three Exhortations to Communion of the 1662 Prayer Book Service which makes the same point, that only Christ's cross and passion obtains remission of sins.

7 A Trental was [a] a set of thirty Requiem Masses, said either on a single or on successive days, or [b] a Mass said at the 'Month's Mind', thirty days after death or burial.

8 Newman is quoting from the third of twenty-one homilies in *The Second Book of Homilies*, of Edward VI. They are listed in article 35 of the Thirty-Nine Articles.

The Truth of these representations cannot be better shown than by extracting the following passage from the Session 22 of the Council of Trent:

> Whereas many things appear to have crept in heretofore, whether by the fault of the times or by the neglect and wickedness of men, foreign to the dignity of so great a sacrifice, in order that it may regain its due honour and observance, to the glory of GOD and the edification of His faithful people, the Holy Council decrees, that the Bishops, ordinaries of each places, diligently take care and be bound to forbid and put an end to all those things, which either *avarice*, which is idolatry, or *irreverence*, which is scarcely separable from impiety, or *superstition*, the pretence of true piety, has introduced. And, to say much in a few words, first of all, as to avarice, let them altogether forbid agreements, and bargains of *payment* of whatever kind, and *whatever is given for celebrating new masses*; moreover importunate and mean extortion, rather than petition of alms, and such like practices, which border on simoniacal[9] sin, certainly on *filthy lucre* [...]. And let them banish from the church those musical practices, *when with the organ or with the chant anything lascivious or impure is mingled*; also all secular practices, vain and therefore profane conversations, promenading, bustle, clamour; so that the house of GOD may truly seem and be called the house of prayer. Lastly, lest any opening be given to superstition, let them provide by edict and punishments appointed, that the priests celebrate it at no other than the due hours, not use rites or ceremonies and prayers in the celebration of masses, other than those which have been approved by the Church, and received on frequent and laudable use. And let them altogether remove from the Church a *set number of certain masses and candles*, which has proceeded rather from *superstitious observance* rather than from true religion, and teach the people in what consists, and from whom, above all, proceeds the so precious and heavenly fruit of this most holy sacrifice. And let them admonish the same people to come frequently to their parish Churches, at least on Sundays and the greater feast, &c.

On the whole, then, it is conceived that the Article before us neither speaks against the Mass in itself, nor against its being [and offering, though commemorative] for the quick and the dead for the remission of sin; (especially since the decree of Trent says, that 'the fruits of the Bloody Oblation are through this most abundantly obtained; so far is the latter from detracting in any way from the former') but against its being viewed, on the one hand,

---

9   Simony was the buying or selling of a church office or ecclesiastical preferment. [See Acts 8:9–24.]

as independent of or distinct from the Sacrifice on the Cross, which is blasphemy; and, on the other, its being directed to the emolument of those to whom it pertains to celebrate it, which is imposture in addition.

Newman, of course, anticipated the Protestant reaction to Tract 90 and so added the following conclusion in the hope that it might go some way to explain his case and assuage the fury.

Conclusion: One remark may be made in conclusion. It may be objected that the tenor of the above explanations is anti-Protestant, whereas it is notorious that the Articles were drawn up by Protestants, and intending for the establishment of Protestantism; accordingly, that it is an evasion of their meaning to give them any other than a Protestant drift, possible as it may be to do so grammatically, or in each separate part.

But the answer is simple:

1. In the first place, it is a *duty* which we owe both to the Catholic Church and to our own, to take our reformed confessions in the most Catholic sense they will admit; we have no duties towards their framers. [Nor do we receive the Articles from their original framers, but from several successive convocations after their time; in the last instance, from that of 1662.]

2. In giving the Articles a Catholic interpretation, we bring them into harmony with the Book of Common Prayer, an object of the most serious moment in those who have given their assent to both formularies.

3. Whatever be the authority of the Declaration prefixed to the Articles, so far as it has any weight at all, it sanctions the mode of interpreting them above given. For its enjoining the 'literal and grammatical sense' relieves us from the necessity of making the known opinions of their framers a comment upon the text; and its forbidding any person to 'affix any new sense to any article' was promulgated at a time when the leading men of our Church were especially noted for those Catholic views which have been here advocated.

4. It may be remarked, moreover, that such an interpretation is in accordance with the well-known general leading of Melanchthon, from whose writings our Articles are principally drawn, and whose Catholic tendencies gained for him that same reproach of popery which has ever been so freely bestowed upon members of our own reformed Church.[10]

---

10 Newman then quotes the historian Mosheim (1694–1755) as declaring that for the sake of reconciliation with Rome, Melanchthon was prepared to give up as 'things indifferent': justification by faith alone, the necessity of good works for salvation, the jurisdiction claimed by the Pope etc.

5. Further: the articles are evidently framed on the principle of leaving open large questions, on which the controversy hinges. They state broadly extreme truths, and are silent about their adjustment. For instance, they say that all necessary faith must be proved from Scripture, but they do not say *who* is to prove it. They say that the Church has authority in controversies, they do not say *what* authority. They say that it may enforce nothing beyond Scripture but do not say *where* the remedy lies when it does. They say the works before grace and justification are worthless and worse, and that works *after* grace *and* justification are acceptable, but they do not speak at all of works *with* GOD's aid, *before* justification. They say that men are lawfully called and sent to minister and preach, who are called and chosen by men who have public authority over them in the congregation to call and send; but they do not add *by whom* the authority is to be given. They say that councils called by princes may err; they do not determine whether councils called *in the name of* CHRIST will err.

6. The variety of doctrinal views contained in the Homilies, as above shown, views which cannot be brought under Protestantism itself, in its widest comprehension of opinions, is an additional proof, considering the connection of the Articles with the Homilies, that the Articles are not framed on the principle of excluding those who prefer the theology of the early ages to that of the Reformation; or rather since both Homilies and Articles appeal to the Fathers and Catholic antiquity, let it be considered whether in interpreting them by these, we are not going to the very authority to which they profess to submit themselves.

7. Lastly, their framers constructed them in such a way as best to comprehend those who did not go so far in Protestantism as themselves. Anglo-Catholics then are but the successors and representatives of those moderate reformers; and their case has been directly anticipated in the wording of the Articles. It follows that they are not perverting, they are using them, for an express purpose for which among others their authors framed them. The interpretation they take was intended to be admissible; though not that which their authors took themselves. Had it not been provided for, possibly the Articles never would have been accepted by our Church at all. If, then, their framers have gained their side of the compact in effecting the reception of the Articles, the Catholics have theirs too in retaining their own Catholic interpretation of them.

An illustration of this occurs in the history of the twenty-eighth article. In the beginning of Elizabeth's reign a paragraph formed part of it, much like that which is now appended to the Communion Service, but in which the Real Presence was *denied in words*. It was adopted by the clergy at the first convocation, but not published.[11]....

What lately has taken place in the political world will afford an illustration in point. A French Minister, desirous of war, nevertheless, as a matter of policy, draws up his state papers in such moderate language that his successor, who is for peace, can act up to them, without compromising his own principles. The world, observing this, has considered it a circumstance for congratulation; as if the former minister, who acted a double part, had been caught in his own snare, It is neither decorous, nor necessary, nor altogether fair, to urge the parallel rigidly; but it will explain what is here meant to convey. The Protestant Confession was drawn up with the purpose of including Catholics; and Catholics now will not be excluded. What was an economy in the reformers, is a protection to us. What would have been a perplexity to us then, is a perplexity to Protestants now. We could not then have found fault with their words; they cannot now repudiate our meaning.

Oxford, The Feast of the Conversion of St Paul, 1841

The aim of the first Tract had been to rouse the clergy and convince them of the Catholic truth that the Church was more than an arm of the State; the effect of this last Tract was to rally most of the nation to its Protestant identity.

The Tamworth Reading Room

On 19 January 1841, Sir Robert Peel, a founder of the modern Conservative Party and of one nation Toryism, opened a Library and Reading Room at Tamworth and used the occasion to give a speech on the power of education to effect moral improvement. Peel's second term as Prime Minister (1841–6) began later that year and was marked by a genuine concern to promote the welfare and interests of the working class. His speech at Tamworth showed that he understood and supported their desire for intellectual and moral self-improvement. For Newman, moral growth was an outcome of Christian holiness, not of a secular education. Peel's speech was published in the Times, *and later revised and issued as a pamphlet. Though Newman was reluctant*

---

11 Newman quotes Burnet on Article 28 here. The whole Tract abounds with quotations and references: there are twenty in one paragraph on *The Visible Church* alone. He is an advocate who has clearly mastered his brief, though the case he argued persuaded few and alienated the majority.

to respond to the speech, the proprietor of the Times, *John Walter, eventually prevailed on him. Newman wrote seven letters to the editor using the pen-name 'Catholicos'. They reveal Newman as a satirist of the first rank; one who relished a fight on paper, and whose quest for personal holiness in no way precluded a don's intellectual pleasure at publicly besting an adversary. Newman's wit, though rarely exercised, could be calculated and cruel. In opposing Peel's hope that institutions like the Tamworth Reading Room would unite everyone in the furtherance of knowledge, Newman shows himself as an anti-liberal sectarian, unwilling to open up Oxford to non-Anglicans. The Tamworth Reading Room reveals Newman at his best and his worst.*

The First Letter: Secular Knowledge in contrast with Religion

Sir, – Sir Robert Peel's position in the country, and his high character, render it impossible that his words and deeds should be other than public property. This alone would furnish an apology for my calling the attention of your readers to the startling language, which many of them doubtless have already observed, in the address which this most excellent and distinguished man has lately delivered upon the establishment of a Library and Reading Room at Tamworth; but he has superseded the need of apology altogether, by proceeding to present it to the public in the form of a pamphlet. His speech, then, becomes important, both from the name and the express act of its author. At the same time, I must allow that he has not published it in the fullness in which it was spoken. Still, it seems to me right and fair, or rather imperative, to animadvert upon it as it has appeared in your columns, since in that shape it will have the widest circulation. A public man must not claim to harangue the whole world in newspapers, and then to offer his second thoughts to such as choose to buy them at a bookseller's.

I shall surprise no one who has carefully read Sir Robert's Address, and perhaps all who have not, by stating my conviction, that, did a person take it up without looking at the heading, he would to a certainty set it down as a production of the years 1827 and 1828 – the scene Gower Street, the speaker Mr Brougham[12] or Dr Lushington, and the occasion, the laying the first stone, or the inauguration, of the then-called London University. I profess myself quite unable to draw any satisfactory line of difference between the Gower Street and the Tamworth Exhibition, except, of

---

12 Henry Peter Brougham, Baron Brougham and Vaux, died 1868. After whom the Brougham carriage is named.

course, that Sir Robert's personal religious feeling breaks out in his Address across his assumed philosophy. I say assumed, I might say affected – for I think too well of him to believe it genuine.

On the occasion in question, Sir Robert gave expression to a theory of morals and religion, which of course, in a popular speech, was not put out in a very dogmatic form, but which, when analysed and fitted together, reads somewhat as follows: Human nature, he seems to say, if left to itself, becomes sensual and degraded. Uneducated men live in the indulgence of their passions; or, if they are merely taught to read, they dissipate and debase their minds by trifling and vicious publications. Education is the cultivation of the intellect and heart, and Useful Knowledge is the great instrument of education. It is the parent of virtue, the nurse of religion; it exalts man to his highest perfection, and is the sufficient scope of his earnest exertions. [...]

And, in addition, it is a kind of neutral ground, on which men of every shade of politics and religion may meet together, disabuse each other of their prejudices, form intimacies, and secure cooperation.

This, it is almost needless to say, is the very theory, expressed temperately, on which Mr Brougham once expatiated in the Glasgow and London Universities. [...]

Mr Brougham laid down at Glasgow the infidel principle, or, as he styles it, 'the great truth', which 'has gone forth to all the ends of the earth, that man shall no more render account to man for his belief, over which he has himself no control'. And Dr Lushington applied it in Gower Street to the College then and there rising, by asking, 'Will any one argue for establishing a *monopoly* to be enjoyed by the few who are of one *denomination* of the Christian Church only?' And he went on to speak of the association and union of all *without exclusion or restriction*, of 'friendships cementing the bonds of charity, and softening the *asperities* which *ignorance and separation* have fostered'. Long may it be before Sir Robert Peel professes the great principle itself! Even though, as the following passages show, he is inconsistent enough to think highly of its application in the culture of the mind. He speaks, for instance, of 'this preliminary and fundamental rule, that no works of *controversial divinity* shall enter into the library [applause]', – of 'the institution being open to all persons of all descriptions, without reference to political opinions, or *religious creed*', and of 'an edifice in which men of all political opinions and *all religious feelings* may unite in the furtherance of knowledge without the *asperities of party feeling*'. Now, that British society should consist of persons of different religions, is this a positive standing evil, to be endured at best as unavoidable, or a topic of exultation? Of exultation, answers Sir Robert; the greater the difference the better, the more the merrier. So we must interpret his tone.

It is reserved to few to witness the triumph of their own opinions; much less to witness it in the instance of their own direct and personal opponents. Whether the Lord Brougham of this day feels all the satisfaction and inward peace which he attributes to success of whatever kind in intellectual efforts, it is not for me to decide; but that he has achieved, to speak in his own style, and is leading in chains behind his chariot-wheels a great captive is beyond question. Such is the reward in 1841 for unpopularity in 1827.

Whatever, however, is a boast to Lord Brougham, is in the same proportion a slur upon the fair fame of Sir Robert Peel, at least in the judgement of those who hitherto have thought well of him. Were there no other reason against the doctrine propounded in the Address which has been the subject of these remarks, (but I hope to be allowed an opportunity of assigning others), its parentage would be a grave *primâ facie* difficulty in receiving it. It is, indeed, most melancholy to see so sober and experienced a man practising the antics of one of the wildest performers of this wild age; and taking off the tone, manner, and gestures of the versatile ex-Chancellor, with a versatility almost equal to his own.

Yet let him be assured that the task of rivalling such a man is hopeless, as well as unprofitable. No one can equal the great sophist. Lord Brougham is inimitable in his own line.

The Second Letter: Secular Knowledge not the Principle of Moral Improvement

A distinguished Conservative statesman tells us from the town-hall of Tamworth that 'in becoming wiser a man will become better', meaning by wiser more conversant with the facts and theories of physical science; and that such a man will 'rise *at once* in the scale of intellectual and *moral* existence'. 'That,' he adds, 'is my belief.' He avows, also, that the fortunate individual whom he is describing, by being 'accustomed to such contemplations, will feel the *moral dignity of his nature exalted*'. [...] It will be difficult to exhaust the reflections which rise in the mind on reading avowals of this nature.

The first question which obviously suggests itself is how these wonderful moral effects are to be wrought under the instrumentality of the physical sciences. Can the process be analysed and drawn out, or does it act like a dose or charm which comes into general use empirically? Does Sir Robert Peel mean to say, that whatever be the occult reasons for the result, so it is; you have but to drench the popular mind with physics, and moral and religious advancement follows on the whole, in spite of individual failures? [...] To know is one thing, to do is another; the two things are altogether distinct. A man knows he should get up in the morning – he lies abed; he knows he should not lose his temper, yet he cannot keep it. A labouring man knows he should not go to the ale-house, and his wife knows she should not filch when she goes out charring, but, nevertheless, in these cases, the consciousness of a duty is not all one with the performance of it. There are then large families of instances, to say the least, in which men may become wiser, without becoming better; what then is the meaning of this great maxim in the mouth of its promulgators? [...]

Now without using exact theological language, we may surely take it for granted, from the experience of facts, that the human mind is at best in a very unformed or disordered state; passions and conscience, likings and reason, conflicting, might rise against right, with the prospect of things getting worse. Under these circumstances, what is it that the School of Philosophy in which Sir Robert has enrolled himself proposes to accomplish? Not a victory of the mind over itself – not the supremacy of the law – not the reduction of rebels – not the unity of our complex nature – not the harmonising of the chaos – but the mere lulling of the passions to rest by turning the course of thought; not a change of character, but a mere removal of temptation. This should be carefully observed. When a husband is gloomy, or an old woman peevish and fretful, those who are about them do all they can to keep dangerous topics and causes of offence out of the way, and think themselves lucky, if, by skilful management, they get through the day without an outbreak. When a child cries, the nurserymaid dances it about, or points to the pretty black horses out of the window, or shows how ashamed poll-parrot or poor puss must be of its tantrums. Such is the sort of prescription which Sir Robert Peel offers to the good people of Tamworth. He makes no pretence of subduing the giant nature, in which we were born, of smiting the loins of the domestic enemies of our peace, overthrowing passion and fortifying reason; but he does offer to bribe the foe for the nonce with gifts which will avail for that purpose just so long as they *will* avail, and no longer.

This was mainly the philosophy of the great Tully, except when it pleased him to speak as a disciple of the Porch. Cicero handed the recipe to Brougham, and Brougham passed it on to Peel. If we examine the old Roman's meaning in 'O *philosophia, vitae dux*', it was neither more no less than this – that *while* we were thinking of philosophy, we were not thinking of anything else; we did not feel grief, or anxiety, or passion, or ambition, or hatred all that time, and the only point was to keep thinking of it. How to keep thinking of it was *extra artem*. If a man was in grief, he was to be amused; if disappointed, to be excited; if in a rage, to be soothed; if in love, to be aroused to the pursuit of glory. No inward change was contemplated, but a change of external objects; as if we were all White Ladies or Undines, our moral life being one of impulse and emotion, not subjected to laws, not consisting in habits, not capable of growth. When Cicero was outwitted by Caesar, he solaced himself with Plato; when he lost his daughter, he wrote a treatise on Consolation. Such, too, was the philosophy of that Lydian city, mentioned by the historian, who in famine played at dice to stay their stomachs. […]

Whether Sir Robert Peel meant all this, which others before him have meant, it is impossible to say; but I will be bound, if he did not mean this, he meant nothing else, and his words will certainly insinuate this meaning, wherever a reader is not content to go without any meaning at all. They will countenance, with his high authority, what in one form or another is a chief error of the day, in very distinct schools of opinion – that our true excellence comes not from within, but from without; not wrought out through personal struggles and sufferings, but following up a passive exposure to influences over which we have no control. They will countenance the theory that diversion is the instrument of improvement, and excitement the condition of right action; and whereas diversions cease to be diversions if they are constant, and excitements by their very nature have a crisis and run through a course, they will tend to make novelty ever in request, and will set the great teachers of morals upon the incessant search after stimulants and sedatives, by which unruly nature may, *pro re natâ*, be kept in order.

Hence, be it observed, Lord Brougham […] tells us, with much accuracy of statement, that 'intellectual occupation made the heart' of Pascal or Cowper '*for the time* forget its griefs'. He frankly offers us a philosophy of expedients: he shows us how to live by medicine. Digestive pills half an hour before dinner, and a posset at bedtime at the best; and at worst, dram-drinking and opium – the very remedy against broken hearts, or remorse of conscience, which is the request among the many, in gin palaces *not* intellectual.

And if these remedies be but of temporary effect at the utmost, more commonly they will have no effect at all. Strong liquors, indeed, do for a time succeed in their object; but who was ever consoled in real trouble by the small beer of literature or science? […]

Such is this new art of living, offered to the labouring classes – we will say for instance, in a severe winter, snow on the ground, glass falling, bread rising, coal at 20d the cwt., and no work.

[…] – that grief, anger, cowardice, self-conceit, pride, or passion, can be subdued by an examination of shells or grasses, or chipping of rocks, or calculating the longitude, is the veriest of pretences which sophist or mountebank ever professed to a gaping auditory. If virtue be a mastery over the mind, if its end be action, if its perfection be inward order, harmony and peace, we must seek it in graver and holier places than in Libraries and Reading Rooms.

The Third Letter: Secular Knowledge not a Direct Means of Moral Improvement

[…] Now independent, of all other considerations, the great difference, in a practical light, between the object of Christianity and heathen belief, is this – that glory, science, knowledge, and whatever other fine names we use, never healed a wounded heart, nor changed a sinful one; but the Divine Word is with power. The ideas which Christianity brings before us are in themselves full of influence, and they are attended with a supernatural gift over and above themselves, in order to meet the special exigencies of our nature. Knowledge is not 'power', nor is glory 'the first and only fair', but 'Grace', or the 'Word', by whichever name we call it, has been from the first a quickening, renovating, organising principle. It has new-created the individual, and transferred and knit him into a social body, composed of members each similarly created. It has cleansed man from his moral diseases, raised him to hope and energy, given him to propagate a brotherhood among his fellows, and to found a family or rather a kingdom of saints all over the earth; it introduced a new force into the world, and the impulse which it gave continues in its original vigour down to this day. Each one of us has lit his lamp from his neighbour, or received it from his fathers, and the lights thus transmitted are at this time as strong and as clear as if 1800 years had not passed since the kindling of the sacred flame. What has glory or knowledge been able to do like this? Can it raise the dead? Can it create a polity? Can it do more than testify man's need and typify God's remedy?

And yet, in spite of this, when we have an instrument given us, capable of changing the whole man, great orators and statesmen are busy, forsooth, with their heathen charms and nostrums, their sedatives, correctives, or restoratives; as preposterously as if we were to build our men of war, or conduct our iron-works, on the principles approved in Cicero's day. […]

In morals, as in physics, the stream cannot rise higher than its source. Christianity raises men from earth, for it comes from heaven; but human morality creeps, struts, or frets upon the earth's level, without wings to rise. The Knowledge School does not contemplate raising man above himself; it merely aims at disposing his existing powers and tastes, as is most convenient, or is practical under the circumstances. [...] It leaves man where it found him – man, and not an Angel – a sinner, not a Saint; but it tries to make him look as much like what he is not as ever it can. [...] 'Temperance topics' stop drinking; let us suppose it; but will much be gained, if those who give up spirits take to opium? *Naturam expellas furcâ, tamen usque recurret*, is at least a heathen truth, and universities and libraries which recur to heathenism may reclaim it from the heathen as their motto.

[...]. I have no fanatical wish to deny to any whatever subject of thought or method of reason a place altogether, if it chooses to claim it, in the cultivation of the mind. Mr Bentham may despise verse-making, or Mr Dugdale Stewart logic, but the great and true maxim is to sacrifice none – to combine, and therefore to adjust, all. All cannot be first, and therefore each has its place, and the problem is to find it. It is at least not a lighter mistake to make what is secondary first, than to leave it out altogether. Here then it is that the Knowledge Society, Gower Street College, Tamworth Reading Room, Lord Brougham and Sir Robert Peel are all so deplorably mistaken. Christianity, and nothing short of it, must be made the element and principle of all education. Where it has been laid as the first stone, and acknowledged as the governing spirit, it will take up into itself, assimilate, and give a character to Knowledge, Knowledge of all kinds will minister to Revealed Truth. [...] But if in education we begin with nature before grace, with evidences before faith, with science before conscience, with poetry before practice, we shall be doing much the same as if we were to indulge the appetites and passions, and turn a deaf ear to the reason. In each case we misplace what in its place is a divine gift. If we attempt to effect a moral improvement by means of poetry, we shall but mature into a mawkish, frivolous, and fastidious sentimentalism – if by means of argument, into a dry, unamiable long-headedness; if by good society, into a polished outside, with hollowness within, in which vice has lost its grossness, and perhaps increased in malignity; if by experimental science, into an uppish, supercilious temper, much inclined to scepticism. But reverse the order of things: put faith first and Knowledge second; let the University minister to the Church, and then classical poetry becomes the type of Gospel truth, and physical science a comment on Genesis or Job, and Aristotle changes into Butler, and Arcesilas into Berkeley. [...]

The Fourth Letter: Secular Knowledge not the Antecedent of Moral Improvement

Human nature wants recasting, but Lord Brougham is all for tinkering it. [...]

I suppose we may readily grant that the science of the day is attended by more lively interest, and issues in more entertaining knowledge, than a study of the New Testament. Accordingly, Lord Brougham fixes upon such science as the great desideratum of human nature, and puts aside faith under the nickname of opinion. I wish Sir Robert Peel had not fallen into the snare, insulting doctrine by giving it the name of 'controversial divinity'.

However, it will be said that Sir Robert, in spite of such forms of speech, differs essentially from Lord Brougham; for he goes on in the latter part of his Address which has occasioned these remarks, to speak of science as leading to Christianity. [...] Depend on it, it is not so safe a road and so expeditious a journey from premise and conclusion as Sir Robert anticipates. The way is long, and there are not a few half-way houses and traveller's rests along it; and who is to warrant that the members of the Reading Room and Library will go steadily on to the goal he would set before them? And, when at length, they come to 'Christianity', pray how do the roads lay between it and 'controversial divinity'? Or, grant the Tamworth readers to *begin* with Christianity as well as science, the same question suggests itself, What is Christianity? Universal benevolence? Exalted morality? Supremacy of law? Conservatism? An age of light? And age of reason? – Which of them all?

Most cheerfully do I render to so religious a man as Sir Robert Peel the justice of disclaiming any insinuation on my part, that he has any intention at all to put aside religion; yet his words either mean nothing, or they do, both on their surface, and when carried into effect, mean something very irreligious.

And now for one plain proof of this.

It is certain, then, that the multitude of men have neither time nor capacity for attending to many subjects. If they attend to one, they will not attend to the other; if they give their leisure and curiosity to this world, they will have none left for the next. We cannot be everything; as the poet says, '*non omnia possumus omnes*'. We must make up our minds to be ignorant of much, if we would know anything. And we must make our choice between risking Science, and risking Religion. Sir Robert indeed says, 'Do not believe that you have not time for rational recreation. It is the idle man who wants time for everything'. However, this seems to me rhetoric; and what I have said to be the matter of fact, for the truth of which I appeal, not to argument, but to the proper judges of facts – common sense and practical experience; and if they pronounce it to be a fact, then Sir Robert Peel, little as he means it, does unite with Lord Brougham in taking from Christianity what he gives to Science.

I will make this fair offer to both of them. Every member of the Church Established shall be eligible to the Tamworth Library on one condition – that he brings from the 'public minister of religion', to use Sir Robert's phrase, a ticket of his proficiency in Christian Knowledge. We will have no 'controversial divinity' in the Library, but a little out of it. If the gentlemen of the Knowledge School will but agree to teach town and country Religion first, they shall have a *carte blanche* from men to teach anything or everything else second. Not a word has been uttered or intended in these Letters against Science; I would treat it, as they do *not* treat 'controversial divinity', with respect and gratitude. They caricature doctrine under the name of controversy. I do not nickname Science infidelity. I call it by their own name, 'useful and entertaining knowledge', and I call doctrine 'Christian knowledge' and, as thinking Christianity something more than useful and entertaining, I want faith to come first, and utility and amusement to follow. […]

However, the Tamworth Reading Room admits of one restriction, which is not a little curious, and has no very liberal sound. It seems that all '*virtuous women*' may be members of the Library; that 'great injustice would be done to the *well-educated and virtuous women* of the town and neighbourhood' had they been excluded. A very emphatic silence is maintained about women not virtuous. What does this mean? Does it mean to exclude them, while *bad* men are admitted? Is this accident, or design, sinister and insidious, against a portion of the community? What has virtue to do with a Reading Room? It is to *make* its members virtuous; it is to exalt *the moral dignity* of their nature; it is to provide 'charms and temptations' to allure them from sensuality and riot. To whom but to the vicious ought Sir Robert to discourse about 'opportunities' and 'access' and 'moral improvement', and who else would prove a fitter experiment, and a more glorious triumph, of scientific influences? And yet he shuts out all but the well-educated and virtuous.

Alas, that bigotry should have left the mark of its hoof on the great 'fundamental principle of the Tamworth Institution'! […]

The Fifth Letter: Secular Knowledge not a Principle of Social Unity

Sir Robert Peel proposes to establish a Library which 'shall be open to all persons of all descriptions, without references to political opinions or to religious creed'. [...]

[...] are religious principles to be put on a level even with political? Is it as bad to be a republican as a believer? ... Is a difference about the Reform Bill all one with a difference about the Creed? Is it as polluting to hear arguments for Lord Melbourne[13] as to hear a scoff against the Apostles? To a statesman, indeed, like Sir Robert, to abandon one's party is a far greater sacrifice than to unparliamentary men; and it would be uncandid to doubt that he is rather magnifying politics than degrading Religion in throwing them together; but still, when he advocates concessions in theology *and* politics, he must be plainly told to make presents of things that belong to him, nor seek to be generous with other people's substance. There are entails in more matters than parks and old places. He made his politics for himself, but Another made theology.

[...] He tells us that his great aim is the peace and good order of the community, and the easy working of the national machine. With this in view, any price is cheap, everything is marketable; all impediments are a nuisance. [...] It is a mistake, too, to say that he considers all differences of opinions as equal in importance; no, they are only equally in the way. [...]

'I cannot help thinking,' he exclaims at Tamworth, 'that *by bringing together in an institution of this kind* intelligent men of all classes and conditions of life, by uniting together, in the committee of this institution, the gentleman of ancient family and great landed possessions with the skilful mechanic and artificer of good character, I cannot help believing that we are *harmonising* the gradations of society, and binding men together by a *new* bond, which will have *more than ordinary* strength on account of the object which unites us.' The old bond, he seems to say, was Religion; Lord Brougham's is Knowledge. Faith, once the soul of social union, is now but the spirit of division. Not a single doctrine but is 'controversial divinity', not an abstraction can be imagined (could abstractions constrain), not a comprehension projected (could comprehensions connect), but will leave out one or other portion or element of the social fabric. We must abandon religion, if we aspire to be statesmen. Once, indeed, it was a living power, kindling hearts, leavening them with one idea, moulding them on one

---

13 Viscount Melbourne (William Lamb), was Prime Minister in a Whig government, briefly, in 1834, when Sir Robert Peel succeeded him. He was Prime Minister again from 1835–41, when Peel again displaced him.

model, developing them into one polity. Ere now it has been the life of morality; it has given birth to heroes; it has wielded empire. But another age has come in, and Faith is effete; let us submit to what we cannot change; [...] Seek we out some young and vigorous principle, rich in sap, and fierce in life, to give form to elements which are fast resolving into their inorganic chaos; and where shall we find such a principle but in knowledge. [...]

The Sixth Letter: Secular Knowledge not a Principle of Action

People say to me that it is but a dream to suppose that Christianity should regain the organic power in human society which it once possessed. I cannot help that; I never said it could. I am not a politician; I am proposing no measures, but exposing a fallacy, [...] The ascendancy of Faith may be impracticable, but the reign of knowledge is incomprehensible. The problem for statesmen of this age is how to educate the masses, and literature and science cannot give the solution.

Not so deems Sir Robert Peel; [...] He certainly thinks that scientific pursuits have some considerable power of impressing religion upon the mind of the multitude. I think not, and will now say why.

Science gives us the grounds or premises from which religious truths are to be inferred; but it does not set about inferring them, much less does it reach the inference – that is not its province. [...] We have to take its facts, and give them a meaning, and to draw out our own conclusions from them. First comes Knowledge, then a view, then reasoning, and then belief. This is why Science has so little of a religious tendency; deductions have no power of persuasion. The heart is commonly reached, not through the reason, but through the imagination, by means of direct impression, by the testimony of facts and events, by history, by description. [...] Many a man will live and die upon a dogma: no man will be a martyr for a conclusion. [...] No one, I say, will die for his own calculations; he dies for realities. This is why a literary religion is so little to be depended upon; it looks well in fair weather, but its doctrines are opinions; and when called to suffer for them, it slips them between its folios, or burns them at its hearth. And this again is the secret of the distrust and raillery with which moralists have been so commonly visited. They say and do not. Why? Because they are contemplating the fitness of things, and they live by the square, when they should be realising their high maxims in the concrete. [...]

I have no confidence, then, in philosophers who cannot help being religious, and are Christians by implication. They sit at home, and reach forward to distances which astonish us; but they have hit without grasping, and are sometimes as confident about shadows as about realities. They have worked out by a calculation the lie of a country which they never saw, and mapped it by means of a gazetteer; [...]

Logic makes but a sorry rhetoric with the multitude; first shoot round corners, and you may not despair of converting by a syllogism. Tell men to gain notions of a Creator from His works, and, if they were to set about it (which nobody does), they would be jaded and wearied by the labyrinth they were tracing. [...] Logicians are more set upon concluding rightly, than on right conclusions. [...] To most men argument makes the point in hand only more doubtful, and considerably less impressive. After all, man is *not* a reasoning animal; he is a seeing, feeling, contemplating, acting animal. [...] It is very well to freshen our impressions and convictions from physics, but to create them we must go elsewhere. [...]

Life is not long enough for a religion of inferences; we shall never have done beginning, if we determine to begin with proof. [...] I would rather be bound to defend the reasonableness of assuming that Christianity is true, than to demonstrate a moral governance from the physical world. Life is for action. If we insist on proofs for everything, we shall never come to action: to act you must assume, and that assumption is faith.

[...]. I have no wish at all to speak otherwise than respectfully of conscientious Dissenters, but I have heard it said by those who are not their enemies, and who had known much of their preaching, that they had often heard narrow-minded and bigoted clergymen, and often Dissenting ministers of a far more intellectual cast; but that Dissenting teaching came to nothing – that it was dissipated in thoughts which had no point, and enquiries which converged to no centre, that it ended as it began, and sent away its hearers as it found them; whereas the instruction in the Church, with all its defects and mistakes, comes to some end, for it started from some beginning. Such is the difference between the dogmatism of faith and the speculations of logic. [...]

The Seventh letter: Secular Knowledge without Personal Religion tends to Unbelief

When Sir Robert Peel assures us from the Town Hall at Tamworth that physical sciences must lead to religion, it is no bad compliment to him to say that he is unreal. He speaks of what he knows nothing about. To a religious man like him, Science has ever suggested religious thoughts; he colours the phenomena of physics with the hues of his own mind, and mistakes an interpretation for a deduction. [...]

[...] to have recourse to physics to *make* men religious is like recommending a canonry as a cure for the gout, [...].

[…] I believe that the study of Nature, when religious feeling is away, leads the mind, rightly or wrongly, to acquiesce in the atheistic theory, as the simplest and easiest. […]

There are two ways, then, of reading nature – as a machine and as a work. If we come to it with the assumption that it is a creation, we shall study it with awe; if assuming it to be a system, with mere curiosity. […] 'When we survey the marvellous truths of astronomy, we are first of all lost in the feeling of immense space, and of the comparative insignificance of this globe and its inhabitants. But there soon arises a *sense of gratification* and of new wonder at perceiving how so insignificant a creature has been *able to reach such a knowledge* of the unbounded system of the universe'.[14] So, this is the religion we are to gain from the study of Nature; how miserable! The god we attain is our own mind; our veneration is even professedly the worship of self.

The truth is that the system of nature is just as much connected with Religion, where minds are not religious, as a watch or a steam carriage. The material world, indeed, is infinitely more wonderful than any human contrivance; but wonder is not religion, or we should be worshipping our railroads. […]

It is observable that Lord Brougham does not allude to any *relation* as existing between his *god* and ourselves. […] What we seek is what concerns us, the traces of a Moral Governor; even religious minds cannot discern these in the physical sciences; astronomy witnesses divine power, and physics divine skill; and all of them divine beneficence; but which teaches of divine holiness, truth, justice, or mercy? Is that much of a Religion which is silent about duty, sin, and its remedies? Was there ever a religion which was without the idea of an expiation?

[…] How melancholy is it that a man of such exemplary life, such cultivated tastes, such political distinction, such Parliamentary tact, and such varied experience, should have so little confidence in himself, so little faith in his own principles, so little hope of sympathy in others, so little heart for a great venture, so little of romantic aspiration, and of firm resolve, and stern dutifulness to the Unseen! How sad that he who might have had the affections of many, should have thought in a day like this, that a Statesman's praise lay in preserving the mean, not in aiming at the high; that to be safe was his first merit, and to kindle enthusiasm his most disgraceful blunder! How pitiable that such a man should not have understood that a body without a soul has no life, and a political party without an idea, no unity.

---

14 Newman is here quoting Lord Brougham

Chapter Six: Newman as a Theologian

Lectures on the Prophetical Office of the Church Viewed Relatively to Romanism and Popular Protestantism

From its beginnings in 1833, to its end with Newman's conversion in 1845, the Oxford Movement can be thought of as a prolonged experiment in ecclesiology. The movement had begun as a 'Catholic' attempt to defend the Church of England as a divine and mystical reality against what was assumed to be the Protestant assumption that it was little more than a social and political institution. At this stage, Newman believed that Anglicanism was a 'Via Media', that is a Middle Way between Rome and the Protestantism of Luther and Calvin. It was a conviction that first found its way into print in two Tracts for the Times *published in August 1834; and an ecclesiology that Newman developed in more detail in his 'Prophetical Office', published on 11 March 1837, and known today as the 'Via Media'.*[1]

Newman's 'Prophetical Office' derived from two sources: his correspondence with the Abbé Jager, and his weekday Parochial Lectures. Had space allowed, the fourteen lectures that made up the work would have embraced the Sacerdotal as well as the Prophetical Office of the Church. It was because Newman believed that the Church of England, as it existed in reality in his day, fell short of embodying his high doctrine of the Church, that he left it for a communion which he believed did, however inadequately.

Introduction

[...] Unhappy is it that we should be obliged to discuss and defend what a Christian people were intended to enjoy, to appeal to their intellects

---

1 The third and final edition of *The Prophetical Office* appeared in 1877 as the second volume of his *The Via Media of the Anglican Church*. It contained a long and important Preface which set out his final contribution to ecclesiology, but this time from a Roman Catholic's point of view. Because 'The author cannot destroy what he has once put into print', Newman included his 'refutation' in the Preface and in various notes.

instead of 'stirring up their pure minds by way of remembrance', to direct them towards articles of faith which should be their place of starting, and to treat as mere conclusions what in other ages have been assumed as first principles. Surely life is not long enough to prove everything which may be made the subject of proof; and, though enquiry is left partly open in order to try our earnestness, yet it is in great measure, and in the most important points, superseded by Revelation – which discloses things which reason could not reach, saves us the labour of using it when it might avail, and sanctions thereby the principle of dispensing with it in other cases. Yet in spite of this joint testimony of nature and grace, so it is, we seem at this day to consider discussion and controversy to be in themselves chief goods. We exult in what we think our indefeasible right and glorious privilege to choose and settle our religion for ourselves; and we stigmatise it as a bondage to be obliged to accept what the wise, the good, and the many of former times have made over to us, nay, even to submit to what God Himself has revealed.

[...] the consequences are undeniable; the innocent suffer by a state of things, which to the self-wise and the carnal is an excuse for their indifference. The true voice of Revelation has been overpowered by the more clamorous traditions of men; and where there are rivals, examination is necessary, even where piety would fain have been rid of it. Thus, in relation to the particular subject which has led to these remarks, that some one meaning was anciently attached to the word 'Church', is certain from its occurring in the Creed; it is certain, for the same reason, that it bore upon some first principle in religion, else it would not have been there. It is certain, moreover, from history, that its meaning was undisputed, whatever that meaning was; and it is as certain that there are interminable disputes and hopeless differences about its meaning now. Now, is this a gain or a loss to the present age? At first sight one might think it a loss, so far as it goes, whatever be the cause of it; in the same sense in which the burning of a library is a loss, the destruction of a monument, the disappearance of an ancient record, or the death of an experimentalist or philosopher. Diminution from the stock of knowledge is commonly considered a loss in this day; yet strange to say, in the instance before us, it is thought far otherwise. The great mass of educated men are at once uneasy, impatient, and irritated, not simply incredulous, as soon as they are promised from any quarter some clear view of the original and apostolic doctrine, to them unknown, on any subject of religion. They bear to hear of researches into Christian Antiquity, if they are directed to prove its uncertainty and unprofitableness; they are intolerant and open-mouthed against them, if their object be to rescue, not to destroy. They sanction a rule of philosophy which they practically refute every time they praise Newton or Cuvier.[2] In truth, they can endure a categorical theory in other provinces of knowledge; but in theology belief becomes practical. They perceive that there, what in itself is but an enquiry into questions of fact, tends to an encroachment upon what they think fit to consider their Christian liberty. They are reluctant to be confronted with evidence which will diminish their right of thinking rightly or wrongly, as they please; they are jealous of being forced to submit to one view of the subject, and to be unable at their pleasure to change; they consider comfort in religion to lie in all questions being open, and in there being no call upon them to act. Thus they deliberately adopt that liberty which God gave His former people in wrath, 'a liberty to the sword, to the pestilence, and to the famine',[3] the prerogative of being heretics or unbelievers.

It would be as well if these men[4] could keep their restless humours to themselves; but they unsettle all around them. They rob those of their birthright who would have hailed the privilege of being told the truth without their own personal risk in finding it; and they force them against their nature upon relying on their reason, when they are content to be saved by faith. Such troublers of the Christian community would in a healthy state of things be silenced or put out of it, as disturbers of the king's peace are restrained in civil matters; but our times, from whatever cause, being times of confusion, we are reduced to the use of argument and disputation, […].

Let this be my excuse for discussing rather than propounding what was meant to be simply an article of faith. We travel by night: the teaching of the Apostles concerning it, which once, like the pillar in the wilderness was with the children of God from age to age continually, is in good measure withdrawn; and we are so far left to make the best of our way to the promised land by our natural resources.

In the following Lectures, then, it is attempted, in the measure which such a mode of writing allows, to build up what man has pulled down, in

---

2 Cuvier, George Léopold Chrétien Frédéric Dagobert, Baron (1769–1832) was the foremost French naturalist and palaeontologist of his day. Newman studied some science as an undergraduate and as an 'educated layman' kept abreast of important scientific developments.

3 Jeremiah 34:17.

4 In what is an extraordinary passage Newman the anti-liberal regrets not only the Reformation and the freedom of intellectual and spiritual enquiry to which it gave rise, but also responds to it with what would nowadays be an unacceptable paternalism. Yet, paradoxically, in his response he often resorts to surprisingly 'liberal' values and tactics.

some of the questions connected with the Church; and that, by means of the stores of Divine truth bequeathed to us in the works of our standard English authors.

The immediate reason for discussing the subject is this: In the present day, such incidental notice of it as Christian teachers are led to take in the course of their pastoral instructions, is sure to be charged with what is commonly called 'Popery', and for this reason – that Roman Catholics have ever insisted upon it, and Protestants have neglected it, to speak of the Church at all, though it is mentioned in the Creed, is thought to savour of Rome. Those then who feel its importance, and yet are not Romanists, are bound on several accounts to show why they are not Romanists, and how they differ from them. [...]

[...] After all, the main object in a discussion should be, not to refute error merely, but to establish truth. [...] It is a poor answer to this enquiry, merely to commence an attack upon Roman teaching, and to show that it presents an exaggerated and erroneous view of the doctrine. [...] we are bound in very shame to state what we hold ourselves, [...].

[...] The question is, what is that sound and just exposition of this Article of faith, which holds together, or is consistent in theory, and, secondly, is justified by the history of the Dispensation, which is neither Protestant nor Roman, but proceeds along that *via media*, which, as in other things so here, is the appropriate path for sons of the English Church to walk in. What is the nearest approximation to that primitive truth which Ignatius and Polycarp enjoyed, and which the nineteenth century has virtually lost?

[...] We have a vast inheritance, but no inventory of our treasures. All is given us in profusion; it remains for us to catalogue, sort, distribute, select, harmonise, and complete. We have more than we know how to use; stores of learning, but little that is precise and serviceable; Catholic truth and individual opinion, first principles and guesses of genius, all mingled in the same works, and requiring to be discriminated. [...]

Lecture 1: *The Nature and Ground of Roman and Protestant Errors*

All Protestant sects of the present day may be said to agree with us and differ from Roman Catholics, in considering the Bible as the only standard of appeal in doctrinal enquiries. They differ indeed from each other as well as from us in the matter of their belief; but they one and all accept the written word of God as the supreme and sole arbiter of their differences. This makes their contest with each other and us more simple; I do not say shorter – on the contrary, they have been engaged in it almost three hundred years, (as many of them, that is, as are so ancient) and there are no symptoms of its ending – but it makes it less laborious. It narrows the ground of it; it levels it to the intelligence of all ranks of men; it gives the multitude a right to take part in it; it encourages all men, learned and unlearned, religious and irreligious, to have an opinion in it, and to turn controversialists. The Bible is a small book; anyone may possess it; and everyone, unless he is very humble, will think he is able to understand it. And, therefore, I say, controversy is easier among Protestants, because anyone whatever can controvert; easier but not shorter, because though all sects agree together as to the standard of faith, viz. the Bible, yet no two agree as to the interpreter of the Bible, but each person makes himself the interpreter, so that what seemed at first sight a means of peace, turns out to be a chief occasion or cause of discord.

It is a great point to come to issue with an opponent; that is to discover some position which oneself affirms and the other denies, and on which the decision of the controversy will turn. It is like two armies meeting, and settling their quarrel in a pitched battle, instead of wandering to and fro, each by itself, and inflicting injury and gaining advantage where no one resists it. Now the Bible is this common ground among Protestants, and seems to have been originally assumed in no small degree from a notion of its simplicity in argument. But, if such a notion has been entertained in any quarter, it has been disappointed by this difficulty – the Bible is not so written as to force its meaning upon the reader; no two Protestant sects can agree together whose interpretation of the Bible is to be received; and under such circumstances each naturally prefers his own – his own 'interpretation', his own 'doctrine', his own 'tongue', his own 'revelation'. Accordingly, acute men among them see that the very elementary notion which they have adopted, of the Bible without note or comment being the sole authoritative judge in controversies of faith, is a self-destructive principle, and practically involves the conclusion, that dispute is altogether hopeless and useless, and even absurd. After whatever misgivings or reluctance, they seem to allow, or to be in the way to allow, that truth is but matter of opinion; that that is truth to each which each thinks to be the truth, provided he really and sincerely believes it; that the divinity of the Bible itself is the only thing that need be believed, and that its meaning varies with the individuals who receive it; that it has no meaning to be ascertained as a matter of fact, but that it may mean anything because it may be made to mean so many things; and hence that our wisdom and our duty lie in discarding all notions of the importance of any particular set of opinions, any doctrines, or any creed, each man having a right to his own, and in living together peaceably with men of all persuasions, whatever our private judgement and leanings may be.

[...] But the case is different as regards Roman Catholics: they do not appeal to Scripture unconditionally; they are not willing to stand or fall by mere arguments from Scripture; and, therefore, if we take Scripture as our ground of proof in our controversies with them, we have not yet joined issue with them. Not that they reject Scripture, it would be very unjust to say so; they would shrink from doing so, or being thought to do so; and perhaps they adhere to Scripture as closely as some of those Protestant bodies who profess to be guided by nothing else; but, though they admit Scripture to be the Word of God, they conceive that it is not the whole word of God, they openly avow that they regulate their faith by something else besides Scripture, by the existing Traditions of the Church. They maintain that the system of doctrine which they hold came to them from the Apostles as truly and certainly as the apostolic writings; so that, even if those writings had been lost, the world would still have had the blessings of a Revelation. Now, they must be clearly understood, if they are to be soundly refuted. We hear it said, that they go by Tradition, and we fancy in consequence that there are a certain definite number of statements ready framed and compiled, which they profess to have received from the Apostles. One may hear the question sometimes asked, for instance, where their professed traditions are to be found, whether there is any collection of them, and whether they are printed and published. Now though they would allow that the Traditions of their Church are in fact contained in the writings of the Doctors, still this question proceeds on somewhat of a misconception of their real theory, which seems to be as follows. By Tradition they mean the whole system of faith and ordinances which they have received from the generation before them, and that generation again from the generation before itself. And in this sense undoubtedly we all go by Tradition in matters of this world. Where is the corporation, society, or fraternity of any kind, but has certain received rules and understood practices which are nowhere put down in writing? How often do we hear it said, that this or that person has 'acted unusually', that so and so 'was never done before', that it is 'against rule', and the like; and then perhaps, to avoid the inconvenience of such irregularity in future, what was before a tacit engagement, is turned into a formal and explicit order or principle. The absence of a regulation must be felt before it is supplied; and the virtual transgression of it goes before its adoption. At this very time a great part of the law of the land is administered under the sanction of such a Tradition; it is not contained in any formal or authoritative code, it depends on custom or precedent. There is no explicit written law, for instance, simply declaring murder to be a capital offence; unless indeed we have recourse to the divine command in the ninth chapter of the book of Genesis.

Murderers are hanged by *custom*. Such as this is the tradition of the Church; Tradition is uniform custom. When the Romanists say they adhere to Tradition, they mean that they believe and act as Christians have always believed and acted; they go by the custom, as judges and juries do. And then they go on to allege that there is an important difference between their custom and all other customs in the world; that the tradition of the law, at least in its details, though it had lasted for centuries upon centuries, anyhow had a beginning in human appointments; whereas theirs, though it has a beginning too, yet, when traced back, has none short of the Apostles of Christ, and is in consequence of divine not of human authority – it is true and intrinsically binding as well as expedient. […]

How then are we to meet the Romanists, […]? We must meet them, and do so fearlessly, on the ground of Antiquity, to which they betake themselves. We accepted the Protestant's challenge, in arguing from mere Scripture in our defence; we must not and need not shrink from the invitation of our Roman opponent, when he would appeal to the witness of Antiquity. Truth alone is consistent with itself; we are willing to take either the test of Antiquity or of Scripture. As we accord to the Protestant sectary, that Scripture is the inspired treasury of the whole faith, but maintain that his doctrines are not in Scripture, so when the controversialist of Rome appeals to Antiquity as our great teacher, we accept his appeal, but we deny that his special doctrines are to be found in Antiquity. […] we challenge our opponent to prove the matter of fact. […] his doctrines are innovations,[5] because they run counter to the doctrine of Antiquity, and because they rest upon what is historically an upstart Tradition.

This view is intelligible and clear, but it leads to this conclusion. The Bible is indeed a small book, but the writings of Antiquity are voluminous; and to read them is the work of a life. It is plain then that the controversy with Rome is not an easy one, not open to everyone to take up. And this is the case for another reason also. A private Christian may put what meaning he pleases on many parts of Scripture, and no one can hinder him. If interfered with, he can promptly answer that it is his opinion and may appeal to his right of Private Judgement. But he cannot so deal with Antiquity. History is a record of 'facts', and facts, according to the proverb 'are stubborn things'. Ingenious men may misrepresent them, or suppress them for a while; but in the end they will be duly ascertained and appreciated. The writings of the Fathers are far too ample to allow of a disputant resting in one or two obscure or ambiguous passages in them, and perma-

---

5 It is just this objection that Newman met in his groundbreaking *Essay On The Development of Christian Doctrine*.

nently turning such to his own account, which he may do in the case of Scripture. For two reasons, then, controversy with Romanists is laborious; because it takes us into ancient Church history, and because it does not allow scope to the off-hand or capricious decisions of private judgement.

[...] Romanism *holds the foundation*, or *is the truth overlaid with corruption*.[6] [...] Such is the relation of Romanism towards true Catholicity. It is the misdirection and abuse, not the absence of right principle.

[...] we Anglo-Catholics do not profess a different religion from that of Rome, we profess their Faith *all but* their corruptions.

Again, this same character of Romanism as a perversion, not a contradiction of Christian Truth, is confessed as often as members of our Church in controversy with it contend, as they may rightly do, that it must be judged, not by the formal decrees of the Council of Trent, as its advocates wish, but by its practical working and its existing state in the countries which profess it. Romanists would fain confine us in controversy to the consideration of the bare and acknowledged principles of their Church; we consider this to be an unfair restriction; why? because we conceive that Romanism is far more faulty in its details than in its formal principles, and that Councils, to which its adherents would send us, have more to do with its abstract system than with its practical working, that the abstract system contains for the most part tendencies to evil, which the actual working brings out, thus supplying illustrations of that evil which is really though latently contained in principles capable themselves of an honest interpretation. Thus, for instance, the decree concerning Purgatory might be charitably made almost to conform to the doctrine of St Austin or St Chrysostom, were it not for the comment on it afforded by the popular belief as existing in those countries which hold it, and by the opinions of the Roman schools.

[...] The best Dissenter is he who is least of a Dissenter; the best Roman Catholic is he who comes nearest to a Catholic.

Lecture 2: On Roman Teaching as Neglectful of Antiquity

[...] Whatever principles they[7] profess in theory, resembling, or coincident with our own, yet when they come to particulars, when they have to prove this or that article of their creed, they supersede the appeal to Scripture and Antiquity by putting forward the infallibility of the Church, thus solving the whole question, by summary and final interpretation both

---

6 Newman would hold to his belief that the Pope was the Antichrist until 1843.
7 i.e. Roman Catholics.

of Antiquity and Scripture. [...]

First, let us understand what is meant by saying that Antiquity is of authority in religious questions. Both the Roman schools and ourselves maintain as follows: That whatever doctrine the primitive ages unanimously attest, whether by consent of the Fathers, or by Councils, or by the events of history, or by controversies, or in whatever way, whatever may fairly and reasonably be considered to be the universal belief of those ages, is to be received as coming from the Apostles. This Canon, as it may be called, rests upon the principle, which we act on daily, that what many independent and competent witnesses guarantee, is true. [...] If it be asked, why we do not argue in this way from the existing as well as from the ancient Church, we answer that Christendom now differs from itself in all points except those in which it is already known to have agreed of old; so that we cannot make use of it if we could. [...] Thus Ancient Consent is, practically, the only, or main kind of Tradition which now remains to us.

... Infant Baptism, for instance, must have been appointed by the Apostles, or we should not find it received so early, so generally, with such a silence concerning its introduction. [...] Universality, of course, proves nothing, if it is traceable to an origin short of Apostolic. [...]

Lecture 3: Doctrine of Infallibility Morally Considered

[...] We must take and deal with things as they are, not as they pretend to be. If we are induced to believe the professions of Rome, and make advances towards her as a sister or a mother Church, which in theory she is, we shall find too late that we are in the arms of a pitiless and unnatural relative, who will but triumph in the arts which have inveigled us within her reach. No; dismissing the dreams which the romance of early Church history and the high doctrines of Catholicism will raise in the inexperienced mind, let us be sure that she is our enemy, and will do us a mischief if she can. In speaking and acting on this conviction, we need not depart from Christian charity towards her. We must deal with her as we would towards a friend who is not himself; in great affliction, with all affectionate tender thoughts, with tearful regret and a broken heart, but still with a steady eye and a firm hand. And in saying this, I must not be supposed to deny that there is any real excellence in the religion of Rome even as it is, or that any really excellent men are its adherents. Satan ever acts on a system; various, manifold, and intricate, with parts and instruments of different qualities, some almost purely evil, others so unexceptionable, that in themselves and detached from the end to which all is subservient, they are really 'Angels of light', and may be found so at the last day. [...] And the points to which I wish to direct attention, as involved in the doctrine of Infallibility, are such as the following: that Romanism considers unclouded certainty necessary for a Christian's faith and hope, and doubt incompatible with practical abidance in the truth; that it aims at forming a complete and consistent theology, and in forming it, neglects authority, and rests upon abstract arguments and antecedent grounds; and that it substitutes a technical and formal obedience for the spirit of love. [...]

The doctrine of the Church's Infallibility is made to rest upon the notion, that any degree of doubt about religious truth is incompatible with faith, and that an external infallible assurance is necessary to exclude doubt. 'Proof', or certainty of things believed, is secured upon two conditions; if there be a God, 'who cannot lie' as the source of Revelation, and if the Church be infallible to convey it. Otherwise, it is urged, what is called faith is merely opinion, as being but partial or probable knowledge. To this statement it is sufficient to reply here, that according to English principles, religious faith has all it needs in having only the former of these two secured to it, in knowing that God is our Creator and Preserver, and that He *may*, if it so happen, have spoken. [...] When we are not personally concerned, even the highest evidence does not move us; when we are concerned the very slightest is enough. [...] Action is the criterion of true faith [...] Nay, doubt in some way or measure may even be said to be implied in a Christian's faith. Not that infallible certainty would take away all trial of our hearts, and force us to obey [...].

[...] When St Thomas doubted of His resurrection, far from justifying his demand for an infallible witness, He declared that he was but diminishing his blessedness by giving him a higher evidence of the miracle than he had already received. [...]

This leads me to notice an important peculiarity of the Roman system, to which such a temper gives rise. According to its *theory*, the Church professes to know only what the Apostles knew, to have received just what they delivered, neither more nor less. But in fact, she is obliged to profess a complete knowledge of the whole Dispensation, such as the Apostles had not. Unless we know the whole of any subject we must have difficulties somewhere or other; and where they are left, there we cannot possess infallible knowledge. [...] there are no degrees in infallibility. [...] Thus, I say, to know all that is revealed with equal clearness, implies that there is nothing not revealed.

This then, is a second and not least observable peculiarity of Roman theology. It professes to be a complete theology. It arranges, adjusts, explains, exhausts every part of the Divine Economy. [...] That feeling of awe which the mysteriousness of the Gospel should excite, fades away under this fictitious illumination which is poured over the entire Dispensation. [...] this technical religion destroys the delicacy and reverence of the Christian mind. ... Rome would classify and number all things, she would settle every sort of question [...]

Lecture 4: Doctrine of Infallibility Politically Considered

If the object of Rome be to teach moral Truth in its highest and purest form, like a prophet or philosopher, intent upon it more than upon those who she addresses, and by the very beauty of holiness, and the unconscious rhetoric of her own earnestness, drawing up souls to her, rather than by any elaborate device, certainly she has failed in that end [...]. But if her one and supreme end is to rule the human mind, if man is the object of her thoughts and efforts, and religion but the means of approaching him, if earth is to be the standard, and heaven the instrument, then we must confess that she is most happy in her religious system. [...] Now the Church of Rome *is* a political power; and, if she stunts, or distorts the growth of the soul in spiritual excellence, it is because, whether unconsciously or not, she has in view political objects, visible fruits, temporal expediency, the power of influencing the heart, as the supreme aim and scope of her system; because she considers unity, peace, the public confession of the truth, sovereignty, empire, the one practical end for which the Church is formed, the one necessary condition of those other and unknown benefits, whatever these be, which lie beyond it in the next world. I am now to illustrate this peculiarity; and in order that there may be no mistake, I will briefly say what I am to do. I do not attempt to prove that Rome is a political power; so well-known a fact may be taken for granted; but I wish to show that those same principles, involved in the doctrine of Infallibility, which distinguish it from our own creed, morally, conduce to that special political character, which also distinguishes it from our own; that what is morally a disadvantage to it, is a political gain; I mean its neglect of the Fathers, its abstract reasonings, and its attention to a system. [...]

[...] We, for our part, have been taught to consider that in its degree, faith, as well as conduct, must be guided by probabilities, and that doubt is ever our portion in this life. We can bear to confess that other systems have their unanswerable arguments in matters of detail, and that we are but striking a balance between difficulties existing on both sides; that we are following as the voice of God, what on the whole we have reason to think such. We are not bent (to God be the praise!) on proselytising, organising, and ruling as the end of life and the *summum bonum* of a Christian community, but have brought ourselves to give our testimony 'whether men will hear, or whether they will forbear', and then leave the matter to God. [...]

Those who are thus minded, will be patient under the inconveniences of an historical controversy. Perceiving that on the whole facts point to certain definite conclusions, and not to their contraries, they will adopt those conclusions unhesitatingly; illuminate what, though true, is obscure, by acting upon it; call upon others to do the same; and leave them to God if they refuse. But it will be otherwise with the man of ardent political temper, and of prompt and practical habits, the sagacious and aspiring man of the world, the scrutiniser of the heart, and conspirator against its privileges and rights. Such a one will understand that the multitude requires a strong doctrine; that the argument, 'it is because it is', a hundred times repeated, has more weight with them than the most delicate, ably connected, and multiplied processes of proof; and that (as is undeniable) investigations into the grounds of our belief, do but blunt and enfeeble the energy of those who are called upon to act. He will feel the truth of this principle of our nature, and instead of acting upon it only so far as Revelation has sanctioned, and dispensing with enquiry within the exact limits in which it is mercifully superseded, he will impatiently complete what he considers to have been left imperfect. He will not be content to take the divine word as it comes to him from above; but he will drug it, as vintners do their wines, to suit the palate of the many. Accordingly, I could almost believe that the advocates of Romanism would easily be reconciled to the loss of all the Fathers (should such a mischance happen), as thinking with a barbarian conqueror, that as far as they agreed with Rome, they were superfluous, and where they disagreed dangerous. [...] I am but speaking of the papist as such, as found on the stage of life, and amid the excitement of controversy, stripped of those better parts of his system, which are our inheritance as well as his; and so contemplating him, surely I may assert without breach of charity, that he would, under circumstances, destroy the Fathers' writings, as he actually does disparage their authority – just as he consents to cut short dispute by substituting the Vulgate for the original inspired Text, and by lodging the gift of Infallibility in the Pope rather than in a General Council.

The same feeling which leads a Roman disputant to shrink from a fair appeal to the Fathers, [...] will also cause him to prefer abstract proofs to argument from fact. Facts, indeed, are confessedly troublesome, and must be avoided as much as possible, by anyone who is bound by his theory to decide as well as dispute, much more if he professes himself infallible. [...] To appeal to facts is to put the controversy out of their own hands, and to lodge the decision with the world at large. [...] When Innocent III, for example, claimed to reign over the kings of the earth, because the sun rules the day, and the moon the night, his argument might be invalid, but it might also be valid, and could not be confuted. [...] But on the other hand, had he, in proof of his pretensions, alleged that St Peter trod upon Nero's neck, he might still have made and enforced them, but he would unnecessarily have subjected himself to an external tribunal.

[...] Rome claims to be infallible, [...] but how does she prove she is so? To speak simply, she does not prove it at all. [...] she acts as if she were infallible, and in this way persuades the imaginations of men [...]. Rome is content to sacrifice logical completeness to secure practical influence. Men act, not because they are convinced, but because they feel; [...]

[...] It is admitted that some of the most interesting questions to the human mind, as the state of the soul immediately upon death, are left in obscurity by Almighty God. Here Rome comes in and contrives to throw the mind upon the Church, as the means by which its wants may be supplied, and as the object of its faith and hope, and thus makes her the instrument of a double usurpation, as both professing to show how certain objects may be attained, and next as presenting herself as the agent in obtaining them. [...]

Lecture 5: On the use of Private Judgement

By the right of Private Judgement in matters of religious belief and practice, is ordinarily meant the prerogative, considered to belong to each individual Christian, of ascertaining and deciding for himself from Scripture what is Gospel truth, and what is not. [...] Rome, as is equally clear, takes the opposite extreme, and maintains that nothing is absolutely left to individual judgement; that is, that there is no subject in religious faith and conduct on which the Church may not pronounce a decision, so as to supersede the private judgement, and compel the assent, of every one of its members. The English Church takes a middle course[8] between these two. It considers that on certain definite subjects private judgement upon the text of Scripture has been superseded, but not by the mere authoritative sentence of the Church, but by its historical testimony delivered down from the Apostles. [...]

The Catholic doctrines, therefore, of the Trinity, Incarnation, and others similar to these, as contained in Antiquity, are, as we maintain, the

---

8 This Tractarian doctrine of Anglicanism as a *Via Media* between 'Romanism' and 'Dissent' goes back to seventeenth-century writers like George Herbert (1593–1633) and Simon Patrick (1625–1707).

true interpretations of the notices contained in Scripture, concerning those doctrines. [...]

Now [...] extreme theories[9] and their practical results are quite intelligible; whatever be their faults, want of simplicity is not one of them. We see what they mean, how they work, what they result in. But the middle path adopted by the English Church cannot be so easily mastered by the mind, first because it is a mean, and has in consequence a complex nature, involving a combination of principles, and depending on multiplied conditions; next, because it partakes of that indeterminateness which [...] is to a certain extent a characteristic of English theology; lastly, because it has never been realised in visible fullness in any religious community, and thereby brought home to the mind through the senses. [...]

The means which are given us to form our judgement by, exclusive of such as are supernatural, which do not enter into consideration here, are various, partly internal, partly external. The internal means of judging are common sense, natural perception of right and wrong, the sympathy of the affections, exercises of the imagination, reason, and the like. The external are such as Scripture, the existing Church, Tradition, Catholicity, Learning, Antiquity, and the National Faith. Popular Protestantism would deprive us of all these external means, except the text of Holy Scripture; as if, I suppose, upon the antecedent notion that, when God speaks by inspiration, all other external means are superseded. But this is an arbitrary decision, contrary to facts; for unless inspiration made use of an universal language, learning at least must be necessary to ascertain the meaning of the particular language selected; and if one external aid be adopted, of course all antecedent objection to any other vanishes. [...]

Most men, I say, try to dispense with one or other of these divine informants; and for this reason − because it is difficult to combine them. The lights they furnish, coming from various quarters, cast separate shadows, and partially intercept each other; and it is pleasanter to walk without doubt and without shade, than to have to choose what is best and safest. The Roman Catholic would simplify matters by removing Reason, Scripture and Antiquity, and depending mainly upon Church authority; the Calvinist relies on Reason, Scripture, and Criticism, to the disparagement of the Moral Sense, the Church, Tradition and Antiquity; the Latitudinarian relies on Reason, with Scripture in subordination; the Mystic on the imagination and affections, or what is commonly called the heart; the Politician takes the National Faith as sufficient, and cares for little else; the

---

9 i.e. The Protestant and the Roman.

man of the world acts by common sense, which is the oracle of the indifferent, the popular Religionist considers the authorised version of the Scripture to be all in all. But the true Catholic Christian is he who takes what God has given him, be it greater or less, does not despise the lesser because he has received the greater, yet puts it not before the greater, but uses all duly and to God's glory.

[...] It is popularly conceived that to maintain the right of Private Judgement, is to hold that no one has an enlightened faith who has not, as a point of duty, discussed the grounds of it and made up his mind for himself. But to put forward such doctrine as this, rightly pertains to infidels and sceptics only; and if great names may be quoted in its favour, and it is often assumed to be the true Protestant doctrine, this is surely because its advocates have not always weighed the force of their own words. Everyone must begin religion by faith, not by controversy [...] it is better for himself that he should do so [...]. If he would posses a reverent mind, he must begin by obeying; if he would cherish a generous and devoted temper, he must begin by venturing something on uncertain information; if he would deserve the praise of modesty and humility, he must repress his busy intellect, and forbear to scrutinise. This is a sufficient explanation, were there no other, of the subscription to the Thirty-Nine Articles, which is in this place exacted of the youth who come hither for education.[10] [...]

Too many suppose that their investigation ought to be attended with a consciousness of making it; as if it was scarcely pleasing to God unless they all along reflect upon it, tell the world of it, boast of it as a right, and sanctify it as a principle. They say to themselves and others, 'I am examining, I am scrutinising, I am judging, I am free to choose or reject, I am exercising the right of Private Judgement'.[11] What a strange satisfaction! Does it increase the worth of our affections to reflect upon them as we exercise them? Would our mourning for a friend become valuable by our saying, 'I am weeping, I am overcome and agonised for the second or third time; I am resolved to weep'? What a strange infatuation, to boast of our having to make up our minds! [...] Is it anything inspiring or consolatory to consider, as such persons do, that Almighty God has left them entirely to their own efforts, has failed to anticipate their wants, [...] Yet such is a commonly received doctrine of this day; against which, I would plainly

10 Oxford ceased to be solely an 'Anglican' university only in 1871. Until that date, all its members were obliged to subscribe to the Thirty-Nine Articles of the Church of England. Newman was totally against relaxing this requirement.
11 Newman is here satirising the more extreme and pious Calvinists, having only fairly recently shed his own Calvinism.

maintain – not the Roman doctrine of Infallibility, which even if true, would be of application only to a portion of mankind, for few comparatively hear of Rome – but generally that, under whatever system a man finds himself, he is bound to accept it as if infallible, and to act upon it in a confiding spirit, till he finds a better, or in course of time had cause to suspect it. [...]

Lecture 6: On the Abuse of Private Judgement

[...] Enough has now been said on the theory of Private Judgement. I conclude then that there is neither natural probability, nor supernatural promise, that individuals reading Scripture for themselves, to the neglect of other means when they can have them, will, because they pray for a blessing, be necessarily led into the knowledge of the true and complete faith of a Christian. I conclude that the popular theory of rejecting all other help and reading the Bible only, though in most cases maintained merely through ignorance, is yet in itself presumptuous. [...]

Lecture 7: Instances of the Abuse of Private Judgement

First might be instanced many of the errors in matters of fact connected with Scripture history, which got current in early times, and, being mentioned by this or that Father, now go improperly by the name of Traditions, whereas they seem really to have originated in a misunderstanding of Scripture. Such, for instance, is the report recorded by Irenaeus, and coming, as he conceived, on good authority, that our Saviour lived to be forty or fifty. Such is Clement's statement that St Paul was married; such is that of Clement and Justin that our Lord was deformed in person. [...]

The controversy about Baptism in which St Cyprian was engaged, and in which, according to our own received opinion, he was mistaken, is a clearer and more important instant in point. Cyprian maintained that persons baptised by heretical clergy, must, on being reconciled to the Church, be re-baptised, or rather that their former Baptism was invalid. The Roman Church of the day held that confirmation was sufficient in such cases; as if that ordinance, on the part of the true Church, recognised and ratified the outward act, already administered by heretics, and applied the inward grace locked up in the Sacrament, but hitherto not enjoyed by the parties receiving it. And she rested her doctrine simply on Apostolical Tradition, which even by itself was a sufficient witness on such a point. Cyprian did not profess any Apostolical Tradition on his side, but he argued from Scripture against the judgement of the Roman See. The argument of himself and his countrymen was of the following kind: '"here is but one Lord, one Faith, one Baptism"; the heretics have not the one Faith, there-fore they have not the one Baptism'. [...] Such are the texts with which the African Church defended itself in Cyprian's day ... Yet, after all, however this be, here is a case, where the mere arguing from Scripture without reference to Tradition (whether voluntarily neglected or not), led to a conclusion which Protestants now will grant to be erroneous. [...]

Newman then goes on to consider Arianism, St Augustine and Predestinarianism, before proceeding to 'tenets which Protestants of every denomination will agree in condemning – Purgatory and the Pope's Supremacy'.

That St Peter was the head of the Apostles and the centre of unity, and that his successors are the honorary Primates of Christendom, in the same general sense in which London (for instance) is the first city in the British Empire, I neither affirm nor deny [...]. But for argument's sake I will here grant that the Fathers assert it. But what there is not the shadow of a reason for saying that they held, what has not the faintest pretension of being a Catholic truth, is this, that St Peter or his successors were and are universal Bishops, that they have the whole of Christendom for their own diocese in a way in which other Apostles and Bishops had and have not, that they are Bishops of Bishops in such a sense as belongs to no other Bishop; in a word, that the difference between St Peter and the Popes after him, and other Bishops, is not one of mere superiority and degree, but of kind, not of rank, but of class. This the Romanists hold; and they do not hold it by Catholic Tradition; by what then? By private interpretation of Scripture.

[...] And this I will say, that if Roman Catholics make converts in this country, it will be more by bold misinterpretation of one or two strong texts, which Protestants have superciliously put aside or explained away, than by any broad recommendations or well-connected arguments which they can produce.

Lecture 8: The Indefectibility of the Catholic Church

[...] Not only is the Church Catholic bound to teach the Truth, but she is ever divinely guided to teach it; her witness of the Christian Faith is a matter of promise as well as of duty; her discernment of it is secured by a heavenly as well as a human rule. She is indefectible in it, and therefore not only has authority to enforce, but is of authority in declaring it. This, it is obvious, is a much more inspiring contemplation than any I have hitherto mentioned. The Church not only transmits the Faith by human means, but has a supernatural gift for that purpose; that doctrine, which is true, considered as a historical fact, is true because she teaches it.

[...] First, in the Twentieth Article we are told that the Church has '*authority* in controversies of faith'. Now these words certainly merely do not mean that she has authority to enforce such doctrines as can historically be proved to be Apostolical. They do not speak of her power of enforcing truth, or of her power of enforcing at all, but say that she has 'authority in controversies', whereas, if this authority depended on mere knowledge of an historical fact, and much more, if only on her persuasion in a matter of opinion, any individual of competent information has the same in his place and degree. The Church has, according to this Article, a power which individuals have not; a power not merely as the ruling principle of a society, to admit and reject members, not simply a power of imposing tests, but simply 'authority in controversies of faith'. But how can she have this authority unless she be so far certainly true in her declaration? She can have no authority in declaring a lie. Matters of doctrine are not like matters of useage or custom, founded on expedience and determinable by discretion. They appeal to the conscience, and the conscience is subject to Truth alone. [...] To say the Church has authority, and yet is not true, as far as she has authority, were to destroy liberty of conscience, which Protestantism in all its forms holds especially sacred [...]

Our reception of the Athanasian Creed is another proof of our holding the infallibility of the Church, as some of our Divines express it, in matters of saving faith. In that Creed it is unhesitatingly said, that certain doctrines are necessary to be believed in order to salvation [*sic*]; they are minutely and precisely described; no room is left for Private Judgement; none for any examination into Scripture, with the view of discovering them.[12] Next, if we enquire the *ground* of this authority in the Church, the Creed answers, that she speaks merely as the organ of the *Catholic* voice, and that the faith thus witnessed, is, as being thus witnessed, such that whoso does not believe it faithfully, cannot be saved. 'Catholic' then, and 'saving' are taken as synonymous terms; in other words, the Church Catholic is pronounced to have been all along, and by implication destined ever to be, the guardian of the pure and undefiled faith, or to be indefectible in that faith. [...] We do not, therefore, set up the Church against Scripture, but we make her

---

12 The Athanasian Creed famously included the words, 'which Faith except everyone do keep whole and undefiled: without doubt he shall perish everlastingly'. Even in Newman's day many clergy omitted the 'damnatory clauses'. Newman, needless to say, would countenance no such thing.

the keeper and interpreter of Scripture.

Such is the doctrine of our most considerable Divines, […] but here we encounter a difficulty. Romanists and Protestant sectaries combine in resisting our interpretation […]. The Protestant sectary alleges that we differ from the Romanists only in minute and unintelligible points; the Romanist retorts, on the other hand, that in heart we are Protestants, but in controversy we are obliged by our theory to profess a devotion while we evade an obedience to the teaching of Antiquity. Such is the position of the *Via Media*.

I have said enough, I hope, in the course of this Lecture, by way of distinguishing between our own and the Roman theology, and of showing that neither our concessions to its advocates are reluctantly made, nor our differences subtle and nugatory, as is objected to us by opponents. Whether we be right or wrong, our theory of religion has a meaning and that really distinct from the Roman theory. […] We hold that the Church Catholic will never depart from those outlines of doctrine which the Apostles formally published; they that she will never depart in any of her acts from that entire system, written and oral, public and private, explicit and implicit, which the Apostles received and taught; we that she has a gift of fidelity, they of discrimination. […]

Lecture 9: On the Essentials of the Gospel

[…] what are the essential doctrines of the Gospel; on determining which will depend the terms of communion, the range of Private Judgement, and the character of the Church's indefectibility.

[…] No one but God can decide what compass of faith is required of given individuals. The necessary Creed varies […] one is bound to know and believe more, or more accurately, another less. Even the minutest and most precise detail of truth may have a claim upon the faith of a theologian; whereas the peasant or artisan may be accepted on a vague and rudimental faith […]

What, then, is the Church's deposit of faith, and how is it to be ascertained? Now, I might answer, in the first place, that the event has determined it. If the Church Catholic is to be indefectible in faith, we have but to enquire what that common faith is, which she now holds everywhere as the original deposit, and we shall have ascertained what we seek. If we adopt this course, we shall find what is commonly called the Creed, to be that in which all branches of the Church agree; and, therefore, that the fundamental or essential doctrines are those which are contained in the Creed. […]

It is known to all who are acquainted with Christian Antiquity, that at Baptism the candidate made a confession of his faith, before he was admissible to it. [...] Whatever this confession might contain, it was, by the force of the terms, the primitive condition of communion, or fundamental faith. Now this confession was what we now call the Creed. [...] In like manner it was called the *Regula Fidei*, or Rule of Faith, as the formulary, by which all statements of doctrine made in the Church, were to be measured and estimated.

Newman then quotes from St Irenaeus (c.130–c.200), Tertullian (c.160–c.225) and the Apostolical Constitutions (c.380), before moving on to the Creed of Pope Pius IV,[13] *which at the time was an important issue between Roman Catholics and other Christian traditions.*

[...] What a contrast to passages such as the foregoing, what a violation of them, is the Creed of Pope Pius, which was the result of proceedings at Trent! whether or not its articles be true, which is a distinct question. Irenaeus, Tertullian, and the rest cite the Apostle's Creed and say, 'This is the faith which makes a Christian, the essentials of revelation, the great truths of which the Gospel consists, the saving doctrine, the treasure committed to the Church'; but in the Creed of Pope Pius, after adding to it the recognition of the seven Sacraments, Transubstantiation, Purgatory, the Invocation of Saints, Image-worship, and Indulgences, the Romanist declares, 'This true Catholic Faith, *out of which no one can be saved*, which I at present freely profess and truly hold, this same do I promise now, and swear by God's assistance, most constantly to retain and confess, whole and inviolate, to the last breath of life'. ... Are we to understand that the words, 'out of which no one can be saved', attaches to every one or any one of those additions? If so, whence is the Roman Catholic or the Church Catholic's power to add to that essential Faith, which St Jude declares, and the Fathers witness, to be once for all delivered to the Saints?

But here we are met with this objection, that the Papal Church has but acted in the spirit of the Nicene Council in its additions to its Creed; that the Council added the celebrated word Homoüsius, or, 'of one substance

---

13 The Creed of Pius IV, also known as the *Professio Fidei Tridentinae*, was, from 1564 to 1967, imposed on everyone appointed to high office in the Roman Catholic Church. It summarised the doctrines promulgated at the Council of Trent (1545–63) and was modified in 1877 to accommodate the decrees of the First Vatican Council (1869–70). In 1967, after the Second Vatican Council (1962–5) it was replaced by a much simplified version.

with the Father', when our Lord's divinity was denied by the Arians, and that Rome has added twelve articles as protests against the heresies of the sixteenth century. To which I answer by asking, is there no difference between adding a word and adding a doctrine, between explaining what is in the Creed and inserting what was not in it? Surely, it was not inconsistent with the reverence due to it, for the Church Catholic, after careful deliberation, to clear up any ambiguity which, as time went on, might be found to exist in its wording. The words of the Creed were not inspired; they were only valuable as expressing a certain sense, and if they were found deficient in expressing that sense, there was as little interference with things sacred, as little real change, in correcting or supplying what was needful, as in completing the lines of a chart or map by the original. That original was the one universally received Faith […].

Newman then goes on to consider the argument that […] the English Church, having drawn up Articles and imposed them on the clergy and others, has in fact committed the same fault which her advocates allege against Rome, viz. of adding without authority to the necessary faith of a Christian. […]

But this is surely a great misconception of the state of the case. The Thirty-Nine Articles are 'Articles of Religion', not of '*faith*'. We do not consider the belief in them necessary to salvation, except so far as they embody in them the Articles of the Creed.

Such, then seems to be the light in which we are to regard our Articles; and till they are imposed on all our members as terms of communion, they are quite consistent with the prerogative accorded, as we have seen, by Antiquity to the Apostolic Creed, quite distinct from the forcible imposition of the Tridentine Articles on the part of Rome.

Lecture 10: On the Essentials of the Gospel

I trust that the foregoing Lectures have disposed us to take a more cheerful view of what the Protestantism of the day considers a hardship. It considers it a hardship to have anything clearly and distinctly told it in elucidation of Scripture doctrine, an infringement on its right of doubting, and mistaking, and labouring in vain. And the violent effort to keep itself in this state of ignorance – this 'unnatural stopping of ears', and 'throwing dust into the air', after the pattern of those Jews who would not hear the voice of Apostles and Martyrs – all this it dignifies by the title of defending the sacred right of Private Judgement, calls it a holy cause, a righteous battle, with other large and senseless epithets. But I trust that we have learned to glory in what the world calls a bondage. We do boast and exult in bearing Christ's yolk, whether of faith or of obedience; and we consider His Creed, not as a tyrannical infliction (God forbid!) or a jealous test, but as a glorious privilege […].

And as they are eager to secure liberty in religious opinions as the right of every individual, so do we make it every individual's prerogative to maintain and defend the Creed. They cannot allow more to the individual in the way of variety of opinion, than we do in that of confessorship. The humblest and meanest among Christians may defend the Faith against the whole Church, if the need arise. He has as much stake in it and as much right to it, as Bishop or Archbishop, and has nothing to limit him in his protest, but his intellectual capacity for making it. The greater his attainments the more serviceably of course and the more suitably he will enter into the dispute; but all that learning has to do for him is to ascertain the fact, what is the meaning of the Creed in particular points, since matter of opinion it is not, any more than the history of the rise and spread of Christianity itself. […]

Now then, having considered in general what the saving Faith is, let us proceed to examine some of the principal objections which are taken to the above view of it.

First, then, it may be urged that the Creed, which I have stated to be the abstract of saving Faith, does not include all doctrines which are essential; especially it does not include any acknowledgement that Scripture is the word of God. It has been asked of us, is belief in Scripture a fundamental of faith or not? If it is, it follows that there are fundamental doctrines besides the articles of the Creed; if it is not, what becomes of the popular notion that the Bible, and the Bible only, is the religion of Protestants. I answer as follows:

If the Roman Catholic asks whether belief in Scripture is an essential part of the faith, which he is apt to do, I ask him in turn, whether the infallibility of the Church is or is not in his system an article of faith. It is nowhere so declared; how then is it less defective in the Creed of Romanism to omit so cardinal a doctrine, than in our own Creed to omit the inspiration and canonicity of the Scriptures. Whatever answer he gives in his own behalf, will serve for us also. […]

That there are greater truths, then, and lesser truths, points which it is necessary, and points which it is pious to believe. Tradition Episcopal and Tradition Prophetical, the Creed and the Decrees of Councils, seems undeniable. But here another object obviously calls for consideration; viz. how the line is to be drawn between them. […] For instance, is the doctrine of original sin to be accounted part of the Creed? Or of Justification by Faith?

Or of Election? Or of the Sacraments? If so is there any limit to that faith which the Creed represents?

I answer, there is no precise limit; nor is it necessary there should be. Let this maxim be laid down concerning all that the Church Catholic holds, to the full extent of her Prophetical Tradition, viz. that her members must either believe or silently acquiesce in the whole of it. Though the meaning of the Creed be extended ever so far, it cannot go beyond our duty of obedience, if not of active faith; and if the line between the Creed and the general doctrine of the Church cannot be drawn, neither can it be drawn between the lively apprehension and the submission of her members in respect to both the one and the other. Whether it be apprehension or submission, it is faith in one or other shape, nor in fact can individuals themselves ever distinguish what they spiritually perceive from what they merely accept upon authority. It is the duty of everyone either to believe and love what he hears, or to wish to do so, or at least, not to oppose, but to be silent.

Lecture 11: On Scripture as the Record of Faith

[...] The Church is not a judge of the sense of Scripture [...] but a witness. If, indeed the word judge be taken to mean what it means in the Courts of Law, one vested with authority to declare the received appointments and useages of the realms, and with power to enforce them, then the Church is a judge – but not of Scripture, but of Tradition. On the contrary, both Protestant sectaries and Catholics of Rome consider their supposed judge to be a judge not merely of past facts, of precedents, custom, belief, and the like, but to have a direct power over Scripture, to contemplate questions of what is true and false in opinion, to have a special gift by divine illumination, a gift guaranteed by promise, of discerning the Scripture sense without perceptible human *Media*, to act under a guidance, and as if inspired, even though not really so. Whether any such gift was once destined for mankind or not, it avails not to enquire; we consider that it is not given in fact, and both Roman Catholics and Protestants hold that it is given. We on the other hand, consider the Church as a witness, a keeper and witness of Catholic Tradition, and in this sense invested with authority, just as in political matters, an ambassador, possessed of instructions from his government, would speak with authority. But, except in such senses as attaches to an ambassador, the Church, in our view of her office, is not a judge.

And if she does not claim for herself any gift of interpretation, in the high points in question, much less does she allow individuals to pretend to it. Explicit as our articles are in asserting that the doctrines of faith are contained and must be pointed out in Scripture, yet they give no hint that private persons may presume to search Scripture, independently of external help when they can obtain it, and to determine for themselves what is saving. The Church has a prior claim to do so, but even the Church asserts it not, but hands over the office to Catholic Antiquity. [...]

We have now cleared the way to another important principle of the Anglo-Catholic system, in which with equal discrimination it takes middle ground between Roman teaching and mere Protestantism. Our Church adheres to a double Rule, Scripture and Catholic Tradition, and considers that in all matters necessary to salvation both safeguards are vouchsafed to us, and both the Church's judgement and private judgement superseded; whereas the Romanist considers that points of faith may rest on Tradition without Scripture, and the mere Protestant that they may be drawn from Scripture without the witness of Tradition. That she requires *Scripture* sanction is plain from the Articles; that she requires *Catholic* sanction is plain from the Athanasian Creed, which, in propounding the necessary faith of a Christian, says not a word about Scripture, resting it upon its being *Catholic*; that she requires both is plain from the Canon quoted [...]

This being the state of the case, the phrase 'Rule of Faith', which is not commonly taken to mean the Bible by itself, would seem, in the judgement of the English Church, properly to belong to the Bible and Catholic Tradition taken together. These two make up a joint rule; Scripture is interpreted by Tradition, Tradition is verified by Scripture; Tradition gives form to the doctrine, Scripture gives life; Tradition teaches, Scripture proves. [...]

If asked, then, how I know that the Bible contains all truth necessary to be believed in order to salvation [*sic*], I simply reply with the first Homily, that the early Church so accounted it, that there is a 'Consent of Catholic Fathers' in its favour. No matter, whether or not we can prove it from reason or Scripture; we receive it simply on historical evidence. The early Fathers so held it, and we throw the burden of our belief, if it be a burden, on them. Stronger evidence for its truth is scarcely conceivable; for if any but the Scriptures had pretensions to be an oracle of faith, would not the first successors of the Apostles be that oracle? [...]

Lastly, it may be asked of us, how it is, supposing Scripture be, as has been here represented, only the doctrine of appeal, and Catholic Tradition the authoritative source of Christian doctrine, that our Articles say nothing of Catholic Tradition, and contemplate Tradition only in its relations to Ceremonies and Rites which are not 'in all places one or utterly alike', 'and may be changed according to the diversity of countries, times and

men's manners'? To which I answer by asking, in turn, why the Articles
contain no recognition of the inspiration of Holy Scripture. In truth, we
must take the Articles as we find them; they are not a system of theology
on whatever view, but protest against certain specific errors, existing at the
time when they were drawn up. There are, as all parties must confess, great
truths not expressly stated in the Articles.

Lecture 12: On Scripture as the Record of our Lord's Teaching

Scripture alone contains what remains to us of our Lord's teaching. If there
be a portion of Revelation, sacred beyond other portions, distinct and
remote in its nature from the rest, it must be the words and works of the
Eternal Son Incarnate. [...] His history is as far above any other possible
revelation, as heaven is above earth; for in it we have literally the sight of
Almighty God in his judgements, thoughts, attributes, and deeds, and His
mode of dealing with us His creatures. Now this special revelation is in
Scripture only; Tradition has no part in it.

To enter into the force of this remark, we should carefully consider the
peculiar character of our Lord's recorded words and works when on earth.
They will be found to come to us even professedly, as the declarations of
a Lawgiver. In the Old Covenant, Almighty God first of all spoke the Ten
Commandments from Mount Sinai, and afterwards wrote them. So our
Lord first spoke His own Gospel, both of promise and of precept, on the
Mount, and His Evangelists have recorded it. Further when he delivered
it, He spoke by way of parallel to the Ten Commandments. And His style,
moreover, corresponds to the authority which He assumes. It is of that
solemn, measured and severe character, which bears on the face of it tokens
of its belonging to One who spoke as none other man could speak. The
Beatitudes, with which His Sermon opens, are instances of this incom-
municable style, which befitted, as far as human words could befit, God
Incarnate.

[...] Surely everything our Saviour did and said is characterised by
mingled simplicity and mystery. His emblematical actions, His typical
miracles, His parables, His replies, His censures, all are evidence of a legis-
lature in germ, afterwards to be developed, a code of divine truth which
was ever to be before men's eyes, to be the subject of investigation and
interpretation, and the guide in controversy. ...

And thus the Fathers speak of His teaching. 'His sayings,' observes St
Justin, 'were short and concise; for He was no rhetorician, but His word
was the power of God.' [...]

Here then is a broad line of distinction between the written and the unwritten word. Whatever be the treasures of the latter, it has not this pre-eminent gift, the custody of our Lord's teaching. I might then, for argument's sake, even grant to Roman Catholics in the abstract all they claim for Tradition as a vehicle of truth, and then challenge them to avail themselves of the allowance; in fact, to add to the sentences of the New Law, if they can. No; the Gospels remain the sole record of Him who spake as never man spake; and it is some kind of corroboration that they are so, that they confessedly contain so much as is really to be found in them. How is it, unless they are the formal record of the New Covenant, that they have in them all the rudiments of Christian Truth as it has ever been received by all branches of the Church, by Roman Catholics as well as ourselves? Their containing so much is, as far as it goes a presumption that they contain all […].

I have said all this by way of refuting what is a favourite theme with the Roman controversialist, that the New Testament consists of merely acci-dental documents, and that our maintenance of its exclusive divinity is gratuitous and arbitrary. […]

Lecture 13: On Scripture as the Document of Proof in the Early Church

We differ, then, from the Roman teaching in this, not in denying that Tradition is valuable, but in maintaining that there is no case in which by itself, and without Scripture warrant, it conveys to us any article necessary to salvation; in other words, that it is not a rule distinct and co-ordinate, but subordinate and ministrative. And this we hold, neither from any abstract fitness that it should be so, nor from the accident that it is so – neither as a mere principle, nor as a mere fact – but as a doctrine taught us and acted on by the Fathers, as proved to us historically, as resting neither on argument nor on experience, but on testimony.

Lecture 14: On the Fortunes of the Church

And now, that our discussions on what may fitly be called the Prophetical Office of the Church draw to a close, the thought, with which perhaps we entered on the subject is not unlikely to recur, when the excitement of the enquiry has subsided, and weariness has succeeded, that what we have said is but a dream, the wanton exercise, rather than the practical conclusion of the intellect. Such is the feeling of minds unversed in the disappointments of the world, incredulous how much it has to promise, how little of substance; what intricacy and confusion beset the most certain truths; how much must be taken on trust, in order to be possessed; how little can be realised except by an effort of the will; how great a part of enjoyment lies in resignation. Without some portion of that Divine Philosophy which bids us consider 'the Kingdom of God' to be 'within us', and which, by prayer and meditation, by acting on what is told us, and by anticipating sight, develops outwardly its own views and principles, and thus assimilates to itself all that is around us – not only the Church in this age and country, but the Church Catholic anywhere, or at any time, Primitive, Roman, or Reformed, is but a name, used indeed as the incentive to action, but without local habitation, or visible tokens, 'here or there', 'in the secret chambers', or 'in the desert'. After all, the Church is ever invisible in its day, and faith only apprehends it.

Under this feeling I proceed, lastly, to consider more attentively this main difficulty in the Anglo-Catholic system, and in doing so shall have opportunity to justify [...] the doctrine which has been suggested, by way of reconciling the mind to it.

The most plausible objection, then urged by the partisans of Rome against the English Church, is, that we are what they call a Parliamentary Church, a State Creation or Establishment, depending on the breath of princes or of populace, and directed towards mere political ends, such as the temporal well-being of the community, or the stability of the Constitution; whereas the True Church is built upon the One Faith, transmitted through successive generations, and simply maintains what it has received, leaving temporal benefits to come and go, to follow or be suspended, as the case may be. The argument comes with the greater force, because Protestants have not unfrequently granted the fact, and only denied its importance. Yet we need not fear to contest the fact itself in spite both of our Roman and our Protestant opponents; and in order to show how little it can be maintained, I will take pains to state it as strongly as I can, before I proceed to reply to it.

It is objected, then, that the Church is by office, and in her very definition, 'the pillar and ground of the Truth', that 'God's Spirit which is upon her, and His words which He has put into her mouth, shall not depart out of her mouth [...]'. In such texts the Faith committed to the Church is represented, not as a secret and difficult doctrine, but as clearly proclaimed, indefectibly maintained, and universally acknowledged. Whatever errors and corruptions there may be in the Church and in her children, so far, it may be argued, is clear, that the true Faith, the one way to heaven, the one message from the Saviour of sinners, the Revelation of the Gospel, will be plain and unequivocal, as the sun in the heavens, from first to last;

so that whoever goes wrong within her pale, will have himself to blame wholly, not his defective light. In the English Church, however, we shall hardly find ten or twenty neighbouring clergymen who agree together; and that, not in the non-essentials of religion, but as to what are its elementary and necessary doctrines; or even as to the fact whether there are any necessary doctrines at all, and distinct and definite faith required for salvation. Much less do the laity receive that instruction in one and the same doctrine, which is a necessary characteristic, as may be fairly alleged, of their being 'taught of the Lord'. They wander about like sheep without a shepherd, they do not know what to believe, and are thrown on their own private judgement, weak and inadequate as it is, merely because they do not know whither to betake themselves for guidance. If they go to one Church they hear one doctrine, in the next they enter into they hear another: if they try to unite the two, they are obliged to drop important elements in each, and thus dilute and attenuate the faith to a mere shadow; if they shrink, as they may naturally do, from both the one doctrine and the other, they are taught to be critical, sceptical, and self-wise; and thus they are sure to be led into heterodoxy in one form or other, over and above the evil whether of arrogance or indifference in themselves. If, again, they are blessed with teachable and gentle minds, such uncertainty makes them desponding and unhappy; they walk in darkness and disquiet, far removed from that 'peace' which the Prophet describes as resulting from the 'teaching' which the children of the True Church receive. [...]

The parallel of the Jewish Church will afford us a sufficient answer to all that has been objected. I need scarcely observe that the Israelites were especially raised up to be witnesses for the One True God against idolatry, and had the doctrine of the Divine Unity set before them, with an injunction upon the fathers ever to teach the children, also that they remained the peculiar people until Christ came; and yet, as everyone knows, there were even long periods in their history during which the whole nation was sunk in idolatry or lingered on in decay, captivity or dispersion. Even then were the English Church, as a Church, to go further than she is ever alleged to have gone, in denying her own powers, were she to put herself on a level with the sectaries round about her, and to consider Ordination as a mere human ceremony, it would not follow that she had lost her gift. [...] Of course there are cases in which a Church incurs more or less of punishment for neglect of its privileges, but even then its state is not the same as if they had never been given; generally speaking, they are but suspended or impaired, not forfeited. Even Samson, after losing his hair upon the lap of Delilah, recovered his strength in his captivity, when his hair grew again. If we have been made God's children, we cannot unmake ourselves; we can never be mere natural men again. There is but the alternative of our being His children still, though erring ones, and under rebuke, or apostates and devils; and surely there is enough on the very face of our Church, as we humbly trust, and as our most bigoted opponents must grant, to show that we are not reprobates, but that, amid whatever scandals, we have faith and love abiding with us. […]

But in truth the whole course of Christianity from the first, when we come to examine it, is but one series of troubles and disorders. Every century is like every other, and to those who live in it seems worse than all times before it. The Church is ever ailing, and lingers on in weakness […]. Religion seems ever expiring, schisms dominant, the light of Truth dim, its adherents scattered. The cause of Christ is ever in its last agony, as though it were but a question of time whether it fails finally this day or another. The Saints are ever all but failing from the earth, and Christ all but coming; and thus the Day of Judgement is literally ever at hand; and it is our duty ever to be looking out for it, not disappointed that we have so often said, 'now is the moment', and that at the last, contrary to our expectation, Truth has somewhat rallied. Such is God's will, gathering in His elect, first one and then another, by little and little, in the intervals of sunshine between storm and storm, or snatching them from the surge of evil, even when the waters rage most furiously. Well may prophets cry out, 'How long will it be, O Lord, to the end of these wonders?' How long will this mystery proceed? How long will this perishing world be sustained by the feeble lights which struggle for existence in its unhealthy atmosphere? God alone knows the day and the hour when that will at length be, which He is ever threatening; meanwhile, thus much of comfort do we gain from what has been hitherto – not to despond, not to be dismayed, not to be anxious, at the troubles which encompass us. They have ever been; they ever shall be; they are our portion. 'The floods are risen, the floods have lift up their voice, the floods lift up their waves. The waves of the sea are mighty, and rage horribly; but yet the Lord, who dwelleth on high, is mightier.'

Lectures on the Doctrine of Justification

Newman's third book, his thirteen Lectures on Justification, *arose out of his controversy with the* Christian Observer *and was published on 30 March 1838. He told his friend Henry Wilberforce that he had taken more trouble over it than with either of his first two books.*

'Justification' was the most fought over doctrine of the Reformation. In the centuries since Luther so much had been written that mastery of the subject

was not easy. The problem for all the churches centred on how sinful human beings could appear in judgement before a righteous God and hope to be acquitted. For the Reformers, the essence of the Gospel was that the Christian was a justified sinner.

 Luther had taught that men and women were justified by grace and through 'faith alone' [sola fides]. When it came to salvation, good works counted for nothing. There was nothing human beings could bring before God that would justify them in His eyes. No less than four, numbered 11 to 14, of the Thirty-Nine Articles of Religion of the Book of Common Prayer are concerned with the doctrine. Article XI seemed to support the Lutheran doctrine of Solafideism: 'We are accounted righteous before God, only for the merit of our Lord and Saviour Jesus Christ, and not for our own works or deservings; wherefore, that we are justified by faith only is a most wholesome doctrine.' To many, however, this seemed to conflict with the Prayer Book's teaching on Baptismal Regeneration. The alternative view seemed to be 'justification by obedience', or 'salvation through works'. In his lectures, Newman attempted to resolve the problem creatively by charting a middle way, an Anglican 'via media', between the faith which justifies (the faith that 'is') and the faith that lives justly (the faith that 'does'). In doing so he anticipated the Ecumenical Theology of the Twentieth Century.

Advertisement to the First Edition

The present volume originated in the following way: it was brought home to the writer from various quarters, that a prejudice existed in many serious minds against certain essential Christian truths, such as Baptismal Regeneration and the Apostolical Ministry, in consequence of a belief that they fostered notions of human merit, were dangerous to the inward life of religion, and incompatible with the doctrine of justifying faith, nay, with express statements on the subject in our Formularies; while confident reports were in circulation that the parties who advocated them could not disguise even from themselves their embarrassment at those statements. Moreover, it was suggested that, though both these lines of doctrine had in matter of fact been continuously followed out by the great body of our divines for two centuries and more, yet such historical considerations did not weigh with men in general against their own impressions; and that nothing would meet the evil but plain statements on the subject argued out from Scripture – statements which, if not successful in convincing those who refused to trust Tradition and the Church, might at least be evidence to the world, that the persons so suspected did themselves honestly believe that the doctrines of our Articles and Homilies were not at variance with what they thought they saw in the services for Baptism, Holy Communion, and Ordination, and in other forms contained in the Prayer Book. [...]

Lecture 1: Faith considered as the Instrument of Justification

Two main views concerning the mode of our justification are found in the writings of the English divines; on the one hand, that this great gift of our Lord's passion is vouchsafed to those who are moved by God's grace to claim it – on the other, to those who by the same grace are moved to do their duty. These separate doctrines, justification by faith, and justification by obedience, thus simply stated, are not at all inconsistent with one another; and, by religious men, especially if not divines, will be held both at once, or either the one or the other indifferently, as circumstances may determine. Yet, though so compatible in themselves, the case is altogether altered when one or other is made the elementary principle of the gospel system – when professed exclusively, developed consistently, and accurately carried out to its limits. Then what seemed at first but two modes of stating the same truth, will be found, the one to be the symbol of what goes by the name of Romanism, the other of what is commonly called Protestantism.

[...] Justification by faith only, thus treated, is an erroneous, and justification by obedience is a defective view of Christian doctrine. The former is beside, the latter short of the truth. The former legitimately tends to the creed of the rigid Lutherans who opposed Melanchthon; the latter to that of Vasquez, Caietan, and other extreme writers of the Roman school. That we are absolutely saved by obedience, that is by *what we are*, has introduced the proper merit of good works; that we are absolutely saved by faith, or by *what Christ is*, the notion that good works are not conditions of our salvation.

[...] This then is peculiarly the Lutheran view, viz. that faith is the proper instrument of justification. That justification is the application of Christ's merits to the individual, or (as it is sometimes expressed) the imparting a saving interest in Him, will not be denied by English divines. Moreover, it will be agreed that His merits are not communicated, or a saving interest secured, except through an instrument divinely appointed. Such an instrument there must be, if man is to take part in the application supposed; and it must be divinely appointed, since it is to convey what God Himself, and He alone, dispenses. It is then a means appointed by God and used by man, and is almost necessarily involved in the notion of justification. All parties seem to agree as far as this; but when we go on to enquire what it is which God has made His instrument, then, as I have said, we find ourselves upon the main subject of dispute between ourselves and the strict followers of the German Reformer. Our Church considers it to be the Sacrament of Baptism; they consider it to be Faith.

[…] Baptism may be considered the instrument on God's part, Faith on ours; Faith may receive what Baptism conveys. But if the word *instrument* be taken to mean in the strictest sense the *immediate* means by which the gift passes from the giver to the receiver, there can be but one instrument; and either Baptism will be considered to convey it (whether conditionally or not, which is a further question), or Faith to seize, or, as it is expressed, to apprehend it – either Faith will become a subordinate means, condition, or qualification, or Baptism a mere sign, pledge, or ratification of a gift which is really independent of it. […]

First then, as to the proper merit of works; it is urged by the school of Luther, that that doctrine is not banished from theology, so long as works are allowed to have any share whatever in our justification, in spite of St James's affirming that they have. While they have any share in it, it is possible to *rest* in our works – they do not imply or remind of Christ's all-sufficiency; but we cannot lean upon our faith, for in fact (as I have said) it has no real substance or strength of its own, nothing to support us; it does but give way and carry us back and throw us on the thought of Christ, in whom it lives. To this argument it may be replied, that since no good works can be done but through the grace of God, those works are but evidence that that grace is with the doer; so that to view them as sharing in our justification tends to elate us, neither more nor less than the knowledge that we are under divine influences is elating. But they answer, that we are not concerned here with formal admissions and distinctions, but with practical impressions; that is to say, that Christ is but the remote source of justification, and that our own doings, though through His grace, are the proximate cause, is in fact to fix the mind on ourselves, not on Him; whereas to teach that He actually in His own person has obeyed the Law for each of us is a most efficacious means of deterring us from thinking about our own obedience to it all, and faith again, however much insisted on, has so little in it to recommend it or to rest in, so little in it holy, precious or praiseworthy, that it cannot seduce us to self-congratulation or spiritual pride or pharisaical exclusiveness, seeing our best doings in the Spirit are neither better nor more acceptable to the Divine Majesty than those natural righteousnesses, which Scripture calls 'filthy rags', and 'an unclean thing'. On the other hand, this doctrine does not tend, they say, to widen the way which Christ has pronounced to be narrow; for though faith is so worthless, and therefore so safe a feeling, yet it is not easy to acquire. […]

And now perhaps enough has been said in explanation of a theology familiar to all ears at present, which differs from our own in these two main points among others – in considering that Faith and not Baptism is the primary instrument of justification, and that this Faith which justifies exercises its gift without the exercise or even the presence of love.

Lecture 2: Love considered as the Formal Cause of Justification

[...] Now I come to consider the opposite scheme of doctrine, which is not unsound or dangerous in itself, but in a certain degree incomplete – truth, but not the whole truth; viz. that justification consists in love, or sanctity, or obedience, or 'renewal of the Holy Ghost'. In describing it then, I am describing not a perversion, but what Saints and Martyrs have in substance held in every age, though not apart from other truths which serve to repress those tendencies to error, which it, in common with every other separate portion of the Scripture creed, contains, not in itself, but when exclusively cherished by the human mind. But in the Roman schools, it has often been thus detached and isolated; to use the technical language which even the Council of Trent has adopted, spiritual renewal is said to be the '*unica formalis causa*',[14] the *one and only* true description of justification; and this seems to be the critical difference between those schools and such divines, whether of the Ancient Church or our own, as seem most nearly to agree with them.

[...] Till the Gospel came, with its manifold gifts of grace, there was a contrariety and enmity between the Divine Law and the heart of man: they confronted each other, the one all light, the other all corruption. They ran parallel to each other, not converging; the Law detecting, condemning, terrifying, not influencing except for the worse; the human heart secretly acquiescing, but not loving, not obeying. In consequence we were unable to please God by what we did, that is, we were unrighteous; for by righteousness is meant obedience such as to be acceptable. We needed then a justification, or making righteous; and this might be vouchsafed to us in two ways, either by our Maker's dispensing with that exact obedience which the Law required, or by his enabling us to fulfil it. In either, but in no other conceivable way, could our moral state, which by nature is displeasing, become pleasing to God, our unrighteousness become righteousness. Now, according to the doctrine I am engaged in expounding, the remedy lies in the latter alternative only; not in lowering the Law, much less in abolishing it, but in bringing up our hearts to it; in preserving,

---

14 The *one formal cause*. *Formal* is here a technical term deriving from Aristotle.

in raising *its* standard, and in refashioning *them*, and so (as it were) attuning them to its high harmonies. As regards the past indeed, since it cannot literally be undone, a dispensation or pardon is all that can be given us; but for the present and future, if a gift is to be vouchsafed us, and we may anticipate what it should be, this is what we have to pray for – not to have the Holy Law taken away, not to be merely accounted to do what we do not do, not a nominal change, a nominal righteousness, and external blessing, but one penetrating inwards into our heart and spirit, joints and marrow, pervading us with a real efficacy, and wrapping us round in its fullness; not a change merely in God's dealings towards us, like the pale and wan sunshine of a winter's day, but (if we may seek it) the possession of Himself, of His substantial grace to touch and heal the root of the evil, the fountain of our misery, our bitter heart and its inbred corruption. As we can conceive God blessing nothing but what is holy, so all our notions of blessing centre in holiness as a necessary foundation. Holiness is the thing, the internal state, because of which blessing comes. He may bless, He may curse, according to his mercy or our deserts; but if He blesses, surely it is by making holy; if He counts righteous,[15] it is by making righteous; if he justifies, it is by renewing; if He reconciles us to Himself, it is not by annihilating the Law, but by creating in us new wills and new powers for the observance of it.

Newman then leads the reader through the Psalms, the Prophets and the Epistles of St Paul arguing his case that by justification is meant 'the washing of regeneration and renewing of the Holy Ghost'. Of the Lutheran doctrine he says: [...] That the scheme of salvation should be one of names and understandings; that we should but be said to be just, said to have a righteousness, said to please God, said to earn a reward, said to be saved by works; that the great wounds of our nature should remain unstaunched; that Adam's old sinfulness should so pervade the regenerate that they cannot do anything in itself good and acceptable, even when it is sprinkled with Christ's blood – all this would of course be a matter of faith, if Scripture declared it; but when merely propounded fifteen centuries after Christ came, it has no claims upon us,

---

15 The orthodox Protestant view was that justification began with our being *reckoned* as righteous because God had *imputed* Christ's righteousness to the unrighteous. This seemed to imply that we were saved by a legal fiction. Protestants also argued that 'being made righteous' as opposed to being 'reckoned righteous' was to confuse justification with sanctification (being made holy).

and might be rejected, even if it were not so very alien as it is to the genius of the Evangelical Covenant. [...] Away then with this modern, this private, this arbitrary, this unscriptural system, which promising liberty conspires against it; which abolishes Christian Sacraments to introduce barren and dead ordinances; and for the real participation of the Son, and justification through the Spirit, would, at the very marriage feast, feed us on shells and husks, who hunger and thirst after righteousness. It is a new gospel, unless three hundred years stand for eighteen hundred; and if men are bent on seducing us from the ancient faith, let them provide a more specious error, a more alluring sophism, a more angelic temper, than this. It is surely too bold an attempt to take from our hearts the power, the fullness, the mysterious presence of Christ's most holy death and resurrection, and to soothe us for our loss with the name of having it. [...]

The main point in dispute is this; whether or not the Moral Law can in its substance be obeyed and kept by the regenerate. Augustine says, that whereas we are by nature condemned by the Law, we are enabled by the grace of God to perform it unto our justification; Luther, that whereas we are condemned by the Law, Christ Himself performed it unto our justification; Augustine, that our righteousness is active; Luther, that it is passive; Augustine, that it is imparted; Luther, that it is only imputed; Augustine that it consists in a change of heart; Luther, in a change of state. Luther maintains that God's commandments are impossible to man; Augustine adds, impossible without His grace; Luther, that the gospel consists in promises only; Augustine, that it is also a law; Luther, that our highest wisdom is not to know the Law; Augustine says instead, to know and keep it; Luther says, that the Law and Christ cannot dwell together in the heart; Augustine says, that the Law *is* Christ; Luther denies, and Augustine maintains that obedience is a matter of conscience; Luther says, that a man is made Christian not by working but by hearing; Augustine excludes those works only which are done before grace given; Luther, that our best deeds are sins; Augustine, that they are really pleasing to God. Luther says that faith is taken instead of righteousness; Augustine, in earnest of righteousness; Luther, that faith is essential, because it is a substitute for holiness; Augustine, because it is the commencement of holiness; Luther says, that faith, as such, renews the heart; Augustine says, a loving faith; Luther would call faith the tree, and works the fruit; Augustine, rather, the inward life, or grace of God, or love, the tree, and renewal the fruit. The school of Luther accuse their opponents of self-righteousness; and they retort on them the charge of self-indulgence: the one says that directly aiming at good works fosters pride; the other that not doing so sanctions licentiousness.

Such are the two views of justification when placed in contrast with each other; and as so placed, I conceive it will be found that the former is false, and the latter is true, but that while the former is an utter perversion of the truth, the latter does in some respects come short of it. What is wanting to complete it we learn from other parts of St Austin's[16] writings, which supply what Luther, not finding perhaps in the theology in which he had been educated, expressed in his own way. I say this, lest I should appear to be setting up any private judgement of my own against a Father of the Church, or to speak of him as I might speak of Luther. St Austin doubtless was but a fallible man, and if in any point opposed the voice of the Catholic Church, so far he is not to be followed; yet others may be more fallible than he; and when it is a question of difference of opinion between one mind and another, the holy Austin will weigh more, even with ordinarily humble men, than their own speculations. St Austin contemplates the whole of Scripture, and harmonises it into one consistent doctrine; the Protestants, like the Arians, entrench themselves in a few favourite texts. Luther, and the rest, men of original minds, spoke as no one spoke before them; St Austin, with no less originality, was contented to minister to the promulgation of what he had received. They have been founders of sects; St Austin is a father in the Holy Apostolic Church.

Lecture 3: *Primary Sense of the Term Justification*

Enough has now been said to make it appear that the controversy concerning Justification, agitated in these last centuries, mainly turns upon this question, whether Christians are not justified by observance of the Moral Law. [...] That in our natural state, and by our own strength, we are not and cannot be justified by obedience, is admitted on all hands, agreeably to St Paul's forcible statements; and to deny it is the heresy of Pelagius. But it is a distinct question altogether, whether *with* the presence of God the Holy Ghost we can obey unto justification; [...].

Now in the foregoing lecture [...] two points were proposed for proof; first that justification and sanctification were in fact substantially one and the same thing; next that in the order of our ideas, viewed relatively to each other, justification followed upon sanctification. The former of these statements seems to me entirely borne out by Scripture; I mean that justification and sanctification are there described as parts of one gift, properties, qualities, or aspects of one; that renewal cannot exist without acceptance, or acceptance without renewal; that Faith, which is the symbol of the one,

---

16 They are the same Saint. Austin is an older, English version of Augustine.

contains in it Love or Charity, which is the symbol of the other. So much concerning the former of the two statements; but as to the latter, that justification *follows* upon sanctification, that we are first renewed, and then and therefore accepted, this doctrine, which Luther strenuously opposed, our Church seems to deny also. I believe it to be true in one sense, but not true in another – unless indeed those different senses resolve themselves into a question of words. […]

If it be asked how I venture, as I do, as regards any proposition which the doctrine of justification involves, to prefer Luther to St Augustine, I answer, that I believe St Augustine really would consider, that in the order of ideas sanctification followed upon justification, though he does so with less uniformity of expression than Luther, and no exaggeration, and a preference of practical to scientific statements. Nor is it in any way wonderful, supposing the two are really united together, and belong to one gift of grace committed to the heart, as its properties or qualities (as light and heat coexist in the sun), that Augustine should not make a point of being logically correct, but should in familiar language speak of the Sun of Righteousness, both as shining on us, in order to warm us, and as shining on us with his genial warmth, that is justifying unto renewal, and justifying by renewing.

In adopting the middle course[17] I have thus prescribed to myself – allowing Luther's statement, and maintaining St Austin's doctrine – I am but following our Articles; which, in one place, speak of justification as synonymous with our being '*counted* righteous before God', or as in being an idea separate from sanctification, following, as I have said above, Luther: and in another as equivalent to 'the *grace* of Christ and the *inspiration of his Spirit*', or as actually consisting in sanctification, following St Austin and the other Fathers. […]

This correspondence between the depth of our misery and the fullness of our recovery will enable us to estimate the wonderful character of the latter. It is an act as signal, as great, as complete, as was the condemnation into which sin plunged us. Whether or not it involves renewal, it is evidently something of a more formal and august nature than renewal. Justification is a word of state and solemnity. Divine Mercy might have renewed us and kept it secret; this would have been an infinite and most

17 Here Newman is deliberately seeking a *Via Media* not only between doctrines, but also between Churches. In the second half of the twentieth century this became the dominant way forward in 'Ecumenical theology'. [See the various ARCIC Reports on official discussions between Anglicans and Roman Catholics.]

unmerited grace, but He has done more. He *justifies* us; He not only makes, He declares, acknowledges, accepts us as holy. He recognises us as His own, and publicly repeals the sentence of wrath and penal statutes which lie against us. He sanctifies us gradually, but justification is a perfect act, anticipating at once in the sight of God what sanctification does but tend towards. In it, the whole course of sanctification is summed, reckoned or imputed to us in its very beginning. Before man has done anything as specimen, or paid anything as instalment, except faith, nor even faith in the case of infants, he has the whole treasures of redemption put to his credit, as if he were and had done infinitely more than he ever can be or do. He is 'declared' after the pattern of his Saviour, to be the adopted 'Son of God' with power, by a spiritual 'resurrection'. His tears are wiped away; his fears, misgivings, remorse, shame, are changed for 'righteousness, and peace, and joy in the Holy Ghost', he is clad in white, and has his crown given to him. Thus justification is at first what renewal could but be at last; and, therefore, is by no means a mere result or consequence of renewal, but a real, though not a separate act of God's mercy. It is a great and august deed in the sight of heaven and hell; it is not done in a corner, but by Him who would show the world 'what should be done unto those whom the King delighteth to honour'. It is a pronouncing righteous while it proceeds to make righteous. [...] The declaration of our righteousness, while it contains pardon for the past, promises holiness for the future.

Lecture 4: *Secondary Senses of the Term Justification*

[...] This, then, is the sense in which we are unrighteous or displeasing to God by nature; and in the same sense, on the other hand, we are actually righteous and pleasing to Him in a state of grace. Not that there is not abundant evil still remaining in us, but that justification, coming to us in the power and 'inspiration of the Spirit', so far dries up the fountain of bitterness and impurity, that we are forthwith released from God's wrath and damnation, and are enabled in our better deeds to please Him. It places us above the line in the same sense in which we were before below it. By nature we were not absolutely devilish, but had a curse within us which so blighted and poisoned our most religious offerings; by grace we are gifted, not with perfection, but with a principle bellowing and sweetening all that we are, all that we do religiously, sustaining, hiding, and (in a sense) pleading for what remains of sin in us, 'making intercession for us according to the will of God'. As by nature sin was sovereign in us in spite of the remains of heaven, so now grace triumphs through righteousness in spite of the remains of sin.

The justifying Word, then, conveys the Spirit, and the Spirit makes our works 'pleasing' and 'acceptable' to God, and acceptablenesss is righteousness; so that the justified are just, really just, in degree indeed more or less, but really so far as this – that their obedience has in it a gracious quality, which the obedience of unregenerate man has not.

Lecture 5: Misuse of the Term Just or Righteous

[…] These conclusions, I doubt not, will be painful to many a man who adopts the principles from which they follow. For we have all been detained by circumstances or, as I may say, are frozen, in an intermediate state between Protestant premises and their rightful inferences. Those circumstances are now, after several centuries, dissolving, and we are gradually gaining a free course, and must choose our haven for ourselves. We must either go forward on a voyage where we can discover only barrenness, or return home to our ancient country, and the sepulchres of the prophets. To see where we shall end, if we go forward, may, through God's mercy, persuade us to go back. […]

Lecture 6: The Gift of Righteousness

[…] In asking, then, what is our righteousness, I do not mean what is its *original source*, for this is God's mercy; nor what is its *meritorious cause*, for this is the life, and above all the death of Christ; nor what is the *instrument* of it, for this (I would maintain) is Holy Baptism; nor what is the *entrance* into it, for this is regeneration; nor what is the *first privilege* of it, for this is pardon; nor what is the *ultimate fruit*, for this is everlasting life. I am not enquiring about anything past, or anything future, or anything on God's part, but of something present and inward. […]

Now to proceed a step further. I have said that, while justification is the application of Christ's *merits* to the individual, that application is the imparting of an inward gift; to this conclusion I have come chiefly by a consideration of the language of St Paul. Now, turning to the gospel we shall find that such a gift is actually promised to us by our Lord; a gift which must of necessity be at once our justification and our sanctification, for it is nothing short of the indwelling in us of God the Father and the Word Incarnate through the Holy Ghost. If this be so, we have found what we sought: *this* is to be justified, to receive the Divine presence within us, and be made a Temple of the Holy Ghost. […]

And this view of the subject enables us to understand how infants may be regenerate, though they give no indications of being so. For as God dwelt secretly in His material Temple, ever Hallowing it, yet only in season giving sensible evidences of what was there, so may He be present with their souls, rescuing them from Satan, and imparting new powers, manifesting new objects, and suggesting new thoughts and desires, without their being conscious, or others witness, of His work.

Moreover, if justification be the inward application of the Atonement, we are furnished at once with a sufficient definition of a Sacrament for the use of our Church. The Roman Catholic considers that there are seven; we do not strictly determine the number. We define the word generally to be an 'outward sign of an inward grace', without saying to how many ordinances this applies. However, what we do determine is, that Christ has ordained two Special sacraments, as *generally necessary to salvation*. This, then, is the characteristic mark of those two, separating them from all others whatever; and what is this but saying in other words that they are the only *justifying* rites, or instruments of communicating the Atonement, which is the one thing necessary to us? Ordination, for instance, gives *power*, yet without making the souls *acceptable* to God; Confirmation gives light and strength, yet is the mere completion of Baptism; and Absolution may be viewed as a negative ordinance removing the barrier which sin has raised between us and that grace, which by inheritance is ours. But the two Sacraments 'of the gospel', as they may be emphatically styled, are the instruments of inward life, according to our Lord's declaration, that Baptism is a new *birth*, and that in the Eucharist we eat the *living* Bread.

Lastly, we now may see what the connection really is between justification and renewal. They are both included in that one great gift of God, the indwelling of Christ in the Christian soul. That indwelling is *ipso facto* our justification and sanctification, as its necessary results. It is the Divine presence that justifies us, not faith, as say the Protestant schools, not renewal, as say the Roman. The word of justification is the substantive living Word of God, entering the soul, illuminating and cleansing it, as fire brightens and purifies material substances. He who justifies also sanctifies, because it is He. The first blessing runs into the second as its necessary limit; and the second being rejected, carries away with it the first. And the one cannot be separated from the other except in idea, unless the sun's rays can be separated from the sun, or the power of purifying from fire or water. I shall resume the subject in the next Lecture.

Lecture 7: The Characteristics of the Gift of Righteousness

It is not uncommon in Scripture, as all readers know, to represent the espe-cial gift of the Gospel as a robe or garment, bestowed on those who are brought into the Church of Christ. [...]

Nor, again, can these expressions be very well taken to mean newness of life, holiness, and obedience; for this reason, if for no other, that no one is all at once holy, and renewed, in that full sense which must be implied if the terms be interpreted of holiness. Baptised persons do not so put on Christ as to be forthwith altogether different men from what they were before; at least this is not the rule, as far as we have means of deciding. Thus there is a call on the face of the matter for some more adequate inter-pretation of such passages of Scripture, than is supplied either by the Roman or the Protestant schools; and this surely is found in the doctrine of the last Lecture. If that doctrine be true, the robe vouchsafed to us is the inward presence of Christ, ministered to us through the Holy Ghost; which, it is plain, admits on the one hand of being immediately vouch-safed in its fullness, as a sort of invisible Shekinah, or seal of God's election, yet without involving on the other the necessity of a greater moral change than is promised and effected in Baptism. [...]

Whatever else, then, Adam had by creation, this seems to have been one main supernatural gift, or rather that in which all others were included, the presence of God the Holy Ghost in him, exalting him into the family and service of His Almighty Creator. This was his clothing; this he lost by disobedience; this Christ has regained for us. [...] For what in truth is the gift even in this our state of humiliation, but a grafting invisibly into the Body of Christ; a mysterious union with Him, and a fellowship in all the grace and blessedness which is hidden in Him? Thus it separates us from other children of Adam, is our badge and distinction in the presence of the unseen world, and is the earnest of greater good in store. It is an angelic glory which good spirits honour, which devils tremble at, and which we are bound reverently to cherish, with a careful abstinence from sin, and with the offering of good works. [...] The Almighty Father, looking on us, sees not us, but this Sacred Presence, even His dearly beloved Son spir-itually manifested in us; with His blood upon our door-posts, in earnest of that final abolition of sin which is at length to be accomplished in us. [...]

[...] On the whole, then, I conclude as follows: that though the Gift which justifies us is, as we have seen, a something distinct from us and lodged in us, yet it involves in its idea its own work in us, and (as it were) takes up into itself that renovation of the soul, those holy deeds and suffer-ings, which are as if a radiance streaming from it.

Lecture 8: Righteousness viewed as a Gift and as a Quality

[...] I proceed, then, to suggest some points of contrast between the two views of justification mentioned, the doctrine of the justifying Presence, which I have been maintaining, and that of justifying obedience, as found among ourselves; for there certainly has been a school of divines in our Church, who by a very different road have practically approached the doctrine of Rome on this subject. What Roman writers have brought about by insisting entirely on the effects of grace, many among ourselves have done by disparaging its sacramental means. The former raise man to the capacity, the latter have reduced him to the necessity, of being justified by his obedience and nothing else. By the latter divines I mean the Arminians who rose in Charles the First's time, and have exercised an extensive influence in our Church since 1688. Those who conceive duly of the gift of justification, exalt the sacramental instrument of possessing it, as feeling that nothing short of means ordained by God can convey what is so much above them. Thus their glowing language about the Sacraments is but a measure of their estimation of their spiritual privileges. And if they go on to say that obedience justifies, it never occurs to them to suppose that they can be taken to be speaking of anything but *the state of soul* in which the heavenly gift resides, and by which it is retained, not that which really causes, or procures, or purchases it. Thus the high doctrine of the Sacraments held by Rome is a safeguard against any such defective or incomplete view of justification as is sanctioned by certain of her writers. But they who see nothing supernatural and mysterious in the Gift, though in words they refer it to the Sacraments, will practically associate it with that which they do see, and which seems to them naturally connected with it, viz. their own obedience. Not believing in any true sense that they are temples of the Holy Ghost, inhabited by Christ, and members of His Body, they consider their justification properly to consist in works, because they do not discern, they do not believe in, anything else, in which it can consist.

Lecture 9: Righteousness the Fruit of our Lord's Resurrection

We know nothing of the reasons of God's wonderful providences; why an Atonement was necessary, why the Son of God was the sacrifice, why that sacrifice must be applied in order to 'wash away the sins' of individuals; let us accept what is given, adore God's wisdom, and be thankful and silent – but, whatever be the deep reasons, this seems to be the rule of His counsel as to our justification; that, as the Atonement was a work of flesh and blood, a tangible, sensible work, wrought out of this material world, not, as the heretics said of old, an imaginary act, the suffering (God forgive the blasphemy!) of a phantom, a mere appearance (for such was the heresy which St John and St Paul especially opposed) – as Christ really 'came in the flesh', which none but deceivers and antichrists can deny, and suffered in the real body and blood of man; so on the contrary the communication of this great and adorable Sacrifice to the individual Christian, is not the communication of that Body and Blood such as it was when offered upon the Cross, but, in a higher, glorified, and spiritual state. [...] the crucified Man, the Divine Son, comes again to us in His Spirit. He came once, then He ascended, He has come again. He came first in the flesh; He has come the second time in the Spirit. He did not come the second time carnally, nor the first time invisibly, but He came first in the flesh, and secondly in the Spirit. As in God's counsels it was necessary for the Atonement that there should be a material, local, Sacrifice of the Son once for all: so for our individual justification, there must be a spiritual, ubiquitous communication of that Sacrifice continually. There was but one Atonement; there are ten thousand justifications. [...] God the Son atoned; God the Holy Ghost justifies.

And here perhaps we may see somewhat of the meaning and depth of the doctrine of justification by *faith* when rightly understood. If justification, or the imparting of righteousness, be a work of the Holy Ghost, a spiritual gift or presence in the heart, it is plain that faith, and faith alone, can discern it and prepare the mind for it, as the Spirit alone can give it. Faith is the correlative, the natural instrument of the things of the Spirit. While Christ was present in the flesh, He might be seen by the eye; but His more perfect and powerful presence, which we now enjoy, being invisible, can be discerned and used by faith only. Thus faith is a mysterious means of gaining gifts from God, which cannot otherwise be gained; according to the text, 'If thou canst believe, all things are possible to him that believeth'. If it was necessary for our justification that Christ should become a quickening Spirit and so be invisible; therefore it was as necessary for the same, in God's providence, that we should believe; as a necessary condition, in St Paul's language, for 'the heart to *believe* unto *righteousness*', as any one thing is a necessary condition of another, as (in this world) eating and drinking are necessary for animal life, or the sun for ripening the fruits of the earth, or the air for transmitting sounds. [...] Faith may be as a key unlocking for us the treasures of divine mercy, and the only key. I say there is no *à priori* improbability in the idea; and we see, from the nature of the case, that Christ could not enter into the hearts of the ten thousand of the true Israel, till He came differently from His coming in the flesh – till He came in the Spirit. And as the Spirit is the only justifier, so faith is the only recipient of justification. [...]

Lecture 10: The Office of Justifying Faith

[…] Faith, then, being the appointed representative of Baptism, derives its authority and virtue from that which it represents. It is justifying because of Baptism; it is the faith of the baptised, of the regenerate, that is, of the justified. Justifying faith does not precede justification; but justification precedes faith, and makes it justifying. And here lies the cardinal mistake of the views on the subject which are now in esteem.[18] In those views faith is considered as the sole instrument, not after Baptism but before; whereas Baptism is the primary instrument, and causes faith to be what it is and otherwise is not, giving it power and rank, and, as it were, constituting it its own successor. […]

Faith, then considered as an instrument, is always secondary to the Sacraments. The most extreme case, in which it seems to supersede them, is found, not in our own, but in the Ancient Church; in which the faith of persons, dying in the state of Catechumens, was held to avail to their reception on death into that kingdom, of which Baptism is the ordinary gate. How different is the spirit of such a guarded exception, from the doctrine now in esteem, that faith, *ipso facto*, justifies, the Sacraments merely confirming and sealing what is complete without them! […]

Enough has now been said upon the symbolical office of faith. If more were needed, it might be further observed that such a view of it is congenial to the tone of thought which the Reformers discover in other matters. As they considered prayers as *lectures*, Absolutions as *declarations*, the Eucharistic Commemoration as a *visible memento*, Mystical Rites as *edifying exhibitions* (which they certainly are also), so they regarded faith as the *symbol* of justification. Of course this is not the highest view of the doctrine; and our own Homilies, in another portion of the Book, go on to the higher, according to which it is an instrument, as has been shown. Well would it have been if all Protestant writers had done the same; but others, following out the view which was more peculiarly their patrimony as Protestants, have ended in the notion that justification is the feeling of satisfaction which belief in God's mercy inspires, and nothing more.

To sum up what has been said: the question has been in what sense faith only justifies, for that it is *necessary* to our justification, all parties allow. I answer, it justifies only, in two ways, as the only inward *instrument*, and as the only *symbol*. Viewed as an instrument, it unites the soul to Christ

---

18 Newman refers here to the Protestant view then dominant in the Church of England. The reality of Baptismal Regeneration was an issue much fought over, occasionally in Ecclesiastical Courts.

through the Sacraments; viewed as a symbol it shows forth the doctrine of free grace. Hence it is the instrument of justification after Baptism; it is a symbol both before and after.

Lecture 11: The Nature of Justifying Faith

After considering the office of Faith, it fitly follows to enquire what it is, both in itself, and as existing in the regenerate. [...] 'Faith is the substance of things hoped for, the evidence of things not seen.'[19] Our Church has nowhere defined faith. The Articles are entirely silent; and though the Homilies contain many popular descriptions, they present, as is natural, nothing consistent and accurate. [...]

It would seem then that Luther's doctrine, now so popular, that justifying faith is trust, comes first, justifies by itself, and then gives birth to all graces, is not tenable; [...] For, as faith cannot exist except in this or that mind, so it cannot be as much as trust, without being also hope, nor hope without having some portion of love. Mere trust as little gives birth to other graces as mere faith. It is common indeed to say that trust in the mercy of God in Christ ensures all other graces, from the fertilising effect of the news of that mercy on the heart. But surely that blessed news has no such effect unless the heart is *softened* to receive it; that softening then is necessary to justification, and by whatever name it is called, religiousness, or love, or renewal, it is something more than trust. That is something more than trust is involved in justifying faith; in other words it is the trust of a renewed or loving heart. [...]

The one view then differs from the other as the likeness of a man differs from the original. The picture resembles him; but it is not he. It is not a reality, it is all surface. It has no depth, no substance; touch it, and you will find that it is not what it pretends to be. When I assign an office to faith, I am not speaking of an abstraction or creation of the mind, but of something existing. I wish to deal with things, not with words. I do not look to be put off with a name or shadow. I would treat of faith as it is actually found in the soul; and I say it is as little an isolated grace, as man is a picture. It has a depth, a breadth, and a thickness; it has an inward life which is something over and above itself; it has a heart, and blood, and pulses, and nerves, though not upon the surface. All these indeed are not *spoken* of, when we make mention of faith; nor are they painted on the canvas; but

---

19 Hebrews 11:1 in the Authorised Version. The Revised Standard Version reads 'Now faith is the assurance of things hoped for, the conviction of things not seen'.

they are implied in the word, because they exist in the thing. What has been observed above, of the distinction between the meaning of a word and the thing, *righteousness*, applies here. Love and fear, and heavenly-mindedness, and obedience, and firmness, and zeal, and humility, are as certainly one with justifying faith, considered as a thing existing, as bones, muscles, and vital organs, are necessary to that outward frame of man which meets the eye, though they do not meet it. Love and fear and obedience are not really posterior to justifying faith for even a moment of time, unless bones or muscle are formed after the countenance and complexion. It is as unmeaning to speak of living faith, as being independent of newness of mind, as of solidity as divisible from body, or tallness from stature, or colour from the landscape. As well might it be said that an arm or foot can exist out of the body, and that man is born only with certain portions, head or heart, and that the rest accrues afterwards, as that faith comes first and gives birth to other graces. This illustration holds with only one limitation; that faith, though connatural with other graces, has a power of reacting upon them, by placing more constraining objects before them, as motives to their more vigorous exercise. [...]

The Apostles then proceeded thus: they did not rest their cause on argument; they did not rely on eloquence, wisdom or reputation; nay, nor did they make miracles necessary to the enforcement of their claims. They did not resolve faith into sight or reason; they contrasted it with both, and bade their hearers believe, sometimes in spite, sometimes in default, sometimes in aid, of sight and reason. They exhorted them to make trial of the Gospel, since they would find their account in doing so. And of their hearers, 'some believed the things which were spoken, some believed not'. Those believed whose hearts were 'opened', 'who were ordained to eternal life', those did not whose hearts were hardened. This was the awful exhibition of which the Apostles and their fellow workers were witnesses; for faith, as a principle of knowledge, cannot be exactly analysed or made intelligible to man, but is the secret, inexplicable, spontaneous movement of the mind (however arising) towards the external world – a movement not to the exclusion of sight and reason, for the miracles appeal to both, nor of experience, for all who venture for Christ receive daily returns of good in confirmation of their choice, but independent of sight or reason before, or of experience after. The Apostles appealed to men's hearts, and, according to their hearts, so they answered them. [...] They came as commissioned from Him, and declared that mankind was a guilty and outcast race, that sin was a misery, that the world was a snare, that life was a shadow, that God was everlasting, that His Law was holy and true, and its sanctions certain and terrible; that He also was all-merciful, that He had appointed a Mediator between him and them, who had removed all obstacles, and was desirous to restore them, and that He had sent themselves to explain how. They said that the Mediator had come and gone; but had left behind Him what was to be His representative till the end of all things, His mystical Body, the Church, in joining which lay the salvation of the world. So they preached, and so they prevailed; [...] They used many arguments, but as outward forms of something beyond argument. Thus they appealed to the miracles they wrought, as sufficient signs of their power, and assuredly divine, in spite of those which other systems could show or pretended. They expostulated with the better sort on the ground of their instinctive longings and dim visions of something greater than the world. They awed and overcame the passionate by means of what remained of heaven in them, and of the involuntary homage which such men pay to the more realised tokens of heaven in others. They asked the more generous-minded whether it was not worthwhile to risk something on the chance of augmenting and perfecting those precious elements of good which their hearts still held; and they could not hide what they cared not to 'glory in', their own disinterested sufferings, their high deeds, and their sanctity of life. They won over the affectionate and gentle by the beauty of holiness, and the embodied mercies of Christ as seen in the ministrations and ordinances of His Church. Thus they spread their nets for disciples, and caught thousands at a cast; thus they roused and inflamed their hearers into enthusiasm, till 'the Kingdom of Heaven suffered violence, and the violent took it by force'. And when these had entered it, many of them, doubtless, would wax cold in love, and fall away; for many had entered only on impulse; many, with Simon Magus, on wonder or curiosity; many from a mere argumentative belief, which leads as readily into heresy as into the Truth. But still, those who had the seed of God within them, would become neither offences in the Church, nor apostates, nor heretics; but would find day by day, as love increased, increasing experience that what they had ventured boldly amid conflicting evidence, of sight against sight, reason against reason, with many things against it, and more things for it, they had ventured well. The examples of meekness, cheerfulness, contentment, silent endurance, private self-denial, fortitude, brotherly love, perseverance in well-doing, which would from time to time meet them in their new kingdom – the sublimity and harmony of the Church's doctrine, the touching and subduing beauty of her services and appointments, their consciousness of her virtue, divinely imparted, upon themselves, in subduing, purifying, changing them, the bountifulness of her alms-giving, her power, weak as she was and despised, over the statesmen and philosophers of the world, her consistent and steady aggression upon it, moving forward in spite of it on all sides at once, like the wheels in the Prophet's vision, and this in contrast with the ephemeral and variable outbreaks of sectarianism, the unanimity and intimacy existing between her widely-separated branches, the mutual sympathy and correspondence of men of hostile nations and foreign languages, the simplicity of her ascetics, the gravity of her Bishops, the awful glory shed around her Martyrs, and the mysterious and recurring traces of miraculous agency here and there, once and again, according as the Spirit willed – these and the like persuasives acted on them day by day, turning the whisper of their hearts into an habitual conviction, and establishing in the reason what had begun in the will. And thus has the Church been upheld ever since by an appeal to the People, to the necessities of human nature, the anxieties of conscience, and the instincts of purity; forcing upon Kings a sufferance or protection which they fain would dispense with, and upon Philosophy a grudging submission and a reserved and limited recognition. [...]

Lecture 12: Faith viewed relatively to Rites and Works

I now proceed to show that though we are justified, as St Paul says, by faith, and, as our Articles and Homilies say, by faith only, nevertheless we are justified, as St James says, by works; and to show in what sense the latter doctrine is true. And that, not only in the case of works of righteousness, but also of ritual services, such as Baptism, as St Paul and St Peter teach. Of course I do not forget St Paul's declaration that 'a man is justified by faith without the deeds of the Law', but he does not thereby assert that justification is independent of the deeds of the gospel [...]

'By works,' says St James, 'a man is justified, and not by faith only.' Now, let me ask, what texts do their opponents shrink from as they from this? Do they even attempt to explain it? Or if so, is it not by some harsh and unnatural interpretation? Next, do they not proceed, as if distrusting their own interpretation, to pronounce the text difficult, and so to dispose of it? Yet who can honestly say that it is in itself difficult? Rather, can words be plainer were it not that they are forced into connection with a theory of the sixteenth century; and then certainly they become as thick darkness [...] If St James is difficult, is St Paul plain? Will anyone say that St Paul is plainer than St James? Is it St James in whose Epistles are 'some things hard to be understood'? What then is this resolute shutting of the eyes to an inspired Apostle, but the very spirit which leads the Socinian to blot out from certain texts, as far as his faith is concerned, the divinity of Christ? If we may pass over, 'By works a man is justified, and not by faith only', why may we not also, 'I and my father are One'? Can we fairly call it self-will to refuse the witness of the latter text, while we arbitrarily take on ourselves to assign or deny a sense to the former? What is meant by maintaining the duty of a man's drawing his Creed from Scripture for himself, and yet telling him it is a deadly heresy to say, just what St James says, and what St Paul (to say the least) does not deny? But in truth, after all, men do not make up their mind from Scripture, though they profess to do so; they go by what they consider their inward experience. They fancy that they have reasons in their own spiritual history for concluding that God has taught them the doctrine of justification without good works; and by these they go. They cannot get themselves to throw their minds upon Scripture; they argue from Scripture only to convince others, but you defeat them again and again, without moving or distressing them; they are above you, for they do not depend on Scripture for their faith at all, but on what has taken place within them. [...]

It seems, then, that whereas Faith on our part fitly corresponds, or is the correlative, as it is called, to grace on God's part, Sacraments are but the manifestation of grace, and good works are but the manifestation of faith; so that, whether we say we are justified by faith, or by works or by Sacraments, all these but mean this one doctrine, that we are justified by grace, which is given through Sacraments, impetrated by faith, manifested in works.

Note on Lecture 12:
On Good Works as the Remedy of Post-Baptismal Sin

From what has been said, it would seem that, while works before justification are but conditions and preparations for that gift, works after justification are much more, and that, not only as being intrinsically good and holy, but as being fruits of *faith*. And viewed as one with faith, which is the appointed instrument of justification after Baptism, they are (as being connatural with faith and indivisible from it, organs through which it acts and which it hallows), instruments with faith of the continuance of justification, or in other words, *of the remission of sin after Baptism*. Since this doctrine sounds strange to the ears of many in this day, and the more so because they have been taught that the Homilies, which our Church has authoritatively sanctioned, are decidedly opposed to it, I make the following extracts from that important work for the accommodation of the general reader who may not have it to hand. Deeply is it to be regretted that a book, which contains 'doctrine' so 'godly and wholesome and necessary for *these* Times', as well as for the sixteenth century, should popularly be known only by one or two extracts, to the omission of such valuable matter as shall now be quoted:

[...] 'For, when both He and his disciples were grievously accused of the Pharisees, to have defiled their soul in breaking the constitutions of the Elders, because they went to meat and washed not their hands before, according to the custom of the Jews, Christ, answering their superstitious complaints, teacheth them *an especial remedy how to keep clean their souls*, notwithstanding the breach of such superstitious orders, "*Give alms*", saith He, "and behold all things are clean unto you."

'He teacheth, then, that to be merciful and charitable in helping the poor, is *the means* to keep the soul pure and clean *in the sight of God*. We are taught therefore by this, that *merciful almsgiving is profitable to purge the soul from the infection and filthy spots of sin* [...]'

Lecture 13: On Preaching the Gospel

[...] But, I must end a train of thought, which, left to itself, would run on into a whole work. And in doing so I make one remark, which is perhaps the great moral of the history of Protestantism. Luther found in the Church great moral corruptions countenanced by its highest authorities; he felt them; but instead of meeting them with divine weapons, he used one of his own. He adopted a doctrine, original, specious, fascinating, persuasive, powerful against Rome, and wonderfully adapted, as if prophetically, to the genius of the times which were to follow. He found Christians in bondage to their works and observances; he released them by his doctrine of faith; and he left them in bondage to their feelings. He weaned them from seeking assurance of salvation in standing ordinances, at the cost of teaching them that a personal consciousness of it was promised to everyone who believed. For outward signs of grace he substituted inward; for reverence towards the Church contemplation of self. And thus, whereas he himself held the proper efficacy of the Sacraments, he has led others to disbelieve it; whereas he preached against reliance on self, he introduced it in a more subtle shape; whereas he professed to make the written word all in all, he sacrificed it in its length and breadth to the doctrine which he had wrested from a few texts.

This is what becomes of fighting God's battles in our own way, of extending truths beyond their measure, of anxiety after a teaching more compact, clear, and spiritual, than the Creed of the Apostles. Thus the Pharisees were more careful of their Law than God who gave it; thus Saul saved the cattle he was bid destroy, 'to sacrifice to the Lord', thus Judas was concerned at the waste of the ointment, which might have been given to the poor. In these cases bad men professed to be more zealous for God's honour, more devotional, or more charitable, than the servants of God; and in a parallel way Protestants would be more spiritual. Let us be sure things are going wrong with us, when we see doctrines more clearly, and carry them out more boldly, than they are taught us in Revelation.

An Essay on the Development of Christian Doctrine[20]

Newman wrote the Essay on Development during his last year as an Anglican, ostensibly for himself, and in one last attempt to justify his defence of the Catholicism of the Anglican Church as a 'via media' between Rome and Canterbury. 'It was,' he said, 'an hypothesis to account for a difficulty.' The difficulty was the old one: that across all the Christian churches there were doctrines which, though they could be supported by the Bible and the teaching of the early Church, were in fact to be found in neither. The Doctrine of the Holy Trinity; the Sufficiency of the Holy Scriptures for Salvation; Transubstantiation, and Purgatory were cases in point. The more theologians attempted to demonstrate that such doctrines had always been believed or were logically implicit in the Bible or the Church Fathers, the less they were able to use them to convince anyone but themselves that their Church was the true Church. And there the matter rested for three hundred years. As Newman struggled to show that the Church of England was, in England, the Church nearest in its Catholicism to the ancient undivided Church of the West, the more keenly he felt the difficulty and the inability of traditional arguments to settle the matter. The problem was of more than academic interest. Newman believed that his spiritual integrity and eternal salvation depended on the issue being resolved. His solution was one which radically transformed the Church's understanding of its beliefs and their history.

Introduction[21]

Christianity has been long enough in the world to justify us in dealing with it as a fact in the world's history. Its genius and character, its doctrines, precepts, and objects cannot be treated as matters of private opinion or deduction, unless we may reasonably so regard the Spartan institutions or the religion of Mahomet. [...] It has from the first had an objective existence, and has thrown itself upon the great concourse of men. Its home is in the world; and to know what it is, we must seek it in the world, and hear the world's witness of it. [....] [69].

---

20 The quotations that follow are from the original 1845 edition but with the text as simplified in quotations and footnotes in J.M. Cameron's, Pelican Books, 1973 edition. The more readily available 1878 edition is so heavily revised and rewritten as to be almost a different work.

21 The text and page numbers are from the 1845 first edition, edited by James Munro Cameron, Pelican Classics, 1973.

[...] Till it is shown why we should view the matter differently, it is natural, or rather necessary, it is agreeable to our modes of proceeding in parallel cases, to consider that the society of Christians which the Apostles left on earth was of that religion to which the Apostles had converted them; that the external continuity of name, profession and communion is a *primâ facie* argument for a real continuity of doctrine; that, as Christianity began by manifesting itself to all mankind, therefore it went on to manifest itself; and that the more, considering that prophecy had already determined that it was to be a power visible in the world and sovereign over it, characters which are accurately fulfilled in that historical Christianity to which we commonly give the name. It is not a great assumption,[22] then, but rather mere abstinence from the wanton admission of a principle which would necessarily lead to the most vexatious and preposterous scepticism, to take it for granted that the Christianity of the second, fourth, seventh, twelfth, sixteenth, and intermediate centuries is in its substance the very religion which Christ and his Apostles taught in the first, whatever may be the modifications for good or evil which lapse of years, or the vicissitudes of human affairs, have impressed upon it. [...] [70].

[...] Whatever be historical Christianity, it is not Protestantism. If ever there were a safe truth, it is this.

And Protestantism has ever felt it. I do not mean that every Protestant writer has felt it; for it was the fashion at first, at least as a rhetorical argument against Rome, to appeal to past ages, or to some of them; but Protestantism, as a whole, feels it, and has felt it. This is shown in the determination already referred to, of dispensing with historical Christianity altogether, and of forming a Christianity from the Bible alone: men would never have put it aside, unless they had despaired of it. It is shown by the long neglect of ecclesiastical history in England, which prevails even in the English Church. Our popular religion scarcely recognises the fact of the twelve long ages which lie between the Councils of Nicaea and Trent, except as affording one or two passages to illustrate its wild interpretations of certain prophecies of St Paul and St John. It is melancholy to say it, but the chief, perhaps the only English writer who has any claim to be considered an ecclesiastical historian, is the infidel Gibbon. German Protestantism, on the other hand, has been of a bolder character; it has calmly faced and carefully

---

22 This is a version of the argument from antecedent probability, which Newman relied on a great deal. The subversion of all common sense arguments in the twentieth century, by concepts such as relativity, indeterminacy and complementarity has rendered it much less attractive to present day Christian apologetics.

surveyed the Christianity of eighteen hundred years, and it frankly avows that it is a mere religion of man and the accident of a period. […] [72].

[…] It is difficult to complete, to finish from history, that picture of the divine religion which, even in its outlines, is sufficient to condemn Protestantism, though not sufficient to imprint upon our minds the living image of Christianity […]. History is not a creed or a catechism; it gives lessons rather than rules […] This must be admitted: at the same time, principles may be laid down with considerable success as keys to its various notices, enabling us to arrange and reconcile them.

Such a key, as regards the teaching of Christianity, it has been imagined was contained in the celebrated dictum of Vincentius,[23] – a method of accounting for whatever variations we may find in the historical testimonies concerning it, of separating authoritative doctrine from opinion, of rejecting what is faulty, and combining and forming a theology. That 'Christianity is what has been held always, everywhere, and by all,' […] [74] Here, then, we have a short and easy method for reconciling the various informations of ecclesiastical history with that antecedent probability in its favour […]

Such is the rule of historical interpretation which has been professed in the English school of divines; and it contains a majestic truth, and offers an intelligible principle, and wears a reasonable air. It is congenial, or, as it may be said, native to the Anglican mind, which takes up a middle position, neither discarding the Fathers nor acknowledging the Pope. It lays down a simple rule by which to measure the value of every historical fact as it comes, and thereby it provides a bulwark against Rome while it opens an assault upon Protestantism. Such is its promise; but the difficulty lies in applying it in particular cases. The rule is more serviceable in determining what is not, than what is Christianity; it is irresistible against Protestantism, and in one sense indeed it is irresistible against Rome also, but in the same sense it is irresistible against England. It strikes at Rome through England. It admits of being interpreted in one of two ways: if it be narrowed for the purpose of disproving the catholicity of the Creed of Pope Pius, it becomes also an objection to the Athanasian; and if it be relaxed to admit the doctrines retained by the English Church, it no longer excludes certain doctrines of Rome which that Church denies. It cannot at once condemn St Thomas and St Bernard, and defend St Athanasius and St Gregory Nazianzen. […] [75].

---

23 The famous Vincentian Canon, *quod ubique, quod semper, quod ab omnibus creditum est,* was laid down by St Vincent of Lérins, (died c. 445 AD) in his *Commonitorium* (II.3). In common with many nineteenth-century writers Newman misquotes it, putting *quod semper* before *quod ubique*.

Newman next explores the limitations of the Vincentian Canon with regard to such doctrines as the apostolical succession and God as Holy Trinity, arguing that it is both futile and contradictory for Anglicans to employ it against Rome when in doing so it undermines their own claims to truth.

[...] I betake myself to one of our altars to receive the Blessed Eucharist; I have no doubt whatever on my mind about the Gift which that Sacrament contains; I confess to myself my belief, and I go through the steps on which it is assured to me. 'The Presence of Christ is here, for it follows upon the Consecration; and Consecration is the prerogative of Priests; and Priests are made by Ordination; and Ordinations come in direct line from the Apostles. Whatever be our other misfortunes, every link in our chain is safe; we have the Apostolical Succession, we have a right form of consecration: therefore we are blessed with the great Gift.' Here the question rises in me, 'Who told you about that Gift?' I answer, 'I have learned it from the Fathers: I believe the Real Presence because they bear witness to it. St Ignatius calls it "the medicine of immortality": St Irenaeus says that "our flesh becomes incorrupt, and partakes of life, and has the hope of the resurrection", as "being nourished from the Lord's Body and Blood"; that the Eucharist is "made up of two things, an earthly and a heavenly"; perhaps Origen and perhaps Magnes, after him, say that It is not a type of our Lord's Body, but His Body: and St Cyprian uses language as awful as can be spoken of those who profane it. I cast my lot with them, I believe as they.' Thus I reply, and then the thought comes upon me a second time, 'And do not the same Ancient Fathers bear witness to another doctrine, which you disown? Are you not a hypocrite, listening to them when you will, and deaf when you will not? How are you casting your lot with the Saints, when you go but half-way with them? For of whether of the two [sic] do they speak more frequently, of the Real Presence in the Eucharist, or of the Pope's Supremacy? You accept the lesser evidence, you reject the greater.' [...] [84].

The following Essay is directed towards a solution of the difficulty which has been stated – the difficulty which lies in the way of our using the testimony of our most natural informant concerning the doctrine and worship of Christianity, viz. the history of eighteen hundred years. The view on which it is written has at all times, perhaps, been implicitly adopted by theologians, and, I believe, has recently been illustrated by several distinguished writers of the continent, such as De Maistre and Möhler: viz. that the increase and expansion of the Christian creed and ritual, and the variations which have attended the process in the case of individual writers and churches, are the necessary attendants on any philosophy or polity which takes possession of the intellect and heart and has had any wide or extended dominion; that, from the nature of the human mind, time is necessary for the full comprehension and perfection of great ideas: and that the highest and most wonderful truths, though communicated to the world once for all by inspired teachers could not be comprehended all at once by the recipients, but, as received and transmitted by minds not inspired and through media which were human, have required only the longer time and the deeper thought for their full elucidation. This may be called the *Theory of Developments* [...] [90].

[...] it is undoubtedly an hypothesis to account for a difficulty. [...] it is an expedient to enable us to solve what has now become a necessary and anxious problem. For three hundred years the documents and facts of Christianity have been exposed to a jealous scrutiny; works have been judged spurious which were once received without a question; facts have been discarded or modified which were once first principles in argument; new facts and new principles have been brought to light; philosophical views and polemical discussions of various tendencies have been maintained with more or less success. Not only have the relative situation of controversies and theologies altered, but infidelity itself is in a different, I am obliged to say, in a more hopeful position, as regards Christianity. The facts of revealed religion, though in their substance unaltered, present a less compact and orderly front to the attacks of its enemies, and allow of the introduction of new conjectures and theories concerning its sources and its rise. The state of things is not as it was, when an appeal lay to the supposed works of the Areopagite, or to the primitive Decretals, or to St Dionysius's answers to Paul, or to the Coeni Domini of St Cyprian.[24] The assailants of dogmatic truth have got the start of its adherents of whatever creed; philosophy is completing what criticism has begun; and apprehensions are not unreasonably excited lest we should have a new world to conquer before we have weapons for the warfare. Already infidelity has its views and ideas, on which it arranges the facts of ecclesiastical history; and it is sure to consider the absence of any antagonist theory as an evidence of the reality of its own. That the hypothesis, here to be adopted, accounts not only for the Athanasian Creed, but for the Creed of Pope Pius, is no fault of those who adopt it. No one has power over the issues of his principles; we cannot manage our argument, and have as much of it as we please and no more. An argument is needed, unless Christianity is to abandon the province of argument; and those who find fault with the explanation here offered of its historical phenomena will find it their duty to provide one of their own.

---

24 These works, once thought genuine, were later revealed to be forgeries.

And as no aim at Roman Catholic doctrine need be supposed to have given a direction to the enquiry, so neither can a reception of that doctrine be immediately based on its results. It would be the work of a life to apply the Theory of Developments so carefully to the writings of the Fathers, and the histories of controversies and councils, as thereby to vindicate the reasonableness of every decision of Rome; much less can such an undertaking be imagined by one who, in the middle of his days, is beginning his life again. So much, however, might be gained even from an Essay like the present – a solution of such a number of the reputed corruptions of Rome, as might form a fair ground for trusting her, where the investigation has not been pursued. [92].

Chapter I: On the Development of Ideas

Section I: On the Process of Development in Ideas

It is characteristic of our minds to be ever engaged in passing judgement on the things that come before them. [...]

Of the judgements thus exercised, some are mere opinions, which come and go, or remain with us only till an accident displaces them [...]. Others are firmly fixed in our minds and have a hold over us, whether they are principles of conduct, or are views of life and the world, or fall under the general head of belief. These habitual judgements often go by the name of ideas, and shall be so called here.

[...] Ideas thus described, being of the nature of judgements, must, properly speaking, be considered as true by those who hold them. [93].

[...] when one and the same idea is held by persons who are independent of each other, and are variously circumstanced, and have possessed themselves of it by different ways, and when it presents itself to them under very different aspects, without losing its substantial unity and identity, and when it is thus variously presented, yet recommended, to persons similarly circumstanced; and when it is presented to persons variously circumstanced, under aspects, discordant indeed at first sight, but reconcilable after such explanations as their respective states of mind require; then it seems to have a claim to be considered the representative of an objective truth. [94].

[...] An idea ever presents itself under different aspects to different minds, and in proportion to that variety will be the proof of its reality and distinctiveness. [95].

[...] if the illustration on which we are proceeding be correct, there is no one idea, no one term or proposition which can duly and fully represent it [...]. [96].

When an idea, whether real or not, is of a nature to interest and possess the mind, it is said to have life, that is, to live in the mind which is the recipient of it. Thus, mathematical ideas, real as they are, cannot be called living, for they have no influence and lead to nothing. But when some great enunciation, whether true or false, about human nature, or present good, or government, or duty, or religion, is carried forward into the public throng and draws attention, then it is not only passively admitted in this or that form into the minds of men, but it becomes a living principle within them, leading them to an ever-new contemplation of itself, an acting upon it and a propagation of it. Such is the doctrine of the natural bondage of the will, or of individual responsibility, or of the immortality of the soul, or of the rights of man, or of the divine right of kings, or of the hypocrisy and tyranny of priestcraft, or of the lawfulness of self-indulgence – doctrines which are of a nature to arrest, attract, or persuade, and have so far the *primâ facie* appearance of reality that they may be looked at on many sides and strike various minds very variously. Let one such idea get possession of the popular mind, or the mind of any set of persons and it is not difficult to understand the effects which will ensue. There will be a general agitation of thought and an action of mind both upon itself and upon other minds. New lights will be brought to bear upon the original idea, aspects will multiply, and judgements will accumulate. There will be a time of confusion, when conceptions and misconceptions are in conflict; and it is uncertain whether anything is to come of the idea at all, or which view of it is to get the start of the others. After a while some definite form of doctrine emerges; and as time proceeds, one view of it will be modified or expanded by another, and then, combined with a third, till the idea in which they centre will be to each mind separately what at first it was only to all together. It will be surveyed, too, in its relation to other doctrines or facts, to other natural laws or established rules, to the varying circumstances of times and places, to other religions, polities, philosophies, as the case may be. How it stands affected towards other systems, how it affects them, how far it coalesces with them, how far it tolerates, when it interferes with them, will be gradually wrought out. It will be questioned and criticised by enemies, and explained by well-wishers. The multitude of opinions formed concerning it, in these respects and many others, will be collected, compared, sorted, sifted, selected or rejected, and gradually attached to it, or separated from it, in the minds of individuals and of the community. It will, in proportion to its native vigour and subtlety, introduce itself into the framework and details of social life, changing public opinion and supporting or undermining the foundations of established order. Thus in time it has grown into an ethical code, or into a system of government, or into a theology, or into a ritual, according to its capabilities; and this system, or body of thought, theoretical and practical, thus laboriously gained, will after all be only the adequate representation of the original idea, being nothing else than what that very idea *meant* from the first – its exact image as seen in a combination of the most diversified aspects, with the suggestions and corrections of many minds, and the illustration of many trials. [97].

This process is called the development of an idea [...]. And it has this necessary characteristic – that, since its province is the busy scene of human life, it cannot develop at all, except either by destroying, or modifying and incorporating with itself, existing modes of thinking and acting. [...] it is carried on through individuals and bodies of men; it employs their minds as instruments, and depends upon them while it uses them.[25] [...] It grows when it incorporates [...]. It is the warfare of ideas, striving for the mastery, each of them enterprising, engrossing, imperious, more or less incompatible with the rest, and rallying followers or rousing foes according as it acts upon the faith, the prejudices, or the interests of individuals. [99].

[...] In time it enters upon strange territory; points of controversy alter their bearing; parties rise and fall about it; dangers and hopes appear in new relations, and old principles reappear under new forms; it changes with them in order to remain the same. In a higher world it is otherwise; but here below to live is to change, and to be perfect is to have changed often. [100].

Section III: On the Corruption of an Idea

Distinctive Tests between Development and Corruption.
Since the developments of an idea are nothing else than its adequate representation and fulfilment, in its various aspects, relations, and consequences, and since the causes which stimulate may also distort its growth, as is seen in the corruptions of truth with which the world abounds, rules are required to distinguish legitimate developments from those which are not such. [116].

Here the most ready test is suggested by the analogy of physical growth, which is such that the parts and proportions of the developed form correspond to those which belong to its rudiments. [...] Unity in type is certainly the most obvious characteristic of a faithful development. [117].

---

25 This is not unlike the suggestion, by Wilson, Dawkins and others, of the existence of the meme as a unit of culture.

Yet this illustration must not be pressed to the extent of denying all variation, [...] changes in outward appearance and internal harmony occur in the instance of the animal creation itself. [...] The butterfly is the development, but not in any sense the image, of the grub. [117].

[...] And, in like manner, real perversions and corruptions are often not so unlike externally to the doctrine to which they belong, as are changes which are consistent with it and true developments. [119].

Nay, one cause of corruption in religion is the refusal to follow the course of doctrine as it moves on, and an obstinacy in the notions of the past. Certainly: as we see conspicuously in the history of the chosen race. The Samaritans who refused to add the Prophets to the Law, and the Sadducees who denied what lay hid in the book of Exodus, were in appearance but faithful adherents to the primitive doctrine. [...]

Natural then as it is at first sight to suppose that an idea will always be the exact image of itself in all stages of its history, experience does not bear out the anticipation. To discover the tests of a true development, as distinguished from a corruption, we must consider the subject more attentively. [120].

...Corruption is a breaking up of the subject in which it takes place, or its resolution into its component parts, which involves eventually a loss of unity [...]. [120].

[...] The corruption of an idea is that state of a development which undoes its previous advances.

If the process is suspended and the state chronic, then it is called decay; but it is called corruption when it hastens to a crisis, as a fever, or the disturbance of system consequent on poisoning, in which the bodily functions are under preternatural influence, whereas in decay there is a loss of activity and vigour.

Thus, without considering the analogy as strict, or sufficient to rest an argument upon, we may use it to introduce several rules for drawing the line between a development and a corruption. That development, then, is to be considered a corruption which *obscures or prejudices its essential idea*, or which *disturbs the laws of development* which constitutes its organisation, or which *reverses its course of development*; that is *not* a corruption which is *both a chronic and an active state*, or which is *capable of holding together* the component parts of a system. From this analysis seven tests of development may be drawn of varying cogency and independence. [121].

The First Test of a true Development; Preservation of Idea
That the essential idea or type which a philosophical or political system
represents must continue under all its developments, and that its loss is
tantamount to the corruption of the system will scarce be denied. When,
for instance, we pronounce a monastic institution to have been in a state
of corruption, we mean that it had departed from the views or professions
in which it was founded. [...] [122].

The Second Test; Continuity of Principles
As in mathematical creations figures are formed on distinct formulae,
which are the laws under which they are developed, so it is in ethical and
political subjects. Doctrines expand variously according to the mind, indi-
vidual or social, into which they are received; and the peculiarities of the
recipient are the regulating power, the law, the organisation, or, as it may
be called, the form of the development. The life of doctrines may be said
to consist in the law or principle which they embody. [...] [124].

Thus the *continuity or alteration of the principles* on which an idea has devel-
oped is a second mark of discrimination between a true development and
a corruption. [...] [127].

Principles are abstract and general, doctrines relate to facts; doctrines
develop, and principles do not; doctrines grow and are enlarged, princi-
ples are illustrated; doctrines are intellectual, and principles more
immediately ethical and practical. Systems live in principles and represent
doctrines. Personal responsibility is a principle, the Being of God is a
doctrine; from that doctrine all theology has come in due course, whereas
that principle is not clearer under the Gospel than in Paradise, and depends,
not on belief in an Almighty Governor, but on conscience. [...] [127].

Again, religious investigation sometimes is conducted on the principle
that it is a duty 'to follow and speak the truth', which really means that it
is no duty to fear error, or to consider what is safest, or to shrink from scat-
tering doubts, or to regard the responsibility of misleading; and thus it
terminates in heresy or infidelity, without any blame to religious investi-
gation itself.[26] [128].

A development to be faithful, must retain both the doctrine and the
principle with which it started. Doctrine without its corresponding prin-
ciple remains barren, if not lifeless, of which the Greek Church seems an
instance; or it forms those hollow professions which are familiarly called
'shams', as a zeal for an established Church and its creed, on merely conser-
vative or temporal motives. [...]

---

26 This paragraph provides an insight into Newman's break with Whately and the
life-long struggle against 'liberalism' that followed.

Pagans may have, heretics cannot have, the same principles as Catholics; if the latter have the same, they are not real heretics, but in ignorance. Principle is a better test of heresy than doctrine. [...][129].

Protestantism, viewed in its more Catholic aspect, is doctrine without principle; viewed in its heretical, it is principle without doctrine. [...] [130].

The Third Test; Power of Assimilation

[...] An eclectic, conservative, assimilating, healing, moulding process, a *unitive power* is of the essence, and a third test, of a faithful development.

Thus, a power of development is a proof of life, not only in its essay, but in its success; for a mere formula either does not expand or is shattered in expanding. A living idea becomes many, yet remains one.

The attempt at development shows the presence of a principle, and its success the presence of an idea. Principles stimulate thought, and an idea keeps it together. [...] [131].

The stronger and more living is an idea, that is, the more powerful hold it exercises on the minds of men, the more able is it to dispense with safeguards, and trust to itself against the dangers of corruption. As strong frames exult in their agility, and healthy constitutions throw off ailments, so parties or schools that live can afford to be rash, and will sometimes be betrayed into extravagances, yet are brought right by their inherent vigour. On the other hand, unreal systems are commonly decent externally. Forms, subscriptions, or Articles of religion are indispensable when the form of life is weakly. Thus Presbyterianism has maintained its original theology in Scotland where legal subscriptions are enforced, while it has run into Arianism or Unitarianism where that protection is away. We have yet to see whether the Free Kirk can keep its present theological ground. The Church of Rome can consult expedience more freely than other bodies, as trusting to her living tradition, and is sometimes thought to disregard principle and scruple when she is dispensing with forms. Thus saints are often characterised by acts which are no patterns for others; and most gifted men are, by reason of their very gifts, sometimes led into fatal inadvertences. Hence vows are the wise defence of unstable virtue, and general rules the refuge of feeble authority. [...] [133].

The Fourth Test; Early Anticipation

Since, when an idea is living, that is, influential and operative in the minds of its recipients, it is sure to develop according to the principles on which they are formed; instances of such a process, though vague and isolated, may occur from the very first, though a lapse of time be necessary to bring it to perfection. [...] [133].

It is certain that,[27] in the idea of Monachism,[28] prevalent in ancient times, manual labour had a more prominent place than study; so much so that De Rancé,[29] the celebrated Abbot of La Trappe, in controversy with Mabillon,[30] maintained his ground with great plausibility against the latter's apology for the literary occupations for which the Benedictines of France are famous. Nor can it be denied that the labours of such as Mabillon and Montaucon are at least a development upon the simplicity of the primitive institution. And yet it is remarkable that St Pachomius,[31] the first author of a monastic rule, enjoined a library in each of his houses, and appointed conferences, disputations, three times a week on religious subjects, interpretations of Scripture, or points of theology. St Basil,[32] the founder of Monachism in Pontus, one of the most learned of the Greek Fathers, wrote his theological treatises in the intervals of agricultural labour. [...] These, indeed, were but exceptions in the character of early Monachism; but they suggest its capabilities and anticipate its history. [...] [135].

The Fifth Test; Logical Sequence
Though it is a matter of accident in what order or degree developments of a common idea will show themselves in this or that place, particular minds or communities taking different courses, yet on a larger field they will on the whole be gradual and orderly, nay in *logical sequence*. It may be asked whether a development is itself a logical process,[33] and if by this is meant a conscious reasoning from premises to conclusion, of course, the answer must be in the negative. [...] [136].

---

27 Newman underlines his argument throughout the Essay with theological and historical examples that demonstrate both his wide reading and his ability to pull appropriate illustrations from his memory and notebooks.
28 Monachism is another word for Monasticism.
29 Armand-Jean Le Bouthillier de Rancé (1626–1700) was a godson of Cardinal Richelieu. Though an able scholar, he was, before a profound deepening of his faith, a very worldly priest. He reformed the monastery of La Trappe along strict Cistercian lines, later known as the Trappist Reform. He was a spiritual director of James II.
30 Jean Mabillon (1632–1707), a Benedictine scholar.
31 St Pachomius (c. 290–346) an Egyptian and Roman soldier who founded Christian monasticism.
32 St Basil the Great (c. 330–379). One of the three Cappadocian Fathers (with St Gregory of Nazianzus and St Gregory of Nyssa). Basil was a great theologian and organiser, noted for his holiness – three attributes not often found together.
33 For a discussion of logical explication as an explanation for undeniable historic changes in Christian teaching see Chapter II of Owen Chadwick's *From Bossuet to Newman* (CUP 1957).

The process of development, thus capable of logical expression, has sometimes been invidiously spoken of as rationalism and contrasted with faith. [...] Rationalism is the preference of reason to faith; but one does not see how it can be faith to adopt the premises, and unbelief to accept the conclusion. [...] to develop is to receive conclusions from received truth, to rationalise is to receive *nothing* but conclusions from received truth; to develop is positive, to rationalise is negative; the essence of development is to extend belief, of rationalism to contract it. [...] [138].

Thus, the holy Apostles would know without words all the truths concerning the high doctrines of theology, which controversialists after them have piously and charitably reduced to formulae, and developed through argument. [...] Thus St Anthony said to the philosophers who came to mock him, 'He whose mind is in health does not need letters'; and St Ignatius Loyola, while yet an unlearned neophyte was favoured with transcendent perceptions of the Holy Trinity during his penance at Manresa. Thus St Athanasius himself is more powerful in statement and exposition than in proof; while in Bellarmine[34] we find the whole series of doctrines carefully drawn out, duly adjusted with one another, and exactly analysed one by one. [...] [139].

The Sixth Test; Preservative Additions

[...] A true development, then, may be described as one which is conservative of the course of development which went before it, which is that development and something besides; it is an addition which illustrates, not obscures, corroborates, not corrects, the body of thought from which it proceeds; and this is its characteristic as contrasted with a corruption. [...] [142].

The Seventh Test; Chronic Continuance

Since the corruption of an idea, as far as the appearance goes, is a sort of accident or affection of its development, being the end of a course, and a transition-state leading to a crisis, it is, as has been observed, a brief and rapid process. [...] Corruption cannot, therefore, be of long standing; and thus *duration* is another test of a faithful development. [...]

The course of heresies is always short. [...] [145].

---

34 The saintly and scholarly Cardinal, Robert Bellarmine (1542–1641), was one of the great apologists for Roman Catholicism at the time of the Reformation. He was canonised in 1930 and declared a Doctor of the Church the following year.

Chapter II: On the Development of Ideas Antecedently Considered

Section I: On the Probability of Developments in Christianity

1. […] And the more claim an idea has to be considered living, the more various will be its aspects; and the more political and social is its nature, the more complicated and subtle will be its developments, and the longer and more eventful will be its course. Such is Christianity; and whatever has been said in the last chapter about the developments of ideas generally, becomes of course an antecedent argument for its progressive development.

It may be objected that inspired documents, such as the Holy Scriptures, at once determine its doctrine without further trouble. But they were intended to create an idea, and that idea is not in the sacred text, but in the mind of the reader; and the question is, whether that idea is communicated to him in its completeness and minute accuracy, on its first apprehension, or expands in his heart and intellect, and comes to perfection in the course of time. […] [149].

4. This moreover should be considered, that great questions exist in the subject-matter of which Scripture treats, which Scripture does not solve; questions too so real, so practical, that they must be answered, and answered, unless we suppose a new revelation, from the revelation which we have, that is, by development. Such is the question of the Canon of Scripture and its inspiration: whether Christianity depends upon a written document as Judaism, if so, on what writings and how many; whether that document is self-interpreting, or requires a comment, and whether any authoritative comment or commentator is provided; whether the revelation and the document are commensurate, or the one outruns the other, that is, whether or not the revelation is partly documentary and partly traditional, and whether or not the document is but partially the revelation, the revelation in an uninspired organ, or the revelation with additions; all these questions surely find no solution on the surface of Scripture, nor indeed under the surface in the case of most men, however long and diligent might be their study of it. Nor were these difficulties settled by authority, as far as we know, at the commencement of the religion; yet surely it is quite conceivable that an Apostle might have dissipated them all in a few words, had Divine Wisdom thought fit. But in matter of fact the decision has been left to time, to the slow process of thought, the influence of mind upon mind, the issues of controversy, and the growth of opinion. […] [152].

Since then Scripture needs completion, the question is brought to this issue, whether defect or inchoateness in its doctrines be or be not an antecedent probability in favour of a development of them. [153].

In whatever sense the need and its supply are a proof of design[35] in the visible creation, in the same do the gaps, if the word may be used, which occur in the original creed of the Church, make it probable that those developments, which grow out of the truths which lie around them, were intended to complete it. [...] [154].

5. [...] Moreover, while it is certain that developments of Revelation proceeded all through the Old Dispensation down to the very end of our Lord's ministry, on the other hand, if we turn our attention to the beginnings of apostolical teaching after His ascension, we shall find ourselves unable to fix an historical point at which the growth of doctrine ceased, and the rule of faith was once for all settled. Not on the day of Pentecost, for St Peter had still to learn at Joppa about the baptism of Cornelius; not at Joppa and Caesarea, for St Paul had still to write his Epistles; not on the death of the last Apostle, for St Ignatius had to establish the doctrine of Episcopacy; not then nor for many years after, for the Canon of the New Testament was still undetermined. [...] The Church went forth from the world, in haste, as the Israelites from Egypt 'with their dough before it was leavened, their kneading troughs being bound up in the clothes upon their shoulders'. [...] [159].

6. It is in point to notice also the structure and style of Scripture, a structure so unsystematic and various, and a style so figurative and indirect, that no one would presume at first sight to say what is in it and what is not. It cannot, as it were, be mapped, or its contents catalogued; but after all our diligence, to the end of our lives and to the end of the Church, it must be an unexplored and unsubdued land [...] [162].

7. Lastly, while scripture nowhere recognises itself, or asserts the inspiration of those portions which are most essential, it distinctly anticipates the development of Christianity, both as a polity and as a doctrine. [...] [163].

Section II: On the Probability of a Developing Authority in Christianity

[...] Reasons shall be given in the present Section for asserting that, in proportion to the probability of true developments of doctrine and practice in the divine scheme, is the probability also of the appointment in that scheme of an external authority to decide upon them, thereby separating them from the mass of mere human speculation, extravagance, corruption, and error, in and out of which they grow. This is the doctrine of the infallibility of the Church; for by infallibility I suppose is meant the power of

---

35 Newman was writing fifteen years [1845] before the publication of Charles Darwin's *Origin of Species* [1859] undermined William Paley's classic statement of the argument from design in *Natural Theology* [1802].

deciding whether this, that, and a third and any number of theological or ethical statements are true. [...] [168].

2. An objection, however, is often made to the doctrine of infallibility *in limine*, which is too important not to be taken into consideration. It is urged that, as all religious knowledge rests on moral evidence, not on demonstration, our beliefs in the Church's infallibility must be of this character; but what can be more absurd than a probable infallibility, or a certainty resting on doubt? I believe, because I am sure; and I am sure, because I think. [...] [169].

3. [...] But why is it more inconsistent to speak of an uncertain infallibility than of a doubtful truth or a contingent necessity, phrases which present ideas clear and undeniable? In truth we are playing with words when we use arguments of this sort. [...] A probable infallibility is a probable gift of never erring; a reception of the doctrine of a probable infallibility is faith and obedience towards a person founded on the probability of his never erring in his declarations or commands. What is inconsistent in this idea? Whatever then be the particular means of determining infallibility, the abstract objection may be put aside.

4. Again, it is sometimes urged that such a dispensation would destroy our probation, as dissipating doubt, precluding the exercise of faith, and obliging us to obey whether we wish it or no; and it is urged that a divine voice spoke in the first age, and difficulty and darkness rests upon all subsequent ones; as if infallibility and personal judgement were incompatible; but this is to confuse the subject. We must distinguish between a revelation and the reception of it, not between its earlier and later stages. [...] [170].

[...] Infallibility does not interfere with moral probation; the two notions are perfectly distinct. It is no objection then to the idea of an arbitrary authority, such as I am supposing, that it lessens the task of personal enquiry, unless it be an objection to the authority of Revelation altogether. [...] [171].

The case then stands thus: that Revelation has introduced a new law of divine governance over and above those laws which appear in the natural course of the world; and we henceforth argue for a standing authority in matters of faith, on the analogy of Nature, and from the fact of Christianity. Preservation is involved in the idea of creation. As the Creator rested on the seventh day from the work which he had made, yet 'He worketh hitherto', so He gave the Creed once for all in the beginning, yet blesses its growth still, and dispenses its increase. [...] As creation argues continual governance, so are Apostles harbingers of Popes. [173].

6. Moreover it must be borne in mind that, as the essence of all religion is authority and obedience, so the distinction between natural religion and

revealed lies in this, that the one has a subjective authority, and the other an objective. Revelations consists in the manifestation of the invisible divine power, or in the substitution of the voice of a lawgiver for the voice of conscience. The supremacy of conscience is the essence of natural religion; the supremacy of Apostle, or Pope, or Church, or Bishop, is the essence of the revealed; and when such external authority is taken away, the mind falls back again upon that inward guide which it possessed even before revelation was vouchsafed. Thus what conscience is in the system of nature, such is the voice of Scripture, or of the Church, or of the Holy See, as we may determine it in the system of revelation. It may be objected, indeed, that conscience is not infallible; it is true, but still it is ever to be obeyed. And this is just the prerogative which controversialists assign to the See of St Peter; it is not in all cases infallible, it may err beyond its special province, but it has in all cases a claim on our obedience. [...] [174].

7. The common sense of mankind does but support a conclusion thus forced upon us by analogical considerations. It feels that the very idea of revelation implies a present informant and guide, and that an infallible one; not a mere abstract declaration of truths not known before to man, or a record of history, or the result of an antiquarian research, but a message and a lesson speaking to this man and that. This is shown by the popular notion which has prevailed among us since the Reformation, that the Bible itself is such a guide; and which succeeded in overthrowing the supremacy of Church and Pope, for the very reason that it was a rival authority, not resisting merely, but supplanting it. [...] We are told that God has spoken. Where? In a book? We have tried it, and it disappoints; it disappoints, that most holy and blessed gift, not from fault of its own, but because it was used for a purpose for which it was not given. The Ethiopian's reply, when Philip asked him if he understood what he was reading, is the voice of nature: 'How can I, unless some man shall guide me?' The Church undertakes that office; she does what none else can do, and this is the secret of the power. 'The human mind,' it has been said, 'wishes to be rid of doubt in religion; and a teacher who claims infallibility is readily believed on his simple word.' We see this constantly exemplified in the case of individual pretenders among ourselves. In Romanism the Church pretends to it; she rids herself of competitors by forestalling them. And probably, in the eyes of her children, this is not the least persuasive argument for her infallibility, that she alone of all churches dares claim it; as if a secret instinct and involuntary misgiving restrained those rival communions which go so far towards affecting it.[36] [175].

---

36 Newman is quoting here from his *Lectures of the Prophetical Office of the Church*, published 1837.

8. [...] The absolute need of a spiritual supremacy is at present the strongest argument in favour of its supply. [176].

[...] By the Church of England a hollow uniformity is preferred to an infallible chair; and by the sects of England, an interminable division. Germany and Geneva began with persecution, and have ended in scepticism. The doctrine of infallibility is a less violent hypothesis than this sacrifice either of faith or of charity. It secures the objects, without, to say the least, violating the letter of the revelation. [177].

9. [...] Gieseler's 'Text Book' bears the profession of being a dry analysis of Christian history; yet on inspection it will be found to be written on a positive and definite theory, and to bend facts to meet it. An unbeliever, as Gibbon, assumes one hypothesis, and an Ultramontane,[37] as Baronius, adopts another. The school of Hurd and Newton consider Christianity slept for centuries upon centuries, except among those who historians call heretics. Others speak as if the Oath of Supremacy or the *congé d'élire*[38] could be made the measure of St Ambrose, and they fit the Thirty-Nine Articles on the fervid Tertullian. The question is, which of all these theories is the simplest, the most natural, the most persuasive. Certainly the notion of development under infallible authority is not a less grave, a less winning hypothesis, than the chance and coincidence of events, or the oriental philosophy, or the working of Antichrist, to account for the rise of Christianity and the formation of its theology. [178].

Chapter III: On the Nature of the Argument in Behalf of the Existing Development of Christianity

Section I: Presumptive Character of the Proof

In proceeding to the consideration of the character of the argument adducible in behalf of the truth of the existing developments of Christianity, we must first direct our attention to the preponderating force of antecedent probability in all practical matters, where it exists. If this probability is great, it almost supersedes evidence altogether. [...] [179].

A further presumption in behalf of these doctrines arises from the general

---

37 The Ultramontanist party in the Roman Catholic Church supported the absolute authority of the Pope in all matters of faith and Church discipline.

38 Congé d'élire [French: 'permission to elect'] refers to the ancient right of English Kings to nominate Bishops. What had been a royal permission to a Dean and Chapter to proceed with the election, became in 1534 a royal command to elect the person nominated by the monarch. Failure to do so was punishable in law. These penalties of praemunire were only abolished in 1967.

opinion of the world about them. Christianity being one, all its doctrines are necessarily developments of one, and, if so, are of necessity consistent with each other, or form a whole. Now the world fully enters into this view of those well-known developments which claim the name of Catholic. It allows them that title, it considers them to belong to one family, and refers them to one theological system. It is scarcely necessary to set about proving what is urged by their opponents even more strenuously than by their champions. [...] [183].

And this general testimony to the oneness of Catholicism extends to its past teaching relatively to its present [...] No one doubts [...] that the Roman Catholic Communion of this day is the successor and representative of the Medieval Church, or that the Medieval Church is the legitimate heir of the Nicene; even allowing that it is a question whether a line cannot be drawn between the Nicene Council and the Church which preceded it. On the whole, all parties will agree that, of all existing systems, the present Communion of Rome is the nearest approximation in fact to the Church of the Fathers, possible, though some may think it, to be nearer to it still on paper.[39] Did St Athanasius or St Ambrose come suddenly to life, it cannot be doubted what communion they would mistake for their own. All surely will agree that these Fathers, with whatever differences of opinion, whatever protests, if we will, would find themselves more at home with such men as St Bernard or St Ignatius Loyola, or with the lonely priest in his lodgings, or the holy sisterhood of mercy, or the unlettered crowd before the altar, than with the rulers or the members of any other religious community. And may we not add, that were the two Saints, who once sojourned, in exile or on embassage, at Treves, to come more northward still, and to travel until they reached another fair city, seated among groves, green meadows, and calm streams, the holy brothers would turn from many a high aisle and solemn cloister which they found there, and ask the way to some small chapel where mass was said in the populous alley or forlorn suburb?[40] And, on the other hand, can anyone who has but heard his name, and cursorily read his history, doubt for one instant how the people of England, in turn, 'we, our princes, our priests, and our prophets', Lords and Commons, universities, ecclesiastical courts, marts of commerce, great

---

39 This whole passage is in many ways the essence of Newman's argument. The Church on 'paper' refers to the Church of England as the 'Via Media'. Newman's tongue is clearly in his cheek here.

40 Newman fails entirely to consider the possibility that these ancient Fathers of the Church might have thought that Eastern Orthodoxy was the Communion nearer to their own.

towns, country parishes, would deal with Athanasius – Athanasius who spent his long years in fighting against kings for a theological term? [184].

Section II: Character of the Evidence

[...] Sometimes when the want of evidence about a series of facts or doctrines is unaccountable,[41] in the course of time, an unexpected explanation or addition is found as regards a portion of them, which suggests a ground of patience as regards the historical obscurity of the rest. Two instances are obvious to mention, of an accidental silence of clear primitive testimony as to important doctrines, and its removal. In the number of the articles of Catholic belief which the Reformation especially resisted, were the Mass and the sacramental virtue of Ecclesiastical Unity. Since the date of that movement, the shorter Epistles of St Ignatius have been discovered, and the early Liturgies verified; and this with most men has put an end to the controversy about those doctrines. What has happened to them, may happen to others; and though it does not happen to others, yet that it has happened to them, is to those others a sort of compensation for the obscurity in which their early history continues to be involved. [191].

Section III: Method of Conducting the Enquiry

[...] If this is, on the whole, a true view of the general shape under which the existing body of developments commonly called Catholic present themselves before us, antecedently to our looking into the particular evidence on which they stand, I think we shall be at no loss to determine what both logical truth and duty prescribe to us as to our reception of them. It is very little to say that we should treat them as we are accustomed to treat other alleged facts and truths, and the evidence for them, which bring with them a fair presumption of evidence in their favour. Such are of every day's occurrence; and what is our behaviour towards them? We do not in the first instance exercise our reason upon opinions which are received, but our faith. We do not begin with doubting, we take them on trust, and we put them on trial, and that, not of set purpose, but spontaneously. [193].

---

41 In setting out his case for 'development' Newman is always very conscious, where certain key doctrines are concerned, of the silence of the early centuries. On page 188 of the Pelican edition, he uses the argument of logical equivalence: 'And thus a converging evidence for facts or doctrines through a certain period may, under circumstances, be as cogent a proof of their presence throughout the period as the *Quod semper, quod ubique, quod ab omnibus*.

Those who will not view the beginning in the light of the result, are equally unwilling to let the whole elucidate the parts. The Catholic doctrines [...] are members of one family, and suggestive, or correlative, or confirmatory, or illustrative of each other. In other words, one furnishes *evidence* to the other, and all to each of them; if this is proved, that becomes probable; if this and that are both probable, but for different reasons, each adds to the other its own probability. The Incarnation is the antecedent of the doctrine of Mediation, and the archetype both of the Sacramental principle and of the merits of the Saints. From the doctrine of Mediation follow the Atonement, the Mass, the merits of Martyrs and Saints, their invocation and *cultus*. From the Sacramental principle come the Sacraments properly so called; the unity of the Church, and the Holy See as its type and centre; the authority of Councils; the sanctity of rites; the veneration of holy places, shrines, images, vessels, furniture, and vestments. [...] You must accept the whole or reject the whole; reduction does but enfeeble, and amputation mutilate. [...] [198].

Section IV: Instances in Illustration

Having set out his arguments and methods of interpretation Newman proceeds next to illustrate them, using as examples Christ's Divinity, the Canon of the New Testament, the reception of the bread only by the laity at the mass, before treating at much greater length the Pope's claim to primacy over all Christendom.

[...] When the Church, then, was thrown upon her own resources, first local disturbances gave rise to Bishops, and next ecumenical disturbances gave rise to Popes; and whether communion with the Pope was necessary for Catholicity would not and could not be debated till a suspension of the communion had actually occurred. It is not a greater difficulty that St Ignatius does not write to the Asian Greeks about popes, than that St Paul does not write to the Corinthians about Bishops. And it is a less difficulty that the Papal Supremacy was not formally acknowledged in the second century, than that there was no formal acknowledgement of the doctrine of the Holy Trinity till the fourth. No doctrine is defined till it is violated. [209].

[...] If the Imperial Power checked the development of Councils, it availed also for keeping back the power of the Papacy. The Creed, the Canon, in like manner, both remained undefined. The Creed, the Canon, the Papacy, Ecumenical Councils, all began to form, as soon as the Empire relaxed its tyrannous oppression of the Church. And as it was natural that her monarchical power should rise when the Empire became Christian so it was natural also that further development of that power should take place when that Empire fell. [210].

Section V: Parallel Instances

Newman was concerned that his methods of reasoning, dependent as they were on degrees of probability, were vulnerable to the charge that they constrained the facts to fit a theory because they were based on neither systematic doubt, nor proof by test and confirmation. His answer was that such strict investigation belonged to the realm of physics. It was not possible with history, ethics or religion. Newman then instances occasions where he believes facts fail to make much sense without the use of antecedent probability.

These instances may suffice in illustration of a method of reasoning, ordinary and necessary when facts are scarce; often easy to handle aright, but very frequently difficult and dangerous; open to great abuse, and depending for its success or failure far more on the individual exercising it than on rules which can be laid down; a method which, if delicate and doubtful when used in proof of the Catholic Church, is far less certain and far less satisfactory in the many instances in which it is applied to scientific and historical investigations. [239].

The remainder of the Essay consists in the application of Newman's seven tests for authentic development throughout a whole range of doctrinal questions. If the depth of treatment through the first six centuries is uneven, the breadth and detail of knowledge employed is considerable. In applying his First Test, Newman discusses at some length: the Arians of the Gothic race; the Nestorians and the Monophysites. In applying his Second Test, he considers: Scripture and its Mystical Sense, and the Supremacy of Faith. Adding the Third Test to the Second, Newman applies them to: The Dogmatic and Sacramental Principles, and the Formation of a Theology by means of them. His method here is cumulative – to convince the reader by demonstrating how authentic development could have given rise to a self-consistent, self-authenticating system whose authority was the sense it made of an original revelation. He continues his tour de force by applying the Fourth Test to the Resurrection and Relics; the Cultus of Saints and Angels; the Merits of Virginity; the Office of Mary and Specimens of Theological Science. The last fifty pages look again at such matters as Christ's Divinity, and the Doctrine of Baptism. Increasingly towards the end, the writing shows signs of being hurried. Newman had convinced himself, laid down his pen, and submitted to the Roman Pontiff.

Such were the thoughts concerning the 'Blessed Vision of Peace', of one whose long-continued petition had been that the Most Merciful would not despise the work of His own Hands, nor leave him to himself; while yet his eyes were dim, and his breast laden, and he could but employ Reason in the things of Faith. And now, dear Reader, time is short, eternity is long. Put not from you what you have found; regard it not as mere matter of present controversy; set not out resolved to refute it, and looking about for the best way of doing so; seduce not yourself with the imagination that it comes of disappointment, or disgust, or restlessness, or wounded feeling, or undue sensibility, or other weakness. Wrap not yourself round in the associations of past years; nor determine that to be truth which you wish to be so, nor make an idol of cherished anticipations. Time is short, eternity is long.

NUNC DIMITTIS SERVUM TUUM, DOMINE,
SECUNDUM VERBUM TUUM IN PACE:
QUIA VIDERUNT OCULI MEI SALUTARE TUUM.[42]

---

42 The opening words of the Canticle *Nunc Dimittis*: 'Lord, now lettest Thou thy servant depart in peace according to thy word, for mine eyes have seen Thy salvation.' [St Luke 2:29.]

Bibliography

The Writings of John Henry Newman

Newman was a prolific writer. The Longmans, Green, and Co. edition of his works (1868–81) ran to thirty-six volumes; while the definitive *Letters and Diaries of John Henry Cardinal Newman (1961–77)* edited by C.S. Dessain, (Associative editors, Ian Ker, Thomas Gorall, Edward E. Kelly and V.F. Behl) runs to thirty-one volumes. [Vols 1–6, Oxford, 1978–84; Vols 11–22, London, 1961–72; Vols 22–31, Oxford, 1973–77.]

Because, when editing, Newman often made extensive revisions to his work, these often need to be taken into account – and here, R. Rickaby's *Index to the Works of John Henry Cardinal Newman* (1914) is indispensable.

The story of Newman's journey to Rome is told in his *Apologia pro Vita Sua* (ed. Martin J. Svaglic, Oxford, 1967), the only spiritual autobiography that can bear comparison to St Augustine's *Confessions*.

Anglican Writings

St Bartholomew's Eve, 1818.
The Arians of the Fourth Century, 1833.
Tracts for the Times [Newman wrote twenty-nine of the ninety], 1833–1841.
Elucidations of Dr Hampden's Theological Statements, 1836.
Lyra Apostolica, 1836. [Contains 109 poems by Newman.]
Verses on Various Occasions, Longman, Green & Co, 1903. [1868.]
Lectures on the Prophetical Office of the Church viewed relatively to Romanism and popular Protestantism, 1837. [Known now as the *Via Media*. [2 vols]]
Lectures on the Doctrine of Justification, 1838.
A Letter to the Rev. Geoffrey Faussett, D.D., 1838.
Church of the Fathers, 1840.
A Letter addressed to the Rev. R.W. Jelf, 1841.
A Letter to the Right Reverend Father in God, Richard, Lord Bishop of Oxford, 1841.
Select Treatises of St Athanasius [2 vols], 1842–1845.

An Essay on the Miracles Recorded in the Ecclesiastic History of the Early Ages,
1843.

Essays Critical and Historical [2 vols.] [from the *British Critic*], 1870.

Parochial and Plain Sermons, 1834–42.

Fifteen Sermons preached before the University of Oxford, 1843.

Essay on the Development of Christian Doctrine, 1845.

*The 'Letters and Correspondence of John Henry Newman, During his Life in the
English Church, with a brief Autobiography, Edited at Cardinal Newman's
Request by Anne Mozley.'* Longman's, Green and Co., London 1891.

Correspondence of John Henry Newman with John Keble and others, 1839–1845,
Longmans, 1917. [Edited at the Birmingham Oratory.]

Selected biographies and studies of Newman's life and writings

The definitive biography is *John Henry Newman*, Ian Ker (Oxford
University Press, 1988). It largely replaces *The Life of John Henry Cardinal
Newman* [2 vols], Wilfred Ward, London 1912.

The Anglican Career of Cardinal Newman, Edwin A. Abbott [2 vols],
Macmillan, 1892.

Contributions chiefly to the Early History of the late Cardinal Newman, W.F.
Newman, Kegan Paul, 1891.

The Mystery of Newman, Henri Bremond, tr. H.C. Corrance, Introduction
by George Tyrrell, Williams and Norgate, 1907.

Oxford Apostles, A Character Study of the Oxford Movement, Geoffrey Faber,
Revised edition 1936. Penguin, 1954.

From Bossuet to Newman, O. Chadwick, 1957.

The Mind of the Oxford Movement, Edited and Introduced by Owen
Chadwick, 1960.

Newman the Theologian, J. H. Walgrave, 1960.

Newman, Meriol Trevor [2 vols], 1962.

God and Myself: The Spirituality of J.H. Newman, H.C. Graef, 1967.

Newman's Spiritual Themes, C.S. Dessain, 1977.

John Henry Newman, C.S. Dessain, [1966, 1971, 1980].

John Henry Newman, His Life & Work, Brian Martin, Continuum, 1982.

Newman and His Age, Sheridan Gilley, Darton, Longman and Todd, 1990.

The Achievement of John Henry Newman, Ian Ker, London, Collins.

Healing the Wound of Humanity, The Spirituality of John Henry Newman, Ian
Ker, Darton, Longman and Todd, 1993.

John Henry Newman: The Resolution of a Dilemma, Richard Harding, Univ.
Com. Inc., 2000.

Index of Names